AN INTRODUCTION TO ART THERAPY:

Studies of the "Free" Art Expression
of Behavior Problem Children and Adolescents
as a Means of Diagnosis and Therapy

*" PSYCHODYNAMIC " APPROACH
TO ART THERAPY*

by

MARGARET NAUMBURG ATR

Psychologist, New York State

Preface to the first edition and
introduction to the revised edition by
MARGARET NAUMBURG

Foreword to the first edition by
NOLAN D. C. LEWIS, M.D.

TEACHERS COLLEGE PRESS
Teachers College, Columbia University
New York and London

Other books by Margaret Naumburg
Dynamically Oriented Art Therapy : Its Principles and Practice, 1966
Psychoneurotic Art : Its Function in Psychotherapy, 1953
Schizophrenic Art : Its Meaning in Psychotherapy, 1950
The Child and the World, 1928

Manufactured in the United States of America

PREFACE TO THE FIRST EDITION

The six studies in this monograph were developed as aspects of a research project at the New York State Psychiatric Institute and Hospital. This research was made possible by the sympathetic interest and active support of Dr. Nolan D. C. Lewis. The aim of the project was the investigation of the possible use of "free" or spontaneous art expression as an aid in both diagnosis and therapy.

While the substance of these studies may be of more immediate interest to those who work in the field of child psychiatry, it is hoped that educators and parents of normal children will recognize that the release of the unconscious into imaginative and spontaneous art projections is also of vital importance for the balanced ego development of the normal child.

Although these papers emphasize the importance of the development of spontaneous art products in the treatment of behavior problem children, the development of such "free" art expression is always associated with a planned use of the transference relationship.

The six studies included in this monograph have previously appeared in psychiatric journals and in a volume on child psychiatry. Acknowledgement and thanks are due to each of these publications for their permission to print the papers in this monograph. Studies I and III appeared in "The Nervous Child"; study II appeared in "The Journal of Nervous and Mental Disease"; study IV appeared in the volume "Modern Trends in Child Psychiatry", International Universities Press; and studies V and VI were published in "The Psychiatric Quarterly".

MARGARET NAUMBURG

New York, April, 1947

FOREWORD TO THE FIRST EDITION

The utilization of drawings for studying the emotional problems of both children and adults is well on its way to become an established useful procedure. Some of the most important and fascinating problems in psychiatry are the most elusive when attempts are made to capture them in a revealing and controlling technique. The special studies described in this monograph were organized to demonstrate, if possible, the emotional factors present in certain personality disorders.

Spontaneous drawings as products of the imagination are satisfactions of wishes. They have the superficial character of the "as if" or of the "make believe", but this manifest content probably always in some respects covers or disguises unconscious underlying motives.

Desires whether frustrated, repressed or partially fulfilled have the tendency to generate dreams, phantasies and various bodily activities some of which take the form of art and other creative expressions. A certain amount of freedom or release of tension is achieved in this way, although its real significance remains unknown to the subject. It is a way of stating mixed and poorly understood feelings in an attempt to bring them into clarity and order in the form of a composition. It is an impulse to express to the self and to communicate to others by means of a special language a partial satisfaction of the underlying wish.

Most drawings of the emotionally disordered express problems involving certain "polarities," e.g. life-death, male-female, father-mother, love-hate, activity-passivity, space, rhythm and color, some being specialized and others generalized in composition. Graphic art affords the opportunity to project all of these trends excessively, and after the student of the productions discovers the key to interpreting them, an opportunity is available to ascertain what occurs under an organized therapeutic procedure.

Without a special technique in the hands of a trained investigator it is difficult or practically impossible to judge what mechanisms are represented when they are incorporated in a complicated drawing, but experience has so far shown that they are usually the expression of the erotic or aggressive drives of the person in the midst of an involved life problem. Psychologically we are dealing with complex problems in which each factor must be segregated, analyzed, studied, evaluated, and then brought again into relationship with the total situation.

The design like its contents has a special personal significance, although it uses a universal language which at certain levels is understood by all. The combinations are largely under the dominance of an unconsciously determined pattern of elements characteristic of phantasies, dreams, childish beliefs and impressions, primitive associations, odd, free and conditioned associations, memories and assortments of free images.

Pictures also show the present state of the relationship between the patient and the therapist, as well as any changes in that relationship that may occur from time to time during treatment. Frequently these transference pictures or the transference content of drawings do not express the whole personality situation, but are filled with the neurotic suppression products of hostility or affection connected with one or more symptomatic trends and historical images which may amuse, haunt or distress the conscious mind of the patient.

The transitional stages as well as the general progress of the emotional disorder are often presented in an interesting manner, becoming intelligible by means of the study of periodic or serial drawings. Through the analysis of the contents of these productions, ways are found of bringing into consciousness the underlying difficulties in a manner that shows the basic drives striving to satisfy the instinctive life, and thus objectification and socialization of previously poorly understood feelings and behavior become possible.

These studies of Miss Naumburg represent progressive steps in a type of research that promises much for the future.

Nolan D. C. Lewis, M.D.

INTRODUCTION TO THE REVISED EDITION

This book, *Studies of the "Free" Art Expression of Behavior Problem Children and Adolescents as a Means of Diagnosis and Therapy*, was first published in 1947. Out of print for some time, it remains the only available book of such illustrated clinical case studies of hospitalized children treated by means of dynamically oriented Art Therapy. Publication of this expanded edition is of interest not only to art therapists but also to artists, students, educators, and other professionals.

Freud's emphasis on the significance of the unconscious image-making power of dreams and fantasies has had an important influence on all forms of modern psychotherapy and clinical psychology. Its value to general education, however, is still being neglected. This image-making power of man's unconscious bypasses the verbal thinking which traditionally and currently is overemphasized in formal educational training. True growth and development of students of all ages has been and continues to be obstructed by the continuous imposition of verbal techniques and knowledge in education. Art educators, for example, have been overconcerned with the correct use of art materials and have paid too little attention to the development of each student's uniqueness. Art Therapy procedures can help to release the imaginative and creative expression of normal pupils and of disturbed patients. Such creativity is routinely tapped by artists, but is not, as yet, sufficiently understood and encouraged by art educators. The Art Therapy approach offers a specialized additional non-verbal technique for releasing, through symbolic imagery, the unconscious, repressed emotions.

Some time ago, "A Report on the Visual Arts," prepared by the Committee of the Visual Arts at Harvard University, pointed out regretfully, "Education was and still remains on a purely verbal level. Great emphasis is laid upon classification, description, explication of nature, of man and his works. The University tends primarily to deal with products rather than with processes, with the fruits of man's creativeness rather than the act of creation" (1956, p. 43). As the committee's statement suggests, we have failed to develop teachers able to train pupils to spontaneous creative expression through which personal insight may be gained. Our failure to develop such teachers has kept our education barren.

It is encouraging that training in methods of dynamically oriented Art Therapy is now expanding in the United States. Leading art educators here and in Canada have, in recent years, become aware of how much Freud has contributed to the understanding of unconscious expression, and a few have made reference to the value of Freud's insights. Their comments, for the most part, however, show little understanding of the true implication of psychoanalysis and its relation to art education. Professor Manuel Barkan, in *A Foundation for Art Education,* writes:

> Freud placed primary emphasis on subconsciously held attitudes and feelings, thus establishing a new direction for understanding the process of internalizing an experience with others. The subconscious is a basic factor in all that a personality does in his personal and social behavior, including his artistic activities. For this reason, Freudian theory makes a significant contribution to art education through encouraging the release of spontaneous expression from the unconscious.[1]

In his book *Icon and Idea,*[2] the late Sir Herbert Read refers only vaguely to the importance of the psychoanalytic approach to art education. He cites Freud's views concerning the unconscious and Jung's emphasis on the "collective" unconscious, but offers no practical suggestions as to how such concepts could be of value in the training of art educators.

Outstanding among professors of higher education (not art education) has been Professor Arthur T. Jersild of Teachers College, Columbia University. In the introduction to his important book *When Teachers Face Themselves*[3] he discusses the implications of psychoanalysis as an influence in the modification of the training of professionals in a number of disciplines.

Freud recognized the importance of training such professionals as educators and pastors in the practical application of psychoanalytic methods. One barrier to incorporation of Freud's insights into the field of education has been the failure of his masterly presentation *The Question of Lay Analysis*[4] to receive in the United States the consideration it deserves. The American Psychoanalytical Association, when it was founded, declared itself opposed to the training of non-medical professionals in psychoanalysis. The Association has modified its original ruling of accepting only physicians for training and is now accepting as members Ph.D. psychologists who have trained at recognized universities.

[1]Barkan, *A Foundation for Art Education,* New York, Ronald Press, 1955, p. 160-163.

[2]Read, *Icon and Idea: the Function of Art in the Development of Human Consciousness,* Cambridge, Harvard University Press, 1955.

[3]Jersild, *When Teachers Face Themselves,* New York: Teachers College Press, 1955 (15th paperback printing, 1973).

[4]Freud, *The Question of Lay Analysis: Conversations with an Impartial Person* (Strachey, trans.), New York: Norton, 1969.

Today, more and more directors of departments of art education at American universities and clinics are establishing courses in Art Therapy training for graduate students, not only in art but also in other disciplines. As a consequence of the growing response to the expansion of graduate Art Therapy training, some chairmen of undergraduate departments of art education have also begun to plan Art Therapy training programs for their students. Whether undergraduate students in art education have as yet had sufficient background in clinical and abnormal psychology to prepare them to begin professional training in Art Therapy deserves serious consideration by professional Art Therapists before policy on such training becomes set. I believe that all Art Therapists should be familiar with the principles and practice of psychoanalysis in order to become psychologically competent in their profession.

As interest in training Art Therapists has grown in recent years, professionals in such disciplines as psychology, social work, and occupational therapy have come to recognize the value of art therapy training as a means of broadening their professional competence. It is also interesting to note that an increasing number of professionals in various disciplines who have had some form of personal psychotherapy have discovered the value of personal training or study of art therapy for increasing their professional competence.

New York City   Margaret Naumburg

June 1973

ILLUSTRATIONS

CASE I.

1. American Flag 9
2. Lucky Strike Advertisement...................................... 10
3. Grant's Tomb and the Viaduct...................................... 12
4. Washington Bridge—A Phantasy of Spring and Winter.............. 13
5. Statue of Liberty, Ferry Boat and Governor's Island.................. 14
6. Downtown New York... 15
7. Parachute Jump, Ferris Wheel and Roller Coaster......... (Frontispiece)
8. Volcano and Earthquake Dream—Exterior View.................... 16
9. Volcano and Earthquake Dream—Interior of Crack................. 17
10. Volcano Drawing with Village Below............................. 18
11. Skeleton Dream 21
12. A Devil 22
13. Butterfly Design and the "Goo-Goo" Phantasy...................... 24
14. Boy Scout Fire... 26
15. Fire in Fireplace... 27
16. City Fire 28
17. Burning of the Normandie....................................... 29
18. Burning Leaves.................................... 30, color plate I
19. Fireworks at the World's Fair.................................... 31
20. Automobile on Fire 32
21. Bozo, the Fire-Eater, and the Big Top Tent....................... 34
22. Trick Dogs 35
23. Shooting Gallery 36
24. Circus Clowns and the Crowd................................... 38

CASE II.

25. The Mountain that "Cracks"..................................... 60
26. The Tree that "Cracks"... 61
27. The Ship that "Cracks" 62
28. Sinking the "Enemy" Ship Containing the Mother's "Men Friends".... 63
29. "The Writer and the Major" 65
30. The Wedding—The Bride and the Steeple that "Cracks"............. 68
31. The Wedding in the Room Below the Church....................... 69
32. The Rainbow and the Cycle of Nature............................ 70
33. The Birth of the Baby at the Hospital............................ 74
34a. First Diagrammatic Drawing of Sex Organs...................... 76
34b. Second Diagrammatic Drawing of Sex Organs..................... 77
34c. Third Diagrammatic Drawing of Sex Organs...................... 78
35. Spring—"The Major Picks a Flower"............................. 80

36. The Statue of Liberty (First Drawing)............................ 83
37. The Statue of Liberty (Second Drawing)......................... 85
38. Washington Bridge at Night 86

CASE III.
39. The Patient's Pet Cat (Second Attempt).......................... 98
40. The Patient's Pet Cat (Third Attempt)........................... 99
41. The Patient's Pet Cat (Fifth Attempt).......................... 100
42. The Patient's Pet Cat (Sixth Attempt)................101, color plate II
43. The Patient Piloting a Plane (First Version)..................... 104
44. The Patient Piloting a Plane (Second Version—First Episode)....... 105
45. The Patient Piloting a Plane (Second Version—Second Episode)...... 106
46. The Patient Piloting a Plane (Second Version—Third Episode)....... 107
47. The Ark Royal... 109
48. War in the Air.. 110
49. War on the Ground.. 111
50. Easter Phantasy 112
51. A Hill with Trees and Multicolored Rocks....................... 115
52. The Hudson with a View of Jersey in the Distance................. 116
53. Engineers 118
54. Infantry 119
55. Cavalry 120
56. Roof Playground—As Seen from Above.......................... 121
57. Baseball 122
58. Football 123
59. Basketball 124
60. Hockey 125
61. Tennis 126
62. Ping-pong 127
63. Clock Golf 128
64. Gun Target Shooting 128
65. Swimming Race 129
66. Automobile Speed Race 129
67. Fencing 130
68. Boxing 130

CASE IV.
69. Head of Hitler.. 140
70. "Daddy and Me"... 141
71. "My House" and Practice Letter A's............................. 142
72. A Ball, Practice Letter A's, a Swastika ("A Man Falling Off a
    Ladder Killed Himself") 143
73. "Shit of Many Colors"............................146, color plate III
74. A Tree, House and Garden...................................... 150
75. A Black Kitten with a Pink Tongue.............................. 151
76. "The Flaming Torch Makes Boo-boo Pops"........................ 152
77. A Dream: "Jimmy goes up to the sky, comes into the house again
    and back into the sky"....................................... 153
78. "My Brother with Boots On".................................... 154

CASE V.

79. Air Battle between Nazis and British.............................. 162
80. A Jap Bomber......................................163, color plate IV
81. A Red House with Red Smoke and Blue Trees...................... 164
82. A Fat, Black Hippopotamus "with a Thing in Front," Behind Bars.... 165
83. Three Cobras with a Glass Case................................... 166
84. Menagerie with Seven Entrances to Animal Houses................. 167
85. Painting of a Brown Dog... 168
86. Three Modelled Figures: a. Pregnant Mother; b. The Mother with
        the Unborn Child; c. The Father.............................. 176
87. The Aztec Goddess of Childbirth................................. 183
88. The Jolly, Handsome Sailor..........................185, color plate V
89. The Beautiful Trained Nurse........................185, color plate VI
90. Another Air Battle between Nazis and British...................... 189

CASE VI.

91. Two Aspects of the Patient's Self....................204, color plate VII
92. "I Feel Like That After Seeing My Doctor. Happy or Depressed".... 205
93. Summer ....211, color plate VIII
94. Aspect of Happiness... 212
95. Happiness 213
96. Happiness 214
97. Depression 215
98. "How I Feel About My Father"................................... 216
99. "Days at Home" (One of seven designs).......................... 217
100. "Days at Home" (One of seven designs)..................color plate IX

CONTENTS

INTRODUCTION TO THE REVISED EDITION viii

I. A STUDY OF THE ART EXPRESSION OF A BEHAVIOR PROB-
LEM BOY AS AN AID IN DIAGNOSIS AND THERAPY...... 1

II. A STUDY OF THE PSYCHODYNAMICS OF THE ART WORK
OF A NINE YEAR OLD BEHAVIOR PROBLEM BOY 49

III. THE PSYCHODYNAMICS OF THE ART EXPRESSION OF A BOY
PATIENT WITH TIC SYNDROME..................... 91

IV. PHANTASY AND REALITY IN THE ART EXPRESSION OF BE-
HAVIOR PROBLEM CHILDREN....................... 133

V. A STUDY OF THE ART WORK OF A BEHAVIOR PROBLEM
BOY AS IT RELATES TO EGO DEVELOPMENT AND SEXUAL
ENLIGHTENMENT 157

VI. THE DRAWINGS OF AN ADOLESCENT GIRL SUFFERING FROM
ANXIETY HYSTERIA WITH AMNESIA................ 196

COLOR PLATES ....following page 50

PARACHUTE JUMP, FERRIS WHEEL AND ROLLER COASTER
(Fig. 7, see p. 13)

This was the first water color made by a nine year old boy; he saw this scene from his home nearby. The colors are clear and bright. An orange parachute jump has blue, green and yellow parachutes; the Ferris wheel is yellow, the roller coaster, black; and the staircase, electric blue. The black boardwalk rail is silhouetted against yellow sand and the sea waves are green and blue. A color reproduction of this water color is found on the cover of this book.

I.

A STUDY OF
THE ART EXPRESSION OF A BEHAVIOR PROBLEM BOY
AS AN AID IN DIAGNOSIS AND THERAPY

INTRODUCTION

This paper will consider the art work of a 9-year-old Jewish boy of illegitimate birth, who was adopted by a middle-aged couple. His difficulties began in early childhood and his symptoms include seclusiveness, hyperactivity, impulsiveness, night terrors, temper tantrums, a compulsive need to collect small objects, and a propensity to steal, lie and play with fire. The patient's condition while at the New York State Psychiatric Institute and Hospital was diagnosed as probably severe compulsive neurosis, but considerable divergence of opinion concerning this diagnosis was evident among the psychiatrists who examined this patient. Such opinions ranged from the postulation of pre-psychotic, probably schizophrenic, to that of severe compulsive neurosis, and the possibility of organic involvement could not be ruled out. A similar division of opinion occurred also among psychiatrists who examined the patient either before his admission or after his dismissal from the hospital.

Frank was hospitalized for a period of 17 months. He had been under treatment for 9 months when he began creative art work with the writer; this continued for the remaining 8 months of his hospitalization.

This particular study of the art work of a single patient is only one of a series now being reported as aspects of a special research project at the New York State Psychiatric Institute and Hospital, in order to investigate the possible use of creative art as an aid in diagnosis and therapy.[1, 2, 3]

The patients included have been selected on the basis of behavior difficulties, without consideration of evident artistic ability. Some of the patients even expressed distaste for art owing to their previous experience in school art classes.

The art periods occur either once or twice a week. How much time each patient may be able to spend in such sessions depends on the opinion of the psychiatrist, the requirements of the educational program and the type of response the patient was capable of making to such activity. But such experimental work in art as was carried out in this research project with a limited number of behavior problem children and adolescents was not related to the group activities of the regular school or occupational therapy program. The length of the art periods depends on both the age and condition of the patient. This does not mean that the art sessions are entirely concerned with art expression. Much time, especially during the early weeks of adjustment to this new creative approach, may be spent in getting acquainted with the patient, by encouraging various types of personal experience in games, play or conversation that develops spontaneously.

All the patients in this study, whatever their individual maladjustments, have held in common the idea that art stems from an ability to trace or copy pictures. This misconception about art and the nature of the creative process is often derived from the kind of teaching still offered in many public schools. While it obviously limits the growth of normal children, and constricts the development of their potentialities, it may do even more harm to children who enter school life without a sound personal orientation. For when art teaching is dealt with as a routine process, it discourages efforts at spontaneous and creative expression and forces pupils into a degree of stereotyped reproduction of known models that encourages regression and evasion of creative effort, even in normal children.

In attempting to get behavior problem patients to express their innermost thoughts and feelings in creative expression as a substitute for the routine of tracing and copying, it is necessary to convince them that their own responses to life are worth while recording. Such children tend to undervalue what they make; they will explain that their pictures are not good because they do not trace from a book or copy them from a chromo on the wall. In order to release such a patient's spontaneous expression, it is essential, whether it takes weeks or months, to convince him that his own emotions and experience, both pleasant and unpleasant, are the stuff from which creative art is made. As soon as such recordings of his inner or outer world begin to appear and win the response of those around him, he gains confidence and usually moves ahead more easily, into unexplored areas of creative experiment. Joy and wonder grow as the patient begins to discover his own original ways of expressing such buried conflicts and repressions. Hidden doubts and fears, unvocalized hates and anxieties, begin to be liberated in both imaginative and objective form through such work.

As aspects of this patient's art expression are described, they will be correlated with the progress notes of the psychiatrist and with information made available through the social worker's record, the nurse's notes and the school's report. This patient's creative expression can be grouped into four major phases that correspond to certain trends in his growth and development during the art sessions. He began his work by making very small stereotyped models of bunnies, turkeys and birds' nests in plastecine, or ruled flags and heads of presidents in pencil. In the next phase he reached out toward a freer and more original expression in objective landscapes, based for the first time on his own observation and experience. Such subjects were soon followed by an intensification of the patient's original expression of his phantasy world; in these designs he began to project his un-vocalized fears, or compulsions and his acute anxiety concerning his illegitimate birth and adoption; in the final phase, the pictures will show how, in the creation of a world of circus people and animals, the patient's ego began, for the first time, to grow and expand in relation to the outer world. This then resulted in drawings of actual places and real events that illustrate his awareness of the difference between the world of phantasy and reality.

When the clinical summary has been presented, a brief report on the patient's further treatment and history after being dismissed from the hospital will be appended, in order to complete the report of the patient's history and adjustment up to the present time.

CLINICAL HISTORY

The knowledge of the family history of this 9-year-old Jewish boy is inadequate. It is known that he was an illegitimate child; his mother was said to be an intelligent 29-year-old Jewish woman of good family background, holding a responsible business position; the father is reported to be a married man, a painter. The family history of both parents is said to be negative as regards nervous and mental diseases.

The patient was placed for adoption, soon after his birth, and was under foster home care up to the age of 5 months, when his present adoptive parents took him. The foster parents had been married 18 years, were in fairly comfortable circumstances, and had been disappointed in having no children of their own. The adoptive mother is 46 years old. She is tense, over-talkative, defensive and emotionally deprived, has frequent crying spells, gets on badly with people, and chooses her few friends from among those who are in need. She emphasizes the patient's intelligence and her love for him, and says that because her husband worked late at night and she was lonely, particularly after the death of her brother, she wanted a child who would be husband, companion and friend. She was originally drawn to this child because his smile reminded her of her dead brother. During the first year he was very frail and required great care. From the time he was a year old he became increasingly hard to manage, and she first tried reasoning, then arguing, as though he were an adult. When these methods had no effect and she became frustrated, she resorted to threatening and physical punishment without result. Considering all that she has done for the patient, she feels that he should not have made her suffer so much.

The adoptive father, a printer, aged 50, seems more stable than the mother, and though somewhat prudish and authoritarian, he appears to be genuinely fond of the patient. He was originally opposed to the adoption. He criticizes the mother for being too harsh, feels the child's problems are the result of poor handling and is reluctant to have him hospitalized. Both parents stated that their only serious marital disagreements were in relation to the patient. When they thought that the patient was asleep they discussed the situation and considered returning him to the agency; the father suspects that the patient may have been awake and listening and may, therefore, have some awareness both of his background (which had never been discussed directly with him) and of his parents' doubts and disappointments concerning him. The home atmosphere has been tense, anxious and full of fears and prohibitions. The mother is said to be very ill at ease when the patient is away, yet when they are together there is constant friction.

The patient is said to have been a full term infant whose earliest development was normal. No history is available. When he was adopted at the age of 5 months, he was critically ill, extremely underweight, and is said to have had rickets. He was a difficult feeding problem and always tended to be underweight and retarded in his general development. As far back as his foster parents can remember, he was a restless, irritable child, who preferred to play by himself, would never share his toys, and wanted the toys of other children whom he tried to dominate.

The patient attended kindergarten before he was 5 years old and during his year there made the best adjustment of his school life. He was promoted regularly during his first two years at school but he had trouble with arithmetic. He became an increasingly severe disciplinary problem at school, developing a propensity to set fires and showing other forms of destructive and aggressive behavior. The school authorities requested his removal from school and neighbors refused to allow their children to play with him. His health was very poor during this and succeeding school years; his illnesses included pneumonia and repeated upper respiratory infections.

In a private boarding school his behavior became worse. After three months of infantile behavior, during which he developed night terrors, screaming that he saw horrible faces on the wall, he had to be removed from the school. The family moved again and placed the patient in a suburban public school. He was then 8 years old and in the third grade. He failed to pass the 3B grade. He continued to be a severe disciplinary problem. In a new public school his behavior was excellent for three weeks and then became worse than ever. He was defiant and totally unmanageable. He always said that he hated his teacher. He showed unpredictable impulsive behavior, climbed the steampipes, spilled ink on the desks, giggled, screamed, crawled around the floor on his hands and knees, exposed himself and masturbated openly in the classroom, showed an exaggerated desire to collect worthless odds and ends, was oblivious of danger, sometimes when over-excited and angry running headlong into the door. It was said that everyone in the neighborhood considered him "crazy." At home he became more stubborn and disobedient, began to "steal things and lie," developed a twitching of the eyes and involuntary movements of his arms and shoulders. He could not sit still for a moment. His teachers reported that he showed initial interest but carried nothing through to completion, that he gave up easily when encountering obstacles, but that he responded to praise and encouragement.

For a period of two months he was under the care of the Bureau of Child Guidance. In play therapy there it was observed that he showed great tenderness to small animals, that he was constantly asking for expressions of love from the examiner; was neat and orderly in putting toys away, was frequently seen looking for something in waste baskets and desks, and when asked about this replied that he was looking for something, he did not know what. In his work with clay he always cut up the clay father and mother, destroying them completely, then quickly punished the clay figure that represented himself. It later came out that the child who was punished was inclined to feel that the punishing parents were not his real parents, but kidnappers who have killed his real parents. It was plain that the patient believed this concerning his adoptive parents. He said that his adoptive mother told him she found him in a milk box, and that other mothers got their babies in a store. As treatment at the Bureau of Child Guidance resulted in no change, hospitalization was recommended.

The patient on admission was tall, underweight, and poorly developed for his age. Exophthalmos and pallor were conspicuous. Physical and neurological examinations were negative.

The patient was given three psychometric examinations while hospitalized — the first in December, 1940, the second in February, 1941, and the third in April, 1942. The first and second tests resulted in IQ ratings of 121 and 120 respectively on the Stanford Binet scale (revision M). These tests placed him in the very superior group as regards general intelligence. He showed excellent reasoning and judgment, good insight into practical problems and excellent rote memory; particular capacity in handling practical situations was evident. His language ability was about average for his chronologic age, but was relatively poor in comparison to other aspects of his intelligence.

Ten months later, by the Stanford Binet test (revision L) he showed an IQ of 112 (plus). The lower score as compared to previous tests, seems to have been due to spottiness of successes on verbal material; his work with concrete manual materials was better. He showed greater interest in the non-verbal materials, made excellent time scores, and demonstrated excellent analytic ability. (Revision L consists of more verbal tests than revision M in which the patient's score was higher.) In the later psychometric tests at both Bellevue Hospital and the Jewish Board of Guardians' school, similar results were obtained; the patient was classified as of superior intelligence, with either weakening or blocking in the verbal field.

The Rorschach record, taken in April, 1942 and interpreted by Z. Piotrowski, indicates either organic cerebral disorder or schizophrenia. The main conclusions are:

1. No drive or ambition for any constructive achievement.
2. Marked anxiety, which seems to be alleviated by preoccupation with disparate details.
3. Marked tendency to intellectual perseveration and emotional lability.
4. Shallow affectivity. (Apparently the child responds to emotional changes, but with inadequate emotions.)
5. Preoccupation with sexual ideas, not without feelings of uneasiness, even fear.

The patient appears to consider himself frustrated emotionally and seems frequently to be thwarted in his desire for friendly and affectionate relationships because of intellectual difficulties and self-centered affectivity that drives others away.

Course in Hospital

The patient remained in the Hospital for 17 months.

Throughout his hospitalization his general condition and behavior changed very little in quality, but fluctuated somewhat in degree. Benzedrine medication was given for several months; later small doses of insulin and Vitamin B1 were given, and more recently the patient has been on luminal. None of these measures have appeared effective.

From the beginning the patient was excluded by other children, was easily reduced to tears by their threats or blows, made no effort to defend himself. He was called by them "crazy," "baby," and "sissy." When his behavior was not excessively infantile his manner was haughty and indifferent. He showed no pleasure in his activities. He was extremely neat about his person, but his drawers were filled with a conglomeration of worthless, hoarded odds and ends. He was possessive and selfish with his belongings. Even during his best periods he was a disturbing influence on the ward.

In his play therapy periods he was hyperactive, indulging in ceaseless, aimless activity for long periods. He often played with such intensity as to appear to exclude the environment entirely. For the most part he showed reluctance to express himself verbally. His play was unproductive, but there were rare flashes of significant and expressive material produced in phantasies. (This will be described as it relates to the art work.)

When the patient had been in the hospital about four months, his behavior became more impulsive and reckless. He narrowly escaped being run over by an automobile and was difficult to manage, not only on walks, but also on the ward, where he frequently struck his teachers. His hoarding tendency increased and he was infantile and provocative, whining much of the time and being more obviously rejected by the other children. About this time he came to use a Teddy bear as an alter ego, and through this medium showed considerable indecision as to whether he was a boy or a girl. From this time on, Teddy made frequent appearances in the playroom, and was always closely identified with the patient's own problems.

For the remainder of the autumn the patient's actions during play therapy were restless and repetitive, and his behavior remained emotionally infantile and hyperactive. This situation has continued from the time when the second examiner began her observation of him. There were, however, brief periods during which his play was relatively productive.

The patient has used toy guns to shoot the examiner repeatedly and has always said that she is not killed but has been gassed; he enjoys frightening her, and gives the impression that he is killing her by inches. For the most part, however, the patient's attitude has been that of infantile affection and dependence. He has cheated in the examiner's favor in games on many occasions, and has always refused to play in the sandbox unless she was sitting on its edge.

On the day before discharge, during his play hour, the patient, in Teddy's voice, told the story of Hänsel and Gretel, completely omitting Gretel after the first sentence, and ending with the statement that after the stepmother died Hänsel came back and he and his father lived happily ever after. Following a brief period of silent play, the patient announced: "Teddy said Frank killed himself. Frank didn't kill himself." Asked why Teddy said that, he replied after considerable silence, "Teddy says he killed Frank or he's going to, I don't know which." He pounded violently on the pounding board and then said, "Now I'm Frank's ghost. Now I'm Frank — now his ghost. I guess I'm both." He was making many weird grimaces and moving his hands in an eerie fashion. There had been no previous expression of suicide ideas by the patient.

Throughout the last six months of the patient's hospitalization his behavior on the ward had become progressively unmanageable. He was provocative with other children, whining in an infantile fashion when they fought him. He was noisy, disturbing, heedless and uncooperative. He had the habit of taking things from other boys' drawers and of collecting all sorts of small gadgets, more avidly than before. He occasionally accused other boys of disturbing him, of staring at him and of opening his door, when they were nowhere near. He became progressively restless, nervous and irritable.

He was discharged to the care of his parents, to be followed weekly in the out-patient department.

In view of the fire that the patient set in his mother's bed at home shortly after his discharge from the hospital, and of the suicide ideas expressed in his phantasy, it was considered advisable to recommend further hospitalization. The family were unwilling to accept the suggestion at the time; but he was examined at Bellevue Hospital the following September.

History Following Discharge from New York Psychiatric Hospital

According to a summary of a report from Bellevue Hospital to the Bureau of Child Guidance after the patient had been examined there during several weeks in 1942, the opinion at first was that he was a child of superior gifts who was suffering from a psychoneurosis with anxiety features. A reconsideration of the case suggested that a better interpretation might be that of psychopathic personality with lack of motivation, poor social insight, inability of relation to other persons and infantile impulsiveness.

The Rorschach test at Bellevue showed an unusually lengthy response for a child — 56 responses — and lack of drive to achievement and flatness of affect, with compulsive features.

The Bellevue Hospital report indicated that he would be a suitable candidate for the Children's Division of Rockland State Hospital, but since there were no vacancies there he was kept at home and attended public school for two terms. In February, in the second school term, difficulties arose in his school adjustment under a new teacher. Again his behavior became infantile and disruptive. The mother went to the school and reported that he was again setting fires at home; it was felt that this was too dangerous a symptom for the school to deal with and he was therefore suspended from school. The mother was anxious to place him away from home.

Transfer to a Social Agency School

The patient was admitted to the school of the Jewish Board of Guardians and had been there for a year and a half when the writer last saw him. A report of his adjustment at this school will follow after the art work has been described.

First Phase of Patient's Art Work: Copying and Tracing

In the first art session Frank gave the impression of a boy younger than 9 years of age. His large head was supported on a delicate body by a slender neck; his dark and sensitive eyes stood out against his sallow skin, and a friendly smile appeared easily in response to sympathy and understanding. Whenever his restless movements ceased, he appeared fatigued. There was, therefore, some truth in his excuse for suspending work after brief periods of concentration; but such pleas had become his habitual method of evading any effort demanded either at home or in school.

FIG. 1. AMERICAN FLAG

Here is an example of a ruled American flag in red, white and blue crayon, typical of the patient's reproductions of similar flags of other nations. Such drawings were varied by the copying of heads of American presidents or the devices of well known advertisements. These were interspersed with the continuous modelling of such small seasonal objects in plastecine as the patient had been taught to make in school, constant repetition of turkeys, Christmas trees and Santa Clauses or Easter rabbits and birds' nests.

In the first art period he chose to model seven small objects in plastecine. His behavior was childishly playful and hyperkinetic. He would break away from his work to hide behind a door or crawl under the table. But when his positive achievements were praised and foolish behavior ignored, he tended to subside and return to whatever he was making.

For weeks he continued to model the usual subjects of public school art; seasonal objects suitable for Thanksgiving, Christmas and Easter were made over and over again. Work in plastecine alternated with crayon copies of heads of American presidents, ruled flags and advertisements. His modelling and drawing were entirely repetitive and lacked expressive significance.

FIG. 2. LUCKY STRIKE ADVERTISEMENT

This reproduction of an advertisement was drawn in one of the first art sessions, before the patient had come to believe that he had anything original within himself that was worthwhile expressing or that would win response from some other person.

Two such stereotypes are illustrated: a ruled American flag in red, white and blue crayon (Fig. 1) and a Lucky Strike advertisement (Fig. 2). These were typical of what the patient produced during the first few weeks of the art sessions, and identical in design with drawings he had made during the previous spring in school. When asked on one occasion whether he could draw something other than an American flag, he smiled brightly and replied, "Oh yes, I could do a Red Cross Flag."

Second Phase: Original Objective Landscapes

Frank was urged in each art period, to try and make something that he had seen in the life about him but had never made before. A tiny figure that he said was the "Statue of Liberty" finally emerged from the plastecine. Beside this he set a small bridge, which he explained was the Washington Bridge as seen from the hospital window. The Statue of Liberty had been observed by the patient from a ferry boat.

This was the boy's first attempt to create from his own experience and observation. In order to develop his efforts, he was urged to model other aspects of the city. To encourage this it was suggested that a large sheet of paper could be used as a map of New York. On this he could place the Statue of Liberty and the Washington Bridge at the opposite ends of the Hudson River; then other landmarks of the city could be added to the plan. Frank responded with enthusiasm to this proposal and before leaving the art room he had suggested how, at the next session, he would make a park with its trees and lake and some of the high buildings downtown.

Frank entered the room for the next art period not only ready to go ahead with the idea but certain now of what he wanted to do; he had planned, he said, to draw large pictures of the Hudson River instead of putting small models on a map. The first design would have the Washington Bridge and the hospital beside it. "Then I'll draw other pieces of the Hudson, one with Grant's Tomb and the viaduct and another with high buildings downtown and then the Statue of Liberty and Governor's Island. I've been there and seen the tents and the stew-house and everything. And when they are all done I'll stick the pieces together in one long picture."

By the time Frank proposed this unexpectedly large scheme, he had begun, however slightly, to free himself from his stereotyped copying; he was now willing to attempt from time to time some small free-hand drawings. A train at a signal crossing in a country landscape showed genuine promise of creative expression.

Although he continued to show signs of fatigue after periods of fifteen or twenty minutes, he nevertheless persisted in his original and ambitious plan, until all four of the large Hudson River and New York City drawings were complete (Figs. 3, 4, 5 and 6). So important became the completion of this project to him that he was willing to continue work on a single design for three or four successive days.

While Frank began to show considerable imagination in the conception of these Hudson River scenes, and a bold directness in creating such designs, he was still unable to use his crayons freely enough to express what he felt. It was then necessary to release his creative expression by overcoming what remained of his stereotyped use of crayons.

When he attempted to fill in the Hudson River in front of Grant's Tomb with a solid mass of straight blue lines, he was asked to stop and feel for a moment, what the water in a river was really like. Was it thick and solid and still, in the way that he had begun to make it? He considered the question and then, moving his hands rhythmically. he described the way in which the river's current flowed. Crayon strokes on paper, he was reminded, could be used as well as his arms to express the rhythmic movement of water. He tried out this new

FIG. 3. GRANT'S TOMB AND THE VIADUCT

These four objective crayon landscapes show how the patient gained the confidence to express himself, and apply his powers of observation and experience to his creative work.

The patient's development of the structure of the viaduct, the movement of the flag, the rhythmic flow of the river, are in striking contrast to the previous inactive stereotypes.

idea on a piece of scratch paper and immediately realized that he could give a live and sinuous quality to the river. Ever since that day he has continued experimenting to find ways of getting the rhythmic feeling of water. Movement began also to appear even in the usually static American flag as it rippled gaily over Governor's Island in one of the Hudson River pictures.

However much satisfaction the patient gained in carrying out these New York City designs, it did not prevent him from sudden relapses into repetitive drawing. Now he began to recopy his original pictures instead of the old school tracings. Urged to find a new theme, he eventually suggested Coney Island. When it was verified that he lived near this place, and was not planning to copy a picture, the new idea was approved.

Only the third and last of the Coney Island pictures will be described (*Frontispiece* Fig. 7). This series was done in water colors

FIG. 4. WASHINGTON BRIDGE — A PHANTASY OF SPRING AND WINTER
This drawing represents a fusion of objective observation and an imaginative expression of phantasy. While making the picture the patient asked whether he might draw a house and garden instead of the playground that was actually there. Making snow on the left side of the bridge (scarcely visible in the reproduction) while the sun was shining and it was spring on the right, caused the patient to laugh and point out the discrepancy.

which the patient began to use for the first time. This large design, 24 by 36 inches, was made in two separate sections. The upper part had been intended originally as the entire picture; but since only the top of the parachute jump, and the upper part of the Ferris wheel and the roller coaster found a place in it, Frank proposed to continue the scene on a second sheet of paper. He therefore added the base of the amusement structures and set the boardwalk, the beach and the sea on the lower section of the picture.

As he learned to control the use of color it became gradually possible to show him how to use the swing of his whole arm in freeing the movement of his timid brush strokes. How effectively he achieved a sense of life and movement is evident in the rhythmic sweep of the black roller coaster tracks and the free curve of the yellow Ferris wheel. The complicated staircase for mounting the Ferris wheel is

FIG. 5. STATUE OF LIBERTY, FERRY BOAT AND GOVERNOR'S ISLAND

In this scene, the patient was again picturing places that he had himself visited on a ferry boat trip.

painted an electric blue and the parachute jump is orange. The sand is golden, the waves of the sea blue and green and the railing of the boardwalk is silhouetted in black against the brightly painted amusement park.

In spite of many pauses for talk and play, as well as some fooling, Frank remained absorbed and carried both the Hudson River and Coney Island series to completion during the first few months of his art work. But no human figures had yet appeared in this phase of his creative expression. Only one phantasy pattern had been produced in the Washington Bridge scene, where winter and spring appear simul-

taneously on opposite banks of the river; it will be described and discussed later in relation to other aspects of his phantasy pictures.

Because of the wealth of· such material, only some typical examples
of phantasy expression will be described. Certain subjects that concern the patient's most acute anxiety had never been verbalized in the
play therapy sessions, but would break through spontaneously in an
art period while he was drawing another subject. It was sometimes
difficult to overcome resistance to the expression of the more fright-

FIG. 6. DOWNTOWN NEW YORK

When this view developed, only one of the skyscrapers was colored
red and the rest were left in outline. As the skyline expanded, what
had started out to be the Chrysler Building became a tall church at
the right. In the center is a building under construction, and beside
the church are billboards with colored advertisements. An airplane,
an automobile and a ferry give an impression of activity, but there
are no people.

ening dreams. On one such occasion the dream was first pantomimed
and only later made into a picture with its disturbing details.

A recurrent volcano dream was an important symbol in the early
expression of the patient's anxiety. On the first day he modelled a
small volcano, after announcing "I want to make a mountain," and
declaring, as he completed it, "It's a volcano." Adding a hole on the

summit, he asked, "How deep is a volcano?" He emphasized the importance of a path that circled around and up the mountain, and showed how someone climbing the path dropped into the hole at the top of the volcano.

Three weeks later Frank volunteered further information about a volcano dream of the previous night. There had been, he said, both a

FIG. 8. VOLCANO AND EARTHQUAKE DREAM — EXTERIOR VIEW
Recurrent anxiety dreams were frequent, but the patient refused to tell about them. Through drawings, they were first projected and then described. This shows the outside of the dream volcano, erupting black lava and below it the great cracks caused by the accompanying earthquake.

volcano and an earthquake in this dream. He described vividly the exterior of the scene, the huge cracks of the earthquake at the foot of the volcano and how he had fallen into one of these open cracks and how he would repeatedly succeed in escaping through another opening in the earth (Fig. 8). After drawing this picture, he made a second small design of the same dream (Fig. 9) elaborating in a diagrammatic fashion the way in which, within the jagged crack, the lava pouring out of the volcano rushed past him, while he was protected from it within a cave. "I lost my little nail on my pinky finger," he said. "And then it grew again. I escape to a ledge and hang on by my hands. Then I come up a stairs," drawing it — "and then I arrive out of the crack in the earth."

FIG. 9. VOLCANO AND EARTHQUAKE DREAM — INTERIOR OF CRACK

This is an enlargement of a single crack in the earth, caused by the earthquake. It illustrates how the patient descended into the earth by means of stairs and escaped from the downpouring lava into a cave, where he hung on by means of his "pinky finger." The swirling lines in the center show how he moved in and out of the earth. The dark, somewhat circular line of his repeated movement covers what was originally drawn as a staircase. The arrow in the lower right corner shows where, as the patient described it, the nurse tickled his feet and woke him.

Again and again he repeated this episode, tracing the movements with his crayon, faster and faster, down into the cave, then up the stairs and back again into the crack of the earth. In continuing this re-creation of a repetitive dream he reached back into an almost self-hypnotic dreamlike state; and as he moved the crayon more and more rapidly in and out of the earth by means of the staircase, his speed changed the steps into a continuous line. Suddenly he stopped this

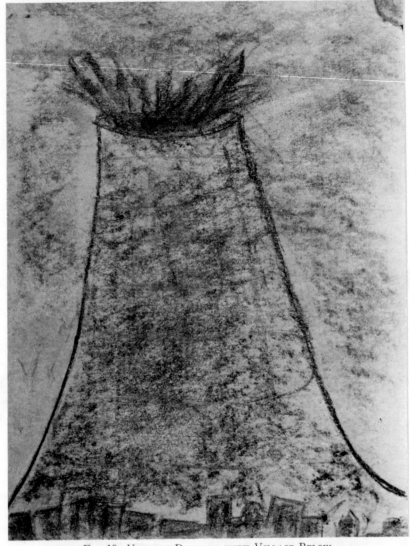

FIG. 10. VOLCANO DRAWING WITH VILLAGE BELOW

This is a large colored chalk drawing made some time after the two
preceding dream pictures. Although it appeared as one of the Fire
Theme Series, it is introduced here because of its close relation to
the dream drawings. It shows the spontaneous transformation of
the volcano theme, starting in the previous drawings as an anxiety
symbol, into this joyous and peaceful scene; the sun is shining, the
sky is blue and a quiet village is silhouetted in gray chalk at the base
of the volcano. Pleased with the effect of this picture, the patient
smiled and said, "Isn't it a lovely day!" There remained no vestige
of the anxiety previously associated with volcanos.

circular movement and marked in the picture a spot where the nurse had tickled his feet and awakened him from the dream. This broke the dream state. This spot is marked by an arrow in the right hand corner of the drawing.

Some months later, similar bad dreams about a volcano with fire and lava pouring forth were reported by the patient to the psychiatrist. But these dreams were vocalized only some time after they had been modelled and drawn in the art sessions.

A transformation of the volcano theme from an expression of anxiety to one of peace and joy occurred spontaneously toward the end of that year. It was one of eight pictures drawn around the theme of fire which will shortly be described. In this large chalk drawing, "Volcano with a Village Below," (Fig. 10) the colors are quite vivid; the sky is bright blue, the sun is shining and a purple path winds up the russet mountain to the crater of the volcano where gray smoke rises from its cone. At the base of this volcanic mountain, Frank drew in gray chalk the silhouette of a peaceful village. Pleased with the effect of the picture, he looked up as he completed it, and said, "Isn't it a lovely day!" There remained, from that time, no vestige of the anxiety previously associated with these volcanos.

THIRD PHASE: PHANTASIES AND DREAMS OF DEVILS AND SKELETONS, GHOSTS AND "GOO-GOOS"

The next group of phantasies and phantasy designs relates to skeletons, devils, ghosts and various forms of death and destruction. While for descriptive convenience certain types of phantasy are here grouped together, they did not appear originally in any such sequence, but were interspersed unexpectedly among various series of pictures already planned.

Skeleton Dreams and Compulsive Repetition

Frank had been coming to the art sessions for five months when the drawing of a skeleton dream was obtained. He had, by that time, developed many original pictures in the Fire Theme and Circus Series, which will be described below. On that day the writer had just praised the circus drawings that the patient had completed. The reason why they were so good, he was told, was that he was using his own ideas and experience and was not just repeating what he had done before. To this Frank replied, "But dreams repeat."

The writer presumed that he was referring to his volcano dreams, but he continued, "Sometimes I'm scared when I dream." When asked what had scared him this time, there was no reply. But instead of speaking, the patient pantomimed his fear; he hung his head, rolling his eyes and running his hand across his neck to suggest throat slitting. Asked what all this action meant, he simply replied, "Dead."

Had he dreamed all this? He replied, "Yes, a skeleton."

He would say no more. So the writer slipped a sheet of paper before him and asked whether he could make a picture of that skeleton. Resistance to the suggestion came in the reply that, "It's invisible."

Inquiry as to how the skeleton looked in this dream finally led him to select a white crayon and draw the skeleton form he had mentioned. He made the skeleton, including all its bones and hat, in a single swiftly drawn line without ever lifting his pencil from the paper. He drew this gun also in white crayon to the right of the skeleton. "He's shot by an invisible man. An invisible man shoots the gun" — this was also drawn in white crayon. "Now the man is dead" — pointing to the skeleton. "The other man"— meaning the one who shot the gun — "is visible now."

Frank then retraced the outline of the man in white crayon as well as the white gun with violet crayon. Then suddenly seizing a round enamel ash tray from the table beside him, he covered over the drawing of the skeleton with three interlocking circles, drawn in violet. He then laughed self-consciously at what he had done, announcing, "See the Ballantine label." Not satisfied with having covered the skeleton with overlapping rings, he then did the same to the violet man and his violet gun (Fig. 11).

Unable to verbalize this anxiety dream, the boy first succeeded in pantomiming it and then expressing his dread concerning death and destruction in a picture. But the overlapping circles appeared to veil again this anxiety that he revealed more completely than he had intended. In dealing with this anxiety dream, he had been able to verbalize for the first time his own awareness of the compulsive repetition of his dreams. About two months later he spoke again of "seeing skeletons in my dreams; they scare me."

In the time between the volcano and skeleton dreams, the patient described another elaborate dream to the psychiatrist; he told how, after falling from one sewer into another and losing various pieces of his body, he finally saw himself as a skeleton. Then, after being buried in a grave, he came out again, whole and alive.

There are many similarities to be found in the phantasy patterns of the skeleton and volcano dreams. All of them are related to the patient's overwhelming anxiety, expressed in symbols of death and destruction; but they are always followed by a safe escape or rebirth.

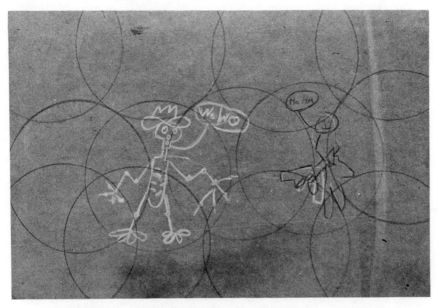

FIG. 11. SKELETON DREAM

This is one of a group of phantasies, relating to skeletons, devils, ghosts and various forms of death and destruction. The skeleton dream was obtained in spite of the patient's refusal to speak of this bad dream of the previous night.

"Sometimes I'm scared when I dream," he stated.

When asked what had scared him, there was no reply. Instead of speaking he pantomimed his fear, with a gesture of throat slitting. Asked whether he had dreamed this, he replied, "Yes, a skeleton."

He would say no more, so the writer slipped a sheet of paper before him and asked whether he could draw the skeleton. Although he declared that it was invisible he finally selected a white crayon and drew the skeleton of this design rapidly, without raising his crayon from the page. As he printed "Wo-wo" at the skeleton's mouth, he emitted the sound himself. As he explained how an invisible man shot an invisible gun at the man who turned into a skeleton, he drew them both in white crayon. After the man was dead the white assailant and his white gun became visible and were retraced in violet as they now appear in this picture. Then seizing a round ash tray, the patient covered over the drawing of the skeleton with three interlocking circles in violet. He laughed self-consciously as he explained this as the "Ballantine Label." Not satisfied with having covered the skeleton with overlapping rings, he then did the same to the violet man and his violet gun. In illustrating this dream, the patient had, for the first time, verbalized his awareness of the compulsive repetition of his dreams.

One of the devil drawings that Frank made without comment is shown (Fig. 12).

The "Goo-goo" Phantasies and the Problem of Adoption

In the fifth art session while carving his initials in a block of plastecine, Frank volunteered, "My hobby is animals." Asked whether he had pets of his own, he replied, "No, but I like all but wild ones."

FIG. 12. A DEVIL

This quick sketch of a devil made by the patient, while developing his Circus Series, represents a sudden breaking through of previous anxiety.

Without preamble, he then announced suddenly, "The 'Goo-goo' man shits at the mother and the lady 'Goo-goo' made piss at the father." He was asked how many "Goo-goos" there were, and replied, "An uncle, an aunt, a father, a mother, children, one teeny-weeny cousin and a baby."

He then broke off a piece of plastecine, rolling it into a ball half an inch in diameter and said, "This is 'Goo-goo' shit. Now I want to make a great big shit." This time the ball was four times as large.

Then he announced, as he rolled out a snake of plastecine, "Now I'll make a great big piss and I'll put the piss around the shit." Having done this, he observed with satisfaction, "See how big the piss is."

He then proceeded to crush what he had made until it was quite formless; the plastecine was then returned to the cabinet. It was evident from the way Frank turned his attention to his box of treasured plastecine models that the episode was over. He was asked how long he had known this "Goo-goo" family. "I just lately made it up," he said. The truth of this statement and the real significance of the "goo-goo" phantasy, as the dramatization of Frank's hostility toward his adoptive parents, was not clarified until months later; then the writer discovered, by a careful check of related dates in the psychiatrist's and social worker's records, that the patient had been officially told of his adoption exactly three days before he had symbolized his resentment against his adoptive parents by the creation of the "Goo-goo" family.

When Frank on the previous Sunday had been officially informed of his adoption by his adoptive parents, the mother had reported that he made no comment and showed no emotional reaction to this news. She therefore concluded that he had not been disturbed by the information. Yet three days later he created the "Goo-goo" man and the "Goo-goo" lady who turned their destructive defecation against the mother and father, who are obviously the patient's adoptive parents in this phantasy.

An original expansion of Frank's creative expression followed this release of his hostility. He asked for crayons, announcing, "Now I'll draw something I don't think I've ever drawn before. But I won't tell you what it will be." A gay multi-colored butterfly pattern appeared (Fig. 13); the wings were variegated but the bodies black, a possible association with the previously modelled "shit." This design was drawn swiftly, with a complete absorption in the work as it developed. When it was finished, Frank was exhilarated by the beauty of his bright butterflies and asked that they be carefully kept for him until the next art session. This was clearly a spontaneous sublimation into satisfying esthetic form of what had begun as a crude release of aggression against the adoptive parents. Similar expressions of hostility concerning the inadequacy of parents have been expressed by other behavior problem children.

Modelling is one of the simplest and most direct channels of expression for encouraging the release of repressed thoughts and feelings associated with prohibitions concerning sexual problems or obscene language. If such outbursts of repressed feelings are permitted by an adult who gives neither undue approval or disapproval to such crude expressions of what has long been buried and forbidden, the patient speedily gains relief and is soon able to make use of this liberated energy in forms of spontaneous and original creative expression. The butterfly design which came after the "Goo-goo" phantasy is a single example of such spontaneous sublimation following the use of excretory symbols. Sublimation through art can sometimes be encouraged by directing the attention of the patient to the possible

FIG. 13. BUTTERFLY DESIGN AND THE "GOO-GOO" PHANTASY

This multi-colored butterfly pattern appeared spontaneously after the patient had released his intense hostility to his adoptive parents by modelling a destructive phantasy about a "Goo-goo" man and lady who hurled "piss" and "shit" at each other. He destroyed these modelled forms of defecation and then created the butterfly design. This is but one example of such sublimation.

use for creative expression of just those themes that he has refused to deal with in either words or play therapy. An example of such art will be discussed later in describing how, when this patient avoided consistently the subject of his fire-setting propensity, he was nevertheless stimulated to produce a series of original designs on the theme of fire.

Two more "Goo-goo" episodes followed later with the psychiatrist. The first one occurred four days after the modelling of the "Goo-goo," "piss" and "shit" and a week after Frank was informed of his adoption. The psychiatrist reports:

> The examiner was represented as being in a house on fire. The patient explained that he had set the house on fire because he did not realize that it was the examiner who lived in the house, but thought rather that it was a certain evil man called the "Goo-goo" man. This person, he said, defecates into the face of people and then kills them. In this manner he killed the Teddy Bear's father and mother.

The Teddy Bear in the play therapy sessions was used as his alter ego and so here we have a direct statement projected onto Teddy, who is Frank, concerning the patient's intense emotion over the loss of his real parents.

A month later, one other reference to the "Goo-goos" was recorded by the psychiatrist:

> Said the patient: "The Teddy bear was found hanged by the neck." He acted out his words by stringing up the Teddy bear with his pants belt. He then took the bear down and stated that Teddy was restored to life. Asked who hanged Teddy, he replied, "I don't know. Teddy is in great danger. He does not realize that his stepmother is a 'Goo-goo' lady."
>
> When the examiner asked what could be done to protect the Teddy bear from his stepmother, the patient answered, "I think he should run away to his home in the hospital where Frank can take care of him." He then explained that he, Frank, was Teddy's new father.

In these three "Goo-goo" phantasies the patient has clearly symbolized his pent-up hostility toward his adoptive parents and thereby released the deep resentment that he never dared express directly to them. Identifying himself with Teddy, who is in great danger, the patient calls the stepmother a "Goo-goo" and describes how Teddy who is rejected, flees to Frank, the new parent for love and protection. Here the two aspects of the patient's personality are dramatized in Teddy and Frank; later, in moments of danger and destruction, another phantasy reported by the psychiatrist, shows the two aspects of himself in the roles of Frank and his ghost.

Apart from these aggressive phantasies directed against the adoptive parents, no overt reference to his adoption or the mystery of his real parents was ever made by the patient during his hospitalization. On only one occasion, during the seventh month of art work, was an oblique reference to the subject recognizable when Frank said, "I know the date of my birthday, but I don't know where I was born."

The writer used this opening to ask him how long he had known of his adoption. "One day," he replied without embarrassment. "A little while ago, they told me in the Park." Relief that this overwhelming problem of his life could now be spoken about openly, was shown in the increased friendliness of the patient during the last part of that day's art session.

FIG. 14. BOY SCOUT FIRE

This is the first of a series of imaginative pictures created around the theme of fire. They were the results of an experiment, ini·iated by the writer in an attempt to release phantasy material that might relate to the patient's fire-setting propensity. No inform·tion concerning this matter had been verbalized by the patient up to that time.

In view of the untrue and contradictory explanations of birth and the frightening threats against masturbation that the mother offered the patient, is it not probable that she also thwarted his earliest childish curiosity and questioning about fire, and punished him physically for his first innocent attempt to strike a match? Required to repress many normal expressions of spontaneous emotion, lied to about birth, frightened about sex, forbidden to fight or play with other children, or to have live pets of his own, it was almost inevitable that, in order to survive, the patient would need to create some phantasy world of his own. That it was filled with skeletons and ghosts and fear of violent destruction by volcanos emitting lava and flames is therefore not too surprising. More intense than even a castration complex was his overwhelming fear of complete annihilation. At 9 years of age he had been given no opportunity to develop his ego; and he had been made to believe that death in his sleep would be the penalty for masturbation. His only release for his frustrated emotions and inhibited activities was found in obstructing the authority of his parents at home and of his teachers in school by the wild and erratic behavior that has been described in the clinical history. Not only did he come to be regarded as "crazy" in school and in the neighborhood where he

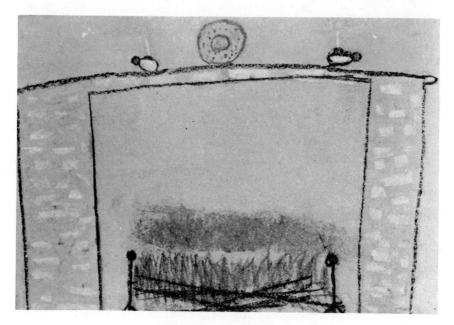

FIG. 15. FIRE IN FIREPLACE

Not only is there a fire in the fireplace, but there are also candles burning on the mantel and a flame design on the center of the plate between the candles.

lived, but his own fears of being "nutty" began to appear in a number of phantasies.

His inability to verbalize his acute anxiety was undoubtedly related to the severe punishments he had received and to the mother's incessant threats of destruction as a punishment for such misbehavior. His phantasies in the play therapy and art sessions therefore began at last to express the intensity of his hostility toward the adoptive mother that he did not dare release in words. The "Goo-goos" expressed aggression against both adoptive parents. But in two other phantasies, the mother was the target of his hostility. In one play session Teddy's mother had been killed by having her throat slashed by her brother, who was then electrocuted for the deed. In another interview with the psychiatrist, Frank modified the story of Hänsel and Gretel by quickly eliminating Gretel. When he ended the story with the death of the stepmother, Hänsel came back home and he and his father lived happily ever after. In a phantasy about burying a dead soldier in the

FIG. 16. CITY FIRE

A fireman is playing a hose on the conflagration, which is breaking forth from all the windows; a man is leaping from a high window and another is jumping into a life net. Human figures appear here for the first time.

sandbox, the boy said that it made no difference that the soldier was lost because he had no friends and his parents who had been his only real friends were dead. Soon after being dismissed from the hospital he set a fire in his mother's bed.

FIRE THEME AS RELATED TO FIRE-SETTING

Two aspects of the fire-setting problem will be dealt with in this paper: first, the series of imaginative pictures created around the theme of fire and second, the way in which the patient, at the end of his period in the hospital, when his behavior had deteriorated on the ward and in the school, expressed his hostility toward the hospital as he had toward his mother, with threats of burning down and exploding the building.

A previous reference has been made to the development of this series of fire pictures as an oblique means of releasing repressed material that the patient was either unable or unwilling to deal with consciously. No information concerning the patient's motivation for fire-setting was derived in either the play therapy or art sessions. As a conscious experiment the writer therefore asked Frank, as he was

FIG. 17. BURNING OF THE NORMANDIE

This design was drawn spontaneously on the day after the news of this disaster. The ship was drawn in dark gray, with three smokestacks against an intense blue sky; the ropes that bind it to the dock are black. Great orange and red flames are bursting from the decks and hull. The drawing has a strength and beauty that are quite dramatic and moving.

completing the Coney Island paintings, whether he thought it might be interesting later to make pictures of the kinds of fires that could be made by man or happen through nature. The patient's response was instantaneous; he suggested that there might be "A boy scout fire built in the woods, a fire in a fireplace, a trolley or an apartment house on fire and many others." It was at the end of an art period that this conversation took place.

In the next art session the Fire Theme series was begun. A new box of vivid chalks was offered to stimulate the work. The first fire pictures executed were those originally planned — "A Boy Scout Fire in the Woods" (Fig. 14), followed by "A Fire in a Fireplace" (Fig. 15). "The Burning of the Normandie" (Fig. 17) was produced spontaneously by Frank the morning after the actual event. The design has an impressive strength and beauty with the gray hulk of the ship

FIG. 18. BURNING LEAVES

This drawing, which the patient called "Burning Leaves," was one of the brightest and most imaginative of his designs. The small house to the left has a green-blue roof of tiles, outlined in red violet; a basketful of gaily colored wash is waiting to be hung on a clothes line; some bright green trees are silhouetted against a blue sky and from a pile of burning leaves gray smoke is rising. See color plate I.

at its dock silhouetted against a bright blue sky, while orange and yellow flames break through its decks. "A City Fire" was the next picture made (Fig. 16). Human figures appear here, the first in any of this patient's art work: a fireman directing a hose on the conflagration that is breaking forth from all the windows, a man leaping from a flaming window, another jumping into a life net far below. "Out of each window a flame was shooting," Frank explained. "All but one, that was closed up."

He had pointed out a similar blocked window in the fireworks picture. There is a possibility that this double symbol related to a window on the postcard picture of the hotel where his adoptive mother had told him he was born.

The volcano design that followed has already been described in connection with the modification of the volcano dreams into a serene and happy picture (Fig. 10).

The drawing that Frank called "Burning Leaves" (Fig. 18) was one of the brightest and most imaginative of his designs. There is a

FIG. 19. FIREWORKS AT THE WORLD'S FAIR

This was again a design that combined direct experience with phantasy. The trylon and perisphere of the World's Fair are in chalky pink on the left, behind the buildings, though they are scarcely visible in this reproduction. The color scheme is striking and quite different from any in this patient's other pictures. He used magenta, lime-green, red, blue, violet, orange and scarlet. These colors repeat in the fireworks across the sky as well as on the striped bands of the turrets on the central building.

small house to the left, with a green-blue roof of tiles, outlined in red violet; a basketful of gaily colored wash, waiting to be hung on a clothes line; some bright green trees against a blue sky and a pile of burning leaves above which gray smoke is rising.

The design of "Fireworks at the World's Fair" (Fig. 19) was unusual in its color scheme. The central building had towers of gaily

FIG. 20. AUTOMOBILE ON FIRE

The final picture in the fire series was done in crayons instead of chalks. It had less esthetic quality but is full of action; it had much significance in relation to one of the patient's immediate problems on that day. It shows a car on fire after hitting a telegraph pole; a little man has been hurled out of the car to the top of the pole. He is crying "Help, help" — printed in a loop coming out of his mouth.

alternating stripes of lime green, magenta, blue and red. The smaller buildings ranged in color from brown and red, to black, white, green and magenta. And the fireworks above the building, made in swirls of mingled blue and violet, orange and green, violet and orange, or scarlet and green, were a source of great delight to the patient. Unfortunately, the chalky pink forms of the trylon and perisphere are scarcely visible in the reproduction beyond the buildings on the left.

The final picture in the Fire Series was done in crayons instead of chalks. It had less esthetic quality, but it was full of action and had much significance in relation to one of the patient's immediate problems on that day. He called it "Automobile on Fire" (Fig. 20). It shows a car on fire after colliding with a telegraph pole; a little man has been hurled out of the car onto the top of the pole. He is crying "Help, help," — the words are printed in a loop coming out of his mouth. His pants hang across a wire and the sun, as Frank explained, is laughing at him from overhead. It was only after the psychiatrist had seen this drawing that it was possible to understand how accurately it depicted the patient's psychological state that morning, for he had been cornered for attempting to let other patients out on the fire escape with a key.

When the fire theme was suggested in an experimental attempt to release the patient's compulsive interest in fire into some form of creative expression, it was impossible to foresee how he might respond. But he seized upon the proposal with enthusiasm and in creating his most imaginative and beautiful pictures on the theme of fire, he began to sublimate aspects of his acute anxiety into satisfying esthetic form.*

Frank's expression of hostility toward the mother, after being dismissed from the hospital, appeared not only in the form of setting a fire in her bed, but also in a symbolic act of aggression against another woman. The patient left his parents in the audience of a movie the-

---

*A summary of the characteristics shown by children who set fires, in a study by H. Yarnell (4) includes many shown by this patient. (a) They set fires with associated phantasies to burn some member of the family who has either withheld love from the child, or become too serious a rival for the love of the parents. (b) The fires are made in or around their own home, cause little damage, are usually put out by the child himself; significance is chiefly symbolic. (c) The children show other types of asocial behavior such as running away from home, truancy, stealing and general hyperkinesis and aggression. (d) Frequently associated are learning disabilities or physical handicaps which further hamper the child in its social adjustment. (e) All children show acute anxiety and suffer from terrifying dreams and phantasies, including vivid attacks by devils, ghosts and skeletons. (f) All children have some sexual conflicts and many tell of active masturbation, sodomy or fellatio; type of activity does not seem to be significant.

atre in order to go to a washroom. Then, instead of carrying out his intention, he urinated out of the window of the toilet upon a young woman passing in the street below. The scene that ensued, when the outraged man friend of the young lady called the manager and Frank and his parents were faced with the consequences of his misbehavior, can be imagined.

THE CIRCUS SERIES AND THE DEVELOPMENT OF THE EGO

When the picture of the automobile on fire had been completed, Frank declared that he would make no more fire scenes. He was ready, however, to make some circus designs. Since this suggestion was known to be related to the circus tracings then being produced in school, this proposal was challenged by the writer. But the patient insisted that he would not copy from his classroom pictures. This circus would be different. It would have side shows that he had never

FIG. 21. BOZO, THE FIRE EATER AND THE "BIG TOP" TENT

This was the first in a long series of circus pictures. Their mood and quality differed from the patient's previous work. These designs are filled with the action of animals and people and a spirit of gaiety and playfulness pervades them. The patient identifies himself consciously or unconsciously, with various human and animal roles. He is the rich and powerful owner of the circus, who also trains performers for their acts, but he admits that he is also sometimes a clown. Unconsciously he also identified with his figure of a tight-rope walker, balancing high in the air above the crowd, for he has been observed also balancing precariously on an imaginary line across the floor of the hall. The right side of this picture was drawn first, with its circus tent, lion cage and balloon aloft. The end of the tent could not be placed on this page and the second sheet was added. When the tent end was complete, the side-show of "Bozo, the Fire-Eater" was drawn. Bozo wears a white hat and green suit, and out of his mouth come the words, "Yum, yum." He is framed in a series of green and red draperies and on the table rests a box from which flames are rising.

drawn before. That Frank could now create original designs based on his own observation of circus life was soon made clear.

The mood and quality of this Circus Series are different from that of any of Frank's previous work. These designs, filled with the action of both animals and people, express a new spirit of gaiety and playfulness. In this circus world he identifies himself first with one and then with another of the human or animal roles. Sometimes he does this consciously, as in pointing to a man in one side show who he says is himself, "I am the richest and most important man and I run and own the whole circus." Again, while drawing "Circus Clowns and

FIG. 22. TRICK DOGS

This sideshow of Toto and Jojo, the trick dogs, is framed in blue curtains and the brown dogs sit obediently on the top of their pyramids of red and blue boxes, embroidered with colored stars. A multi-colored umbrella covers the admission stand which bears a legend that adults pay 50 cents and children 15 cents.

The Crowd" (Fig. 24) he whispers confidentially to the writer, "I am sometimes also a clown." This is an accurate description of himself, when he plays for a laugh from his companions on the ward. Again, while creating the side show of "The Trick Dogs" (Fig. 22) he explains, "I train the trick dogs and everybody else in the circus."

In the "Shooting Gallery" (Fig. 23) design Frank has given quaint expression to the moving targets of little ships, pumpkin faces, swinging stars and balls, pushed up by water-jets which could only have been drawn by one who had observed closely the apparatus of such a shooting gallery. But unconscious as well as conscious identification with circus parts are shown in Frank's drawings of the "greatest show on earth." In his design of a tightrope walker, balancing in space above a crowd, he has made a vivid dramatization of an aspect of his present life problem; he has often been seen acting out this role by balancing precariously on an imaginary line across the hall floor. But he also identifies with the humbler roles of circus

FIG. 23. SHOOTING GALLERY

This expression of the moving targets of little ships, pumpkin faces, swinging stars and balls pushed up by waterjets could have been drawn only from keen personal observation of the details of such a shooting gallery.

animals; this may be either conscious or unconscious. He drew a chained elephant on the day his parents took him to the circus and added a projectile that the elephant hurled against his keeper. For many months Disney's *Dumbo* which touched him deeply has been a source of delight and comment. The baby elephant with the large pink ears was modelled and drawn a number of times before the circus series developed. When asked to tell about *Dumbo* he said, "It's both funny and sad. The sad part is where everyone was leaving Dumbo because he was different." In the elephant Dumbo the patient had found his counterpart, one who is also rejected and misunderstood.

When Frank began the circus, he drew a picture of the "Big Top Tent"; he then continued it on another paper, and added his first side show. This, he explained, was a "Fire Eater" (Fig. 21). Not only did this man have a box of fire on the table before him with which he performed, but in a loop beside his mouth was printed in large letters, "Yum yum." Frank had recently set aside the theme of fire, only to have it reassert itself unconsciously in the circus pictures.

The sense of his own importance as owner of the circus was strengthened by his announcement, "I own all the money in the world." This statement he quickly confirmed by creating a quantity of hundred and thousand dollar bills. "I am the president of the whole world," he stated on another occasion. "Everyone can have whatever they need for nothing, except the robbers."

Here he seemed to hint at a Robin Hood role for himself. In his phantasies in the play therapy and art sessions, he liked to associate himself with those whom he regards as rich and powerful, especially Roosevelt, LaGuardia and Churchill. Identification with this increasing number of rôles permitted aspects of his long stifled ego development to appear, for the first time. It is evident that now, at least, in his circus world of phantasy, he has become a very important and many-sided man.

In the midst of his dramatic identification with the action of human performers such as the clown, the tightrope walker and the fire-eater, a new theme now emerged. As he drew a second version of the "big top" he commented, "There are people waiting outside the tent," and made some small circles in black to represent them. "Is it all right," he stopped to ask, "if I just leave these black rings, without filling them in, to be a crowd?"

Assured that he might make his picture as he chose, he added dozens more of these massed circles to represent people waiting in line behind a rope. Thus was the first crowd picture drawn spontaneously. Later, others followed in which he contrived to symbolize a crowd by a mass of these small clustered circles. Such a crowd is reproduced in the "Circus Clowns and the Crowd" (Fig. 24). In this picture, the crowd sitting in the bleachers is described by the patient as, "Three-fourths of the whole world," who had come to see the show he both ran and owned.

In this spontaneous development of the theme of the crowd as audience may be found the beginning of the patient's attempt to pit his expanding ego against the larger world that still lies beyond him. Had it been possible to continue this type of creative art expression beyond the term of the patient's hospitalization, it might have become a means of returning him to a more active group life. For, in these circus pictures it is apparent that Frank's inner world of phantasy could now create an initial bridge to the outer world. With the assertion and strengthening of his own ego, he had been drawing closer to participation in the lives of other people. Had time permitted this would probably have resulted, before long, in the re-creation not only

FIG. 24. CIRCUS CLOWNS AND THE CROWD

The clowns are set on a diagonal below the bleachers, where a crowd consisting of "three-fourths of the whole world" are watching them. A section of the circus ring in red, orange and blue is visible in the foreground to the right. The foremost clown, garbed in red with a high blue hat, plays on a white bass drum decorated with a green border. The second clown, wearing a towering red and blue headdress, plays a trombone. Behind them, follows a rickety train for their coming performance. An unusual aspect of this design is the depiction of a crowd by the massing of myriad black circles. This symbolic method of expressing a crowd was first used by the patient quite spontaneously to show people waiting outside of the "big top." This was the fourth circus picture in which he drew such a crowd. In creating his circus world, the patient's conscious and unconscious identification with a number of human and animal roles was related to a growth and expansion of his still immature ego; now in the creation of the crowd, the patient began for the first time to pit his own ego development against a larger world of people.

of a circus but also of the boy's own life in a series of imaginative pictures.

Contrast Between Regression in Ward Behavior and Improvement in Art Expression

A disparity between the patient's responses in the art sessions and the rest of his ward life had been evident for some months. In order to clarify this discrepancy between the growth and expansion of the boy's personality through his art expression and his apparent regression in ward behavior, it is necessary to review briefly some aspects of his history up to the time of his admission.

Before reaching the hospital, Frank had failed to make a satisfactory adjustment at any school unless he was given particular attention by a teacher. While he was a child of superior intelligence, advanced in reading and history, he was always retarded in arithmetic. The same variability in meeting grade requirements was also evident in his studies in the hospital school. While his teacher there stated that the patient had the capacity to do the work of the older group, his disruptive and infantile behavior made it necessary to allow him to return to the younger class. Acting foolishly, crawling on the floor and clowning were typical ways in which he won attention from his classmates. He preferred to play with younger children and could easily be dominated and led into mischief by a more aggressive companion.

The clinical history suggests that the patient has never been permitted to live through certain normal phases of emotional and physical growth. The middle-aged adoptive parents, particularly the mother, not only prevented him from playing with other children, but she was also compulsive about his cleanliness and order, forbade him to fight, and after spoiling him in infancy proceeded to discipline him severely in later life for childish misdemeanors. The mother reported to the social worker that having adopted the patient at such an early age, she had believed that she could readily mold him to her will. Punishments for his shortcomings were constantly heaped upon him. Conferences with the social worker seem to have done little to alter the mother's rigid attitude in her treatment of the boy. The father blamed difficulties with the child on his wife's severity. While these talks revealed the adoptive mother's inability to understand the child, or to allow him adequate opportunities to develop his own initiative or satisfy his own need for love and sympathy through pet animals or other people, she seemed unable to change her methods of handling him.

The good opinion of their neighbors was more important to this middle-aged couple than the needs of the child. They would worry, especially the mother, as to how people would criticize his childish attachment to stuffed animals; the mother also feared criticism of the boy's demonstrativeness in public. When he expressed a spontaneous impulse, it was often rejected or misunderstood; he had to give up a stray kitten that he fed and longed to keep because his father did not like animals around the house; he was laughed at by his mother for calling a bunch of dandelions that he had picked for his teacher "a bouquet." A careful consideration of the basis of the mother's accusations against the child makes it seem probable that by blocking spontaneous childish impulses to collect bright and shiny objects, and by severe and incessant prohibitions against fighting or playing with other children, she had helped to set the pattern for his later behavior difficulties.

The boy's inclination to play with fire may well have been stimulated by the mother's original mishandling of all his spontaneous questionings about life and sex and her repression of all his positive efforts at independence. The patient's deep resentment against the mother's many lies, prohibitions and unreasonable punishments came out in various phantasies and dreams about the destruction of the mother.

The wild and reckless behavior of the patient, at home, in school and on the city streets, appears to have been intensified by the repressive measures of the adoptive mother. Could the failure of the patient to adjust to the requirements of ward life be related to his apparent inability, at that time, to meet the requirements of any formal group or of community living?

Is it not possible also that this patient's expansion of personality through his art work was an outcome of the opportunity it opened to him to develop a form of expression suitable to an immature ego that had, up to that time, been crushed by the too repressive environment of home and school? Would not the intensification of the patient's hostility and destructiveness on the ward, during the final weeks of hospitalization, be simply a repetition of his protest against the previous restrictions of school and home? Is it not possible, therefore, that with the first release of unexpressed anxiety and hostility through creative art he was, temporarily at least, unable to meet such minimum conditions of group life as a schoolroom or a hospital ward imposed?

Such an assumption would then give special significance to the patient's increasingly aggressive and destructive behavior during the final weeks of his hospitalization — to his open hostility as manifested in window breaking and other forms of destruction. It would also make comprehensible his threats to stab a nurse with a wooden knife and his avowal of an intention to burn down or explode the hospital with a bomb. However disturbing such actions and words might be in relation to ward life, might they not be correlated with positive improvement in the art sessions as a sign of an expansion of the ego and therefore a trend toward ultimate recovery?

The cumulative threats to this patient's ego development have been reviewed. Anxiety concerning his illegitimate birth and subsequent unexplained adoption, dread concerning the consequences of masturbation and inability to meet the severe standards of the adoptive mother — all these helped to motivate the patient's escape into a phantasy world. What sensitive child could face such overwhelming threats alone, without fear not only of castration but of utter annihilation?

As this unsympathetic and threatening environment forced the patient back within himself, his buried phantasy life did go on. His art work shows that, though deeply repressed, his inner life did not die; his terrors, his dreams, his hopes and his wishes can be seen to emerge gradually into channels of creative expression. He began to find release from those phantasies of death and destruction so long sealed up within. As the patient gained assurance in the use of both color and form, he was able at last to find a way to build up his ego from within, so that eventually he might be able to meet the world on more equal terms; in time the external world might even cease to threaten and overwhelm him.

Such questions and speculations were raised by the writer in reading this paper, three years ago. But not until two years later was confirmation of such a possibility received through the patient's later successful adjustment in a social agency school.

After this paper had been read at a general staff conference of the New York State Psychiatric Institute and Hospital, Dr. Nolan D. C. Lewis formulated his impression of the patient's creative expression as follows: "There is a definite sequence in this patient's art work from stereotypy to originality. He began to make ordinary things, the landscapes first — the phantasy came after that; then comes the destruction, followed by the expansion of the ego. The patient feels himself on top of the world, he has all the money to distribute, he is the chief owner of the circus.

"First there is the deep regression and then he works through to more normal expansion of the ego. The ego may even become hypertrophied. This may be a phase in getting well in adult schizophrenia; some of the craziest activity may be a healing process, the individual using it to pull himself up. As in other psychic problems, it may cause, at first, great distortions and later we see it is being used toward healing. In respect to this, time is the main thing — in estimating whether the distortion is followed by healing. We do not know yet on which side of the ledger to place these reactions — whether to the left or the right, regarding them as destruction or as healing."

Here Dr. Lewis suggested the possibility that the patient's apparently destructive behavior on the hospital ward, might be only a preamble to the interior process of healing and recovery, which has now been borne out by recent reports of the patient's successful social and academic adjustment at a country boarding school, conducted under the direction of a social agency.

ART EXPRESSION AND THE PROBLEM OF REALITY

When the examples of this patient's art work, that have just been described, were presented before the general staff conference at the New York Psychiatric Institute, the psychiatrists present agreed that, on the basis of his creative expression, the patient could not be considered schizophrenic. For they recognized that, however varied his phantasy life as expressed in the art work, he never failed to make a distinction between the imagined and the actual. This was evident in the volcano and skeleton dreams. In making pictures of objective experience, as in the case of the Hudson River and Coney Island scenes, he would sometimes stop in the middle of his work and ask, "Is it alright if I add something make-believe?"

A few examples of Frank's conscious awareness of this difference between his world of inner imagination and outer experience will be cited. For instance, in drawing the "Washington Bridge" of the Hudson River Series (Fig. 4) he referred to the actual existence of a playground on the right bank below the bridge; but he wished to know whether he could substitute a house and garden instead. Assured that he was free to decide, he made it spring, with flowers blooming on the right side of the bridge, while it was winter with snow on the left. He laughed as he pointed out the absurdity of having two opposite seasons in a single picture.

On many other occasions, the writer was able to test the patient's awareness of the difference between fact and phantasy. In making a picture of Niagara Falls, he said that it was based on a photograph that he had seen; before allowing free rein to his imagination, he wanted to know whether it would be all right to color the rocks on the sides of the falls in bright colors that were not at all like the real ones.

As another example, when Frank chose to draw the Lincoln Memorial in Washington, which he explained he had seen pictured on a postage stamp, he let his imagination develop the color scheme but held to the original structure of the building in his design. When asked about an iron rail with which he had decorated the steps of the memorial, he admitted, "It's not really there. I just made that up." The grill had improved the esthetic balance of his design, but it had not interfered with his awareness of the actual form of the structure.

In concluding the discussion on this paper at the Institute general staff conference, Dr. Lewis stated: "Certainly this patient is not schizophrenic — the dream distortion in this patient tends more into compulsive childhood anxiety."

SUBSEQUENT ADJUSTMENT IN A SOCIAL AGENCY SCHOOL

In order to complete this study, a brief report will be added tracing the patient's adjustment, both academically and socially, during a year and a half at a special school conducted under the auspices of the Jewish Board of Guardians.

Two visits were made by the writer to the school while the boy was there, in order to gather a first hand impression of his development and adjustment and also to obtain an evaluaton of his behavior from those who were in direct contact with him in that institution.*

The patient entered this school in the spring of 1943 after further difficulties in his public school adjustment because of infantile and disruptive behavior. The mother had, at that time, reported a renewal of his fire-setting at home and so the school authorities decided to suspend him. These difficulties were apparently not in evidence in his adjustment at the agency school. According to the social worker's report:

> The boy presents absolutely none of the behavior picture known to us at the time of referral. He is an active, restless, infantile youngster, but there are no temper tantrums, conspicuous attention-getting behavior, instability or withdrawal. I am the only one who has noticed any interest in fire and this came out through the boy's repeated insistence that he light my cigarette for me during interviews. The boy has not been destructive nor particularly aggressive. There is no evidence of sex play. He is compliant, friendly and sociable.

In relation to school work and behavior, the social worker reports:

> In school, in both his academic and junior group classes, the teachers say he behaves as well as any other child in the class and is not regarded as different by anyone.

The writer who checked up on his academic work, was told that he did excellently, was in fact one of the best pupils in the class and was

*Through the courtesy and interest of Mr. Herschel Alt, director of the Jewish Board of Guardians, the confidential reports on this patient's case were made available and permission was granted to use any of the data in this report. A word of appreciation is also due the staff of the school, including the principal, teachers, social workers and house mother, for their cooperation in making this information available.

doing fifth grade work; he had been recommended for shop because his academic work was outstanding; after that he was promoted to the sixth grade. A visit by the writer to his classes found Frank interested and absorbed in his studies.

In regard to his adjustment in the cottage life with other boys of his own age, the social worker reports:

> The cottage mother indicated that the boy is making a very satisfactory adjustment here. He is very cooperative and helpful in the cottage, relates nicely to the other children and gets along with them in their play and is not involved in any misconduct. He is quite attached to the house mother in a clinging and dependent fashion, apparently enjoying the chance to be near her and receive some recognition and approval. He likes to do things for her and goes out of his way to do so.

An interview by the writer with the house mother corroborated this report. Frank's own behavior, when showing the school buildings and grounds, was evidence of how well he had adapted himself to this new environment. Not only did he enjoy showing the school, the farm, the chicken houses, the swimming pool and his own cottage, but he gave the impression of really belonging to the place, emanating a sense of pride and satisfaction in sharing this life with both the children and the adults of the school.

When Frank showed the writer the playroom in the cottage where he lived, a group of boys were playing Ping-pong and carrying on other informal activities. "These are my friends," he explained; calling them over, he introduced them with the manner of a host. Frank and the writer were immediately included in the game of Ping-pong. The atmosphere remained friendly and natural. Only later was it discovered that this group of nine and ten year-old boys had been left in their cottage alone, to take care of themselves on their honor, while the house mother was away on an emergency call.

On the writer's first visit, Frank showed her a series of tiny pencil drawings which he admitted, when questioned, had been copied. He expressed an interest in having paints of his own and in trying to make something original. On the writer's second visit an experiment was made with water colors. It became evident that with a little encouragement the boy would again be able to return to a more creative and original expression.

A little later that year he illustrated some of his dreams and phantasies with pencil drawings for the social worker. One of them concerned a skeleton that said "Woo," and a haunted house at midnight; a second drawing, done on the same day, consisted of two skulls. To questioning on the meaning of these pictures he gave no reply. They were reminiscent of the ghosts and skeletons drawn with the writer. Further creative art work might now bring out the significance of the unconscious in these recent phantasies and dreams.

Frank also told the worker a dream about his mother, who was lying on a couch, and how he discovered that she was dead. After a trip in a rocket plane he had returned with his boy friend and, going back home, found the mother still dead. After telling the dream he became silent. Asked what the dream had made him think of he replied, "I didn't think of anything. I had a vision — a woman bending over."

He then drew a picture, which the writer saw. It was a caricature of a witch-like female with an excessively long and ridiculous nose. He was asked why he had drawn the picture that way.

"Well, she had a long nose," he said.

"Why?"

"Well, you know the story about Pinocchio — he had a long nose. Every time he lied the nose grew longer."

"Did anyone ever lie to you?" the worker asked.

"My mother, she always promised things and she didn't keep her promises."

Frank was now able to verbalize his hostility toward his mother, which he had buried for so many years.

He showed much greater articulateness also, according to the social worker's report, in his ability to discuss his interest in collecting:

> Frank was glad that he could bring all kinds of things into the cottage, and no one here would object and throw them away. Asked by the social worker what his parents said about his collecting, he explained that his father did not mind much, but it was his mother who yelled at him particularly. She used to insist that he get rid of these worthless things; every once in a while she would force him to clear out his collection. He didn't like that at all, because he had taken a lot of trouble to get these things together and wanted to keep them as his prized possessions.

This comment of Frank's on his impulse to collect those things that had been forbidden and denied him by his mother, here reveals a central point around which he had been attempting to express his immature ego feelings. The school had respected this impulse and allowed him a place for whatever he chose to gather together in his own cupboard.

In the year and a half that the patient has now spent in this agency school, the change and improvement have been outstanding. He has become a leader among his companions and there has been no evidence of fire-setting, seclusiveness, night terrors or tendency to steal or lie.

His still active interest in collecting things has been offered justifiable expression; his compulsiveness about neatness and order has been directed into socially useful channels; and his interest in studying and examining small objects is applied to collecting unusual information on special school subjects.

He has lived here within the stable setting of a family group, with a cottage mother who has given him the understanding and affection he craves and for whom he has seemed eager and ready to carry out useful housework. He has stated that now, for the first time in his life, he really likes school. He has also, for the first time, made many friends with whom he has seemed to adjust without difficulty. He has been able also to enjoy the intimacy with pets he has always longed for. A single reservation concerning his acceptance of the new life was given the writer in these words: "I sometimes miss the noise of the city." Yet he declares that he wants to live the rest of his life in the country.

The school reported that the attitude of the parents, especially of the mother, towards their adoptive son has not changed. But it now seems possible that Frank, with his roots established, for the first time, in a well harmonized school and community life, may now be in the process of developing his ego to such a degree that he may eventually cease to be overwhelmed by the over severity and rigidity of his adoptive mother.

CONCLUSION

Throughout this paper the significance of the unconscious and the important role of phantasy expression through the use of free art expression have been stressed as an aid in diagnosis and therapy. The gradual projection of the patient's acute anxiety into changing art forms that were related to the fears and threats of a restrictive and overwhelming environment has been correlated with the psychological records of the art sessions, the record of the treatment by the psychiatrist and the reports from nurses, psychologist, social workers and teachers in the hospital.

It has been shown how the patient's awareness of the difference between phantasy and reality, in the evolution of his art expression, played a part in the diagnosis of his case. The patient's recent successful adjustment in an agency school, where in his second year, he has become a leader both in the academic studies and in community life, suggests a degree of recovery from his psychoneurosis that corresponds to those signs of improvement that had already become evident in the patient's art work, three years earlier, while he was still hospitalized. The recent changes in the patient suggest continued growth and development of his immature ego, in the boarding school environment that has been able to protect him, to some degree, from the impact of the adoptive parents, while it creates an environment of greater security and sympathy.

Changes that appeared in the development of the patient's immature ego as he moved away from stereotyped forms, devoid of personal content, to wider areas of personal expression, based on both subjective and objective experience, have been presented. From these, certain implications as to the nature of the process of creativity began to emerge. There comes to the fore a conflict between the mechanisms of repetitive response and those of spontaneous behavior. Whether the repetitive actions of an individual are induced by the demands of educational procedure or are due to neurotic compulsions has not as yet been sufficiently considered. Kubie, in his paper, "The Repetitive Core of the Neurosis" [5] has offered some important material on the nature of repetitiveness in the psychic life of the normal as well as of the abnormal individual that should effect a revision of the demand for repetitiveness that still blocks the development of individuality in many of our school programs today.

The value and place of spontaneity, not only in creative art expression but in all aspects of personality development, have been fully expressed in the writings of Meyer [6] and Fromm.[7] But Freud pays less attention to this factor. He tends rather to emphasize the protective value to the individual of the mechanism of repetition and the necessity of accepting education as of use in order to "inhibit, forbid and suppress." [8]

The future demands a re-examination of the nature of the creative process. Should spontaneity be accepted as playing a more decisive role in the growth of the individual than was formerly recognized, this would lead, inevitably, to certain modifications in our educational procedures for the re-integration of personality in behavior problem children.

BIBLIOGRAPHY

[1] Naumburg, Margaret: "Children's Art Expression and War," The Nervous Child, Vol. 2, No. 4, pp. 360-373, 1943.

[2] Naumburg, Margaret: "The Drawings of an Adolescent Girl Suffering from Conversion Hysteria with Amnesia," The Psychiatric Quarterly, Vol. 18, No. 2, pp. 197-224, 1944.

[3] Naumburg, Margaret: "A Study of the Psychodynamics of the Art Work of a Nine Year Old Behavior Problem Boy," The Journal of Nervous and Mental Disease, Vol. 101, No. 1, Jan. 1945.

⁴ Yarnell, Helen: "Firesetting in Children," American Journal of Orthopsychiatry, Vol. X, pp. 272-286, 1940.

⁵ Kubie, Lawrence S.: "The Repetitive Core of Neurosis," Psychoanalytic Quarterly, Vol. X, No. 1, pp. 23-43, 1941.

⁶ Meyer, Adolf: Originally published in a pamphlet: "A Contribution of Mental Hygiene to Education," Chicago; Illinois Conference on Public Welfare, Oct. 1933, "Spontaneity," Sociometry, IV; 159, 1941.

⁷ Fromm, Erich: "Escape From Freedom," Farrar & Rinehart, 1941.

⁸ Freud, Sigmund: "New Introductory Lectures in Psychoanalysis," W. W. Norton and Co., 1933.

II

A STUDY OF THE PSYCHODYNAMICS OF THE ART WORK OF A NINE YEAR OLD BEHAVIOR PROBLEM BOY

INTRODUCTION

There is, today, an increase of interest in the use of the creative arts with mental patients as a means of both exploring and reintegrating human personality. Recognition of the validity of measuring personality by means of such tests as the Rorschach and Thematic Apperception, as well as scientific analyses of individuality through handwriting and gesture has stimulated the use of the arts as supplemental projective techniques.[1, 2]

In the encouragement of art expression for the purpose of either diagnosis or therapy, there still remains considerable divergence of approach. Some psychiatrists recognize the value of such art for both purposes; some find it useful for diagnosis and others only for therapy. The test of the wider potentialities of such art expression lies still in the future.

When the art work of mental patients is considered diagnostically, it reveals little, unless it is of a type that is spontaneous and quite free from formal direction. But if art is employed as therapy, two quite different approaches are possible; both are valid and useful, but they serve different objectives. The more formal and traditional approach is represented by the occupational therapists, who have been most effective, with mental patients, in developing an acquisition of skills in various crafts. Such training is carefully graded and planned in order to assist the patient in attaining technical mastery of the tools and materials in a chosen activity. The emphasis in occupational therapy, as in academic art teaching, is on the technique of the craft or art to be mastered, rather than on the self-expression of the patient.

Spontaneity and originality of expression are advocated by those who give precedence in therapeutic work to what has been called "free" expression. Since the term is neither adequate nor accurate, but useful for lack of better, it requires some definition. By "free" art expression is meant an authentic and original response to life (either inner or outer) made in some chosen art form; it does not mean a reproduction of models or stereotypes such as are often followed in formal art teaching or occupational therapy. One danger in using the term "free" expression is that it suggests to the uninitiated that those who accept it imagine that such a condition as absolute and unconditioned freedom can exist. But those who advocate the encouragement of creative expression are fully aware of the limitations of such freedom; for the mental patient, like every other individual, is conditioned by factors working upon him from both within and without his personality. Among dominant influences radiating from the environment are those related to the general cultural and economic milieu, the parental attitudes and the school experience. All of them play a part in either stimulating or deflecting what spontaneity the patient is able to release, in his first attempt at "free" expression in art.

While full credit must be given to occupational therapy for what it has accomplished with mental patients, there remains an important area in the development of spontaneous creativity as a means of diagnosis and therapy which it has not entered. This field includes original work in the practical as well as the fine arts. For when emphasis is placed on the release of the patient's personality through his art, and not on any technical proficiency attained, it serves a different therapeutic purpose. For the patient, it helps to release unexpected capacities which bring confidence and provide satisfaction; and to the psychiatrist, it offers a revealing projective technique for both diagnosis and therapy. When the patient has been helped to overcome his inhibitions and is able to express his deepest fears, wishes and phantasies on paper or in clay, he is tapping the unconscious in the symbolic language of images, which will often bring to the surface what he dare not or can not say in words.

This method of supplementing the psychiatric interview with the use of "free" art expression, as a projective technique, demands some reconsideration of the role of imagination and phantasy in the course of treatment. As soon as original art work is encouraged, instead of dependence on models and specific techniques, the focus of a patient's art activity is modified. He will begin to draw on his own inner resources and this will inevitably lead to some expression of the conflicts within the personality, which may reveal aspects of the pattern of his mental disease as well as the specific insecurities or traumatic experiences within the patient. Such release, drawn from both the conscious and unconscious levels, may, in itself, have a distinctly therapeutic effect on the patient, while it offers to the psychiatrist another avenue of approach in the treatment.

When such a patient is encouraged to express imaginatively and freely whatever interests him, the themes chosen are likely to range over many subjects; such work may deal with the actual happenings of the personal life, treated as either inner or outer events; or it may recreate either factual or phantasy experiences of childhood; or dram-

I. Burning Leaves. See page 30.

II. Cat: Sixth Attempt. See page 101.

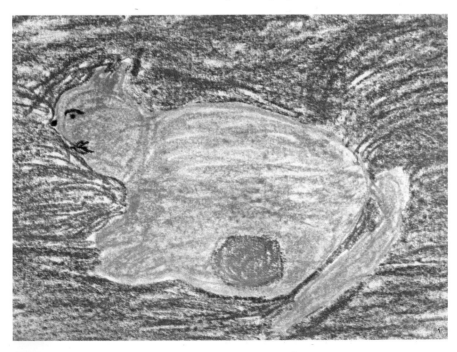

III. Shit of Many Colors. See page 146.

IV. A Jap Bomber. See page 163.

V. The Jolly, Handsome Sailor.
See page 185.

VI. The Beautiful Trained Nurse.
See page 185.

VII. Opposing Aspects of the Patient. See page 204.

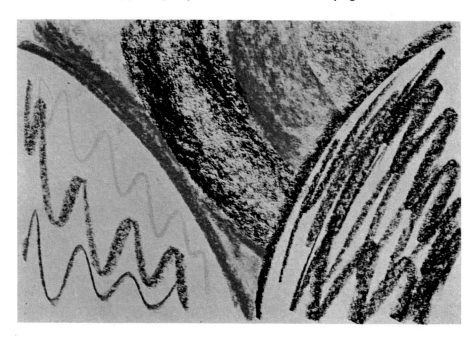

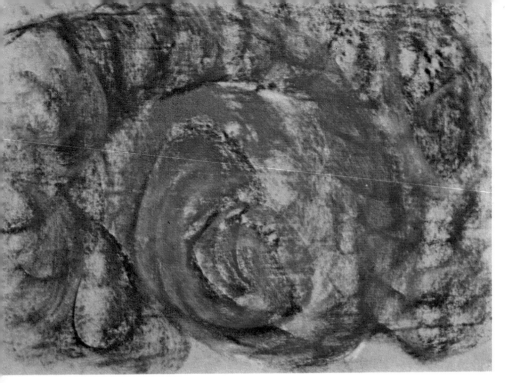

VIII. Summer. See page 211.

IX. Days at Home (one of seven designs). See page 217.

atize wishes and daydreams about the present or the future. Dreams also are likely to be included in some of these spontaneous art forms.

Since the language of images is the speech of the unconscious, it serves as a more primitive and direct mode of personal expression than words. Such personality patterns as are revealed through spontaneous art have been more thoroughly studied with psychotic than with neurotic patients.[3, 4] Further cultivation of "free" expression as a projective technique may became increasingly useful as a supplement to the psychiatric interview. Research in this field will probably develop more rapidly in the future as an aspect of the psychosomatic study of personality.

Since all aspects of the adult personality are bound up with the earlier childhood influences, the preliminary steps of a study of the spontaneous use of the creative arts with mental patients belongs to an investigation of such art expression in children. As an initial move in this direction, the research project of which this study is a part was begun in 1942 at the New York State Psychiatric Institute, in order to discover to what extent the use of free art expression might be of supplementary aid in diagnosis and therapy in the treatment of behavior problem children and adolescents.[5, 6]

Phantasy has been found to play an important part in this research of the spontaneous art expression of children. But the imaginative life revealed seems to combine aspects of both the Freudian[7] and Jungian[9] interpretation of phantasy. At times it represents, in unmistakable Freudian terms, an attempt to "escape from reality," at others it becomes a projection of "a unifying function" that deals with a collective past or an individual future, in the Jungian sense.

The detailed study of this nine-year-old behavior problem boy, which follows, will illustrate the various ways in which the life of phantasy can be employed, either to escape from, meet or transform reality.

In the treatment of children, projective techniques become even more important than with adults, because children are less able to express their thoughts and feelings in words and are closer to the more primitive expression of themselves through the language of images and play. This fact has been widely recognized in the constant use, today, of one form or another of play therapy in the treatment of children who are mentally ill. While dramatics and music and art have also been used to a lesser degree for this purpose, the techniques, so far described, have often had a somewhat limited and narrow purpose in view. There remains much pioneer work to be done in this field, in order to discover how projective methods can be most effectively developed to reveal the repressed and distorted aspects of personality in childhood.

Because art work has never been associated in the minds of behavior problem children with either disciplinary or therapeutic measures, they are ready to respond with a minimum of suspicion and distrust when opportunity for creative activity is offered.

When such children are institutionalized for the first time they are inevitably on the defensive. For months and even years, they have been regarded as "bad" or intractable at home and in school. They usually realize that they are placed in a hospital as the last resort of distracted parents or hopeless teachers and such patients are, therefore, bound to react with some degree of hostility and distrust to this new experience in a mental hospital.

Approach of the Patient to "Free" Expression in Art

When Nick, who was a nine-year-old boy of German-Italian parents, was brought to the hospital for treatment, it was stated that for the past five years he had been running away from home occasionally and for the past three years had been showing progressive symptoms of untrustworthiness, fantastic lying, conspicuous need for attention, prolonged absences from home and truancy from school; he comes from a home in which the father's work has caused him to be absent much of the time and the mother has been sexually promiscuous and neglectful of the child. The diagnosis was primary behavior disorder, neurotic type. The clinical summary will make clear how this patient's symptoms developed after the mother first left home with a lover.

The art periods with this patient began two months after hospitalization; they continued once a week, during five and a half months. Hour sessions did not seem too long, as is the case with many behavior problem children. Nick was encouraged to create spontaneously with any of the available art materials. These included crayons, paints and plastecine. While he remained tense and hyperkinetic, he was always eager and interested in the art work. He would usually open a session by announcing what he would make that day. Subjects in the ascendant, during the first few weeks, were jungle wars, sea fights and air-battles. His ceaseless commentary was filled with garbled versions of movies and comics adapted to his own phantasy life. While making these early war scenes, his speech was as explosive and fragmentary as the bombs and flames that filled them.

War games on similar themes, with equally vivid and episodic speech, were reported by the psychiatrist in her progress notes of the play sessions.

As Nick's confidence in his own powers to create on paper what was still buried within him grew, his preference for war scenes diminished. This symbolic release, in art form, of long repressed conflicts, brought a degree of relief from the pressure of his anxiety and also led, with the help of accompanying conversations, to a growth of insight concerning his own problems. No interpretation was, in this case, given to the patient at any time about the meaning of his symbolic drawings. For, to the writer, the therapeutic value of such art expression does not depend on interpretation, but rather on its value as an image language of the unconscious.

Nick became increasingly interested in the growth of his ability to use crayons and paints so as to express his own inner feelings and ideas. When this improvement in his work was noted and praised, he was much pleased and responded with the ambitious announcement, "I'm going to be the best artist in the hospital."

What Nick is not yet able to state in words, he now projects in the unconscious symbolism of his art. Here in battle scenes, the pressure of his anxiety first forces the expression of his hostility and insecurity into pictures of war. Gradually the deeper aspects of this boy's traumatic experience, which had long been inaccessible to verbalization, begin to be released in the unconscious imagery of his design. As Nick gained confidence in his ability to express his buried thoughts and feelings in the safe disguise of pictures, he grew gradually more able, through accompanying talk and questioning, to approach the inner source of his conflicts.

Nick's art work will, therefore, be considered as it developed through four of its phases: first, those designs that deal with war; then those that express aspects of his problems about love, marriage, birth and sex; thirdly, those which approach his running away adventures; and finally the landscapes that are concerned with nature or the cosmos. The subjects of life and death appear from time to time, in both talks and art work, but their deeper meaning as related to the patient's anxiety is only verbalized by him at the end of his hospitalization. Nick's own words will be quoted whenever space permits to give added significance to the meaning of his art work as it is described.

Records were kept of the patient's running commentary as he made pictures or modelled. These were written down after each art session. Brief excerpts from the writer's notes, as well as those of the psychiatrist, will be introduced to show what this art expression meant to the patient.

When the clinical summary of this patient's history has been presented, Nick's art work will be considered from several viewpoints; after describing the pictures and the patient's comments, the manner in which these art products confirm the data obtained by the psychiatrist in the play session will be considered; secondly, various forms of unconscious material derived through the creative imagery of the art periods will be described to show how this spontaneous art spoke through the language of the unconscious what the patient was either unable or unwilling to verbalize in the play therapy sessions. The full import of these designs can only be grasped when they are regarded, simultaneously, from the symbolic and the realistic level; for only then is the complex mingling of conscious and unconscious impulses in the psyche of the patient brought into focus.

CLINICAL HISTORY

The information for this clinical summary was obtained from the patient's father who had not been in direct contact with the child while away for six months on convoy duty. The mother had deserted her husband and child to go away with another man a month before the patient was brought to the hospital by the father.

There is no history of mental illness in the patient's background, but indication of neurotic trends on both sides of the family. The patient's father is of Italian and his mother of German parentage. The father is unstable, idealistic, completely dominated by his wife who is also highly neurotic, erratic and unpredictable in her behavior which includes sexual promiscuity. Six years ago she fell in love with another man with whom she left her home. Since then she has gone out with many men, has taken alcohol excessively and has been sexually promiscuous. In October 1942 she deserted her husband and her only child to live with a married man who has two children and does not propose a divorce. She is said to have returned to her husband's home, but not to the marital relationship, a month after the patient had been hospitalized.

The patient has been exposed to the constant severe quarrelling in the home since, at least, his fourth year.

An only child, the patient was said to have had devoted care from his mother during the first four years of his life. He was active, domineering and destructive with his toys, always preferring to play with younger boys, and was unafraid. After the onset of his difficulties, his symptoms included over-activity, marked sensitiveness, distractibility, tenseness, great need for attention and many fears, particularly in relation to physical injury. He began, at about four years of age, to tell fantastic tales and run away from home. These episodes increased in frequency and length as he grew older and truancy began to develop also. This behavior, it would appear, was a direct reaction to the catastrophic situation at home at the time when his mother had her first affair with another man. The parents were then on the verge of separation, but the mother refused to leave without her child and the father refused to give him up. From this time on the mother became progressively neglectful of the patient, often leaving him alone all night or keeping late hours to entertain many men friends.

The patient started kindergarten at the age of six and seemed to make a good adjustment, showing fondness for his teacher. During this year he was not afraid to fight with boys his own age, even taking on several at a time. When the patient was promoted to 1A, he refused to go to the new teacher and when taken to her he would cry, beg to get excused and not return to school. He would go for a walk and return home when school was dismissed. The father, coming home from a travelling job at eight o'clock one morning, found his wife asleep after a gay party and the patient greatly upset. The patient told his father that he had been unable to sleep, because there were people all over his bed and because his mother had been in bed with some other man.

The patient was studied at the Bureau of Child Guidance when he was six years old and was described as consistently negativistic, sensitive and hyperactive, showing great curiosity and destructiveness and resisting most attempts to work with him in play therapy. He gave the impression at that time of high average or slightly superior intelligence and showed unusual ability with manipulative materials, had a good grasp of number concept, but had not yet learned to read or spell. He was defensive about talking about any of his inner feelings, would not discuss school and said he did not know why he ran away. He showed unusual tenseness and presented a more severe picture than the parents' story had indicated.

From the age of seven until the date of admission, the patient's behavior became progressively worse. His school attendance became more irregular and his absences from home grew longer. He had twice to repeat school grades so that he is now only in 3A.

The patient's father, when he returned home unexpectedly after a six months absence on convoy duty, found his wife with another man and the patient locked in an upstairs room, screaming. On the following day the patient ran away from home. He returned at three in the morning just as his mother was leaving home with her lover. His father told him the circumstances; the patient showed great distress but was indifferently treated by his mother.

During the father's absence, he understands that the patient has been away from home for as long as forty-eight hours at a time on several occasions and with progressive frequency. Since the beginning of the school term he has attended school for not more than two weeks in all. During the month before admission, after the mother's desertion and while the patient was staying with his father, he ran away from home four times. When the patient was found he was always exhausted, having been long without sleep and without food, torn and dirty as though he had not washed at all. He greeted his father with indifference and communicated very little of his adventures. When the parents visited the hospital together, the child made a great fuss over the mother to the exclusion of the father whom he appeared to resent deeply.

On admission, the patient was a well-developed, well-nourished 9½-year-old child with no remarkable physical or neurological findings. Laboratory tests were negative. Electro-encephalogram showed no abnormal electrocortical activity.

The psychometric test resulted in an IQ of 96 on the Revised Stanford Binet. His performance test scores were very superior, suggesting special aptitude for an interest in working with manual materials. Attentional difficulties were marked, as was emotional reaction to the possibility of failure. Therefore his mental level was thought to be considerably higher than was evident on this test.

On the ward the patient appears unhappy, often preoccupied, seclusive, afraid of the older boys, unable to defend himself, constantly seeking the company of the younger children, unable to join in group activity, wandering restlessly around the ward. He is heedless and forgetful, often disobedient, unreliable, telling many fantastic stories to the other children and making efforts to get attention from both patients and nurses. He requires constant supervision, races about at the times when the other children are performing their chores, hiding and refusing to do the smallest tasks. He cries easily and is a poor loser at games. He always remained a difficult supervisory problem but later showed a somewhat better adjustment and told fewer fantastic tales.

In the playroom he is superficially friendly with the examiner, is curious about the contents of the playroom drawers, restless and distractible, uncommunicative both about his feelings and his play efforts. He excluded the examiner from play, gravitated most often to soldiers and airplanes, and is destructive in his treatment of toys. At one time he said he would stay in the hospital until he was 14, when he would join the Marines and go and be killed by having his head shot off in the war. At the mention of either his father or his mother, he became silent or evasive, and was totally inattentive whenever an effort was made to talk with him about his problems.

During his Christmas holidays with his parents, the patient ran away twice from an intolerable home situation; his acceptance of the hospital and his somewhat better adjustment here seems to date from that time.

On the basis of this clinical summary it becomes evident that a major catastrophe had befallen this patient when he was four years old; what had been for the child, up to the time of the mother's desertion, a happy and protected home, suddenly shattered and fell apart. From that event dates the onset of disturbing changes in his behavior. Fantastic lying and running away from home began at this time; these symptoms were apparently ignored by his parents until they became so severe as to result in constant truancy from school.

As the mother grew more promiscuous during the father's prolonged absences she not only entertained many men in the home, but exposed the patient to many of these intimate situations. The mounting rate of the patient's disappearances while the mother was again away from home with a man seems to have finally forced the father to bring the boy to the hospital.

When the art work was begun with this patient, he had already been under psychotherapeutic treatment for two months. His response in the hospital as reported in the clinical summary was similar to that given at the Bureau of Child Guidance, five years previously. He was still unable or unwilling to talk of his inner feelings, he would not discuss home or parents or his running away from home and school. Nor was he ever able to offer any reason for such escapades.

When the writer began art sessions with Nick, the inner conflicts that were known to be related to his outward behavior in running away and telling fantastic stories, had still been consistently evaded by the patient. How this boy's phantasy life and traumatic experiences were gradually projected into his art expression will become evident as the aspects of his unconscious life are revealed.

Since the purpose of these art sessions, carried out with a number of behavior problem patients, has been to discover whether such expression can be of aid in diagnosis and therapy, it is essential to encourage these patients to find ways of expressing in art what concerns their lives and interests. When or how this will begin to take place varies with each individual patient. Sometimes comments about a pet animal may be the starting point for a first attempt to make a picture that relates to some object or experience out of his own world. When free expression of his own life begins to replace copies of airplanes and comics or the replicas of school art, it is possible, for the first time, to come closer to this patient's inner problems through his own creative work. When such spontaneous outpourings first reveal aspects of the patient's family difficulties, it is certain also to include some symbolic, if not realistic, expression of his unresolved sex problems.

SERIES OF WAR PICTURES

The patient had already been in the hospital two months when he began art work with the writer. He was eager to come and at the first

session announced: "I like to draw and can make all kinds of things
— planes." For a number of art periods bombing planes dominated
his designs. There were air battles between the "enemy" which was
Japanese or German and the Americans, sometimes joined by Aus-
tralians. There were many scenes in which bombers dropped their
loads from the air, to sink ships or wipe out enemies or explode ammu-
nition dumps. Outbursts of flame, terrific explosions of TNT, black
swirling hurricanes increased the holocaust. The sounds of bursting
bombs, whizzing airplanes, martial music and the "drip, drip" of
blood, accompanied the making of these war pictures.

Sensitive, tense and hyperkinetic, this patient was forced by the
overwhelming pressure of his anxiety to escape into his own phantasy world. Nick worked quickly and explosively when he had focussed on the idea for a picture. Impatient of delay, he was unwilling
to linger over filling-in his outlines with solid color. These rapidly
sketched battle scenes, however loaded with the patient's anxiety,
showed a rare sensibility and dramatic power in their evocation of
twisted planes and sudden explosions. When he had begun to project
his inner conflicts into the expression of these art forms, he achieved
both satisfaction and relief. And what was of added importance, he
would then begin to voice, in the symbolic language of art, those inner
conflicts which he had been unable up to that time to bring forth in the
language of words.

The human battle scenes were frequently interspersed with jungle
and undersea struggles in which crocodiles and snakes as well as
imaginary creatures and magicians fought to overcome each other.
In such combats, whether of men or animals, on land or sea or in the
air, Nick was clearly projecting his own conflicts. While war games
remained the chief theme in the play therapy sessions throughout his
hospitalization, these became less important as the art sessions progressed. In the battle pictures several significant themes began to
appear. The nature of the "enemy," still unidentified in relation to
his personal conflicts, was drawn as being extremely large and powerful. But in the midst of this destructive war a theme of rebirth became
evident in a garden which was burnt by fire in the midst of battle, but
which "would grow again with all kinds of roses and flowers." In
later pictures that deal with marriage, birth and sex, flames and explosions also occur, but always the people that are symbols of what
concerns Nick's own life escape unhurt and are saved.

The art work had continued some weeks before either of the two
outstanding symbolic patterns, now to be described, had begun to

emerge in Nick's war pictures. The first design was directly linked to the traumatic shock caused by the mother's desertion; the second pattern was also associated with the rejection of the patient by the mother, yet it was diverted from the mother and turned against her "men friends."

The first of these unconscious symbols did not emerge clearly until it had been repeated in several battle pictures. Only then did a recurrent cleft, made by means of two parallel saw-toothed lines, become weighted with additional meaning. Whenever Nick created one of these jagged splits in some part of a picture, he would print beside the object, the single word "crack." Then he would continue the shooting and the breaking forth of flames in the battle scene.

The clinical history of this patient leaves little doubt as to the meaning of this recurrent schism in the pattern of his life. At the age of four his childhood world had shattered, when his mother left home with a lover. So speaks, consistently, the recurrent image of the great "crack"; in one picture it divides a mountain, in another it splits a tree-trunk, in a third, it tears a ship apart, while in yet a fourth it shatters the steeple of the church where the bride(who is also the mother) is about to be married. (Figs. 25, 26, 27 and 30).

The patient did not elaborate on the meaning of these rifts. But in placing the single printed word "crack" across the life pattern of these pictures, the unconscious had spoken in no uncertain terms.

To bring out the significance of this recurrent image of the "crack" as the symbolic representation of this patient's traumatic experience, these designs that showed the split are described in detail beneath the accompanying pictures. (Figs. 25, 26, 27, 28 and 30). The patient's own comments will be quoted whenever space permits.

The next battle scene, in which the crack appeared, came two weeks later. For this see "The Tree That 'Cracks'" with its accompanying description (Fig. 26). In this scene, an unusual number of this patient's often repeated anxiety symbols were combined within a single picture. Not more than one or two such images usually appeared in one design. But on this occasion there were eight such symbols. Besides the splintered tree there were consuming red flames, spiralling black hurricanes, airplanes dropping bombs, explosions of TNT and the supportive use of camouflage and other protective techniques to guard against danger. The final and outstanding anxiety symbol was described by Nick as "a torpedo hanging up there in the sky. It is on four cords." How this was drawn and the episode dram-

The War Series (Figs. 25, 26, 27 and 28)

In many of the patient's war pictures there appeared a significant symbol of two parallel, saw-tcothed lines beside which was always printed the word "crack," without any comment. He would then continue the picture — dramatizing the shootings, bombings and explosions with the accompaniment of appropriate sound effects.

FIG. 25. THE MOUNTAIN THAT "CRACKS"

In the upper left hand corner of this crayon drawing is shown the "crack" that divides the mountain. Across the mountainous scene there are evident several groupings of red flames and in the lower right hand corner is drawn a pile of red boxes marked TNT that are exploding in flames. The flames and the dynamite, because of their strong red color, dominate the scene in the original picture. For all else in this drawing, including the "crack," the trees, rivers, mountains, flags, tcmmy guns, as well as the Japs and Americans, who fight on opposing' mountains, are all outlined only in brown crayon.

While innumerable brown tommy-guns have been drawn, only two of these are manned by figures of soldiers. Yet the feel of battle going on between armies is created in the placement of these symbolic guns. "See," says Nick, "in the jungle a little fire starts and then it starts growing. It's going to do a lot of damage. The Americans couldn't get out of here at this fire. But they could get out by the river in their diving suits." He illustrates how the Americans are saved by a swimming gesture. "Then the mountain cracks — there's melted brick." Nick then prints "crack" for the first time. "See the trees burning!" and he draws more flames. He counts aloud as he makes "eleven boxes of TNT." A shot from the battle explodes the dynamite and it too goes up in flames.

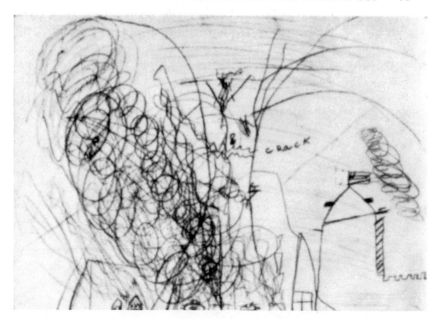

FIG. 26. THE TREE THAT "CRACKS"

The large tree, in brown, in the center of this drawing, shows the jagged double line, labelled "crack." The story of the battle taking place concerns bombings and air battles of Americans against a jumble of Germans and Japanese. The lightly made cross lines in red, green, yellow and pink across the tree trunk represent camouflage. On the base line are a row of tiny tanks, jeeps, army tents, KP and TNT houses that were bombed from the air. Great red flames and coils of black smoke rise from this bombing. A plane is visible in the air behind the flames. This drawing contains an unusual number of anxiety symbols. "Two machine gunners are up in the tree to watch in case airplanes come. Inside of the tree is a red airport. I think there'll be some firing." "There's pursuit planes and everything protecting this place. There's a captured German airplane up inside the tree. Now the tree opens and the plane flies out. You won't believe it, this wall is so thick, that not even a bomb can break it. These men here are very armed, aren't they?" He draws them inside of the fort, in front of the tree. "Now I'll camouflage the tree." For this he seized in one hand four colors, selected at random — red, green, yellow and pink — and drew lines across the entire tree, announcing, "It will look like a rainbow with this camouflage." "Do you know what that is," making a sizzling sound, "That's fire. The Japs set the fires. The fort, though, is fireproof. Good-bye airplane hangar. Good-bye automobile — all goes up in flames!" A third of the picture is now filled with fire. The outstanding anxiety symbol is the black torpedo drawn as "Hanging up there in the sky. It is on four cords." The patient has drawn this so that it shows against the upper part of the tree trunk, above the "crack." Dramatically he explains how "If one goes, then two goes, then three goes — there's only one left. It depends on which side the cords go, where the torpedo will fall. And when the torpedo drops the whole thing will explode. Then there are flames, black smoke, a big storm. a black hurricane. Then the fire goes out."

atized is described beneath the reproduction of this scene (Fig. 26). When Nick here speculates concerning the suspended black torpedo and wonders which cords may break first and send it hurtling through space to cause destruction, he has produced an image that is more than an expression of his own acute anxiety. For the pattern of that suspended torpedo is really a modernized version of that classical and universal symbol of anxiety — the suspended sword of Damocles.

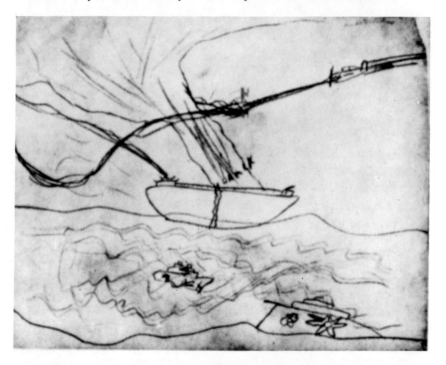

FIG. 27. THE SHIP THAT "CRACKS"

This oil tanker which "cracks" when it is bombed from the air by planes goes up again in red flames. The rest of the picture is drawn in blue crayon. Only the sea consists of a mingling of green and blue waves. This patient's father was then on convoy duty on such a tanker and had previously described to his son the harrowing details of the bombing and sinking of his ship and his rescue from the icy sea. The patient frequently expressed anxiety concerning the safe return of his father.

Without taking the time to consider the deeper meaning of these supportive anxiety symbols in this war scene, it is clear that such comments by Nick as "You wouldn't-believe the walls are so thick no bomb can break them," and "These men are very armed, aren't they?", as well as the significance of the camouflaging of the tree, are all symbolic measures of self-protection against his acute anxiety.

Throughout the art sessions these and other anxiety symbols may reappear suddenly and unexpectedly in scenes where they interrupt the natural sequence of the story.

In order to bring out more clearly the nature and meaning of this "crack" symbol, several of the other scenes that show this jagged split are reproduced (Figs. 27 and 30). No attempt will be made, however, in this paper to interpret more deeply the evident sexual symbolism expressed in the cracking of the mountain, the tree, the ship and the church steeple.

The second outstanding symbolic pattern that the patient developed did not emerge as swiftly and sharply as this recurrent image of the

FIG. 28. SINKING THE "ENEMY" SHIP CONTAINING THE MOTHER'S "MEN FRIENDS"

Designs of ships being bombed from the air by swooping planes appeared frequently in this patient's war pictures. But the symbolic meaning of this pattern only became evident after several months of art work. As the patient became able gradually to verbalize more freely, he dared to draw this picture which describes the bombing of three German sailors whom he called "my mother's men friends." These sailors on the green battleship are bombed by the plane which sets the ship afire with bright red flames. "Just what I'd like to do to those sailors, lay their boat six feet under. You're going to see nothing but ashes in the ocean," commented the patient. From this time on he grew gradually able to verbalize his hostility and jealousy toward the mother's lovers.

"crack." It was not until several months after Nick had started the art work that he began to verbalize more freely about his own problems. Then only did he begin to explain to the psychiatrist who his real "enemies" were. In two succeeding play therapy sessions he expressed hostility against "enemies." The psychiatrist reported that he threw lumps of clay fiercely at the walls, trying to hit an imaginary target. He admitted these enemies to be Hitler and Hirohito. Later in the session when asked who his own enemies could be, he replied: "They could be friends of my mother's." He then proceeded to name and describe his mother's friends. A few days later, when modelling fights between enemy snakes and crocodiles, he repeated that his enemies were "Friends of my mother. I want them out of this world."

The following week, the same subject of his mother's friends who were his "enemies" was now expressed in a picture in the art session. He told of three brothers, German sailors, who were friends of his mother. He was asked if he would like to make a picture about them. He drew a green battleship and said the three sailors were on it. Above the ship he made a plane, bombed the ship and set it afire. "Just what I'd like to do to those sailors, lay their boat six feet under. You're going to see nothing but ashes in the ocean!" (Fig. 28).

In the fifth month of hospitalization, this patient began to be able to express openly in both play therapy and art sessions his jealousy and resentment towards his specific "enemies," his mother's friends, whom he had destroyed so frequently before under the guise of Japs and Germans in the battle pictures.

The Love, Marriage, Birth and Sex Cycle

The pictures in this series that concern love, marriage, birth and sex began with a drawing of "The Writer and the Major" (Fig. 29). In the third art session, after drawing a battle scene, Nick announced: "Now I'll do a picture of you. Keep your glasses on. I'll make you standing. Stand up please. Put your hand out on your hip, and the other hand across." The writer posed as requested. "You've got short sleeves," he commented as he drew. "Now I'll do your feet." The result of Nick's efforts was a quickly drawn front view figure of a woman outlined in orange, with a blue blouse and a purplish skirt.

"Now I'll draw a man — a major," announced Nick. "His overcoat and head blue." After drawing a profile of the figure of the major he placed a gun with bayonet in his hand and a pistol in his belt. Then a hat with a feather, which he described as he worked. He elaborated the major's costume with an epaulet. The sounds of martial music were being hummed as Nick completed the major's portrait.

At this point his whole manner changed. He had been absorbed and quite happy while making these two figures. Now he drew back

THE LOVE, MARRIAGE, BIRTH AND SEX CYCLE (INTERSPERSED WITH
COSMIC LANDSCAPES) (FIGS. 29, 30, 31, 32, 33, 34 AND 35)

FIG. 29. "THE WRITER AND THE MAJOR"

within himself and began suddenly to whisper anxiously: "If I told you what the major says, you'd punish me." Assured that he would not be punished, he still insisted in a whisper: "You'd be angry." After further assurance and more hesitation, Nick came close to the writer, and in her ear he whispered very softly, "The major marries you."

On the back of this drawing, when he signed his name, Nick writes: "Will you marry me?" Before finishing the picture, he tells the writer, significantly, that the social worker always kisses him when she leaves. But no response is made to this remark.

It was evident that, in this picture of "The Writer and the Major," the patient was expressing his transference. But besides using the writer as a mother substitute, he was now approaching symbolically, for the first time, the problem of marriage and sex as it related to himself, his parents and the extra-marital relations of his mother. It was going to be necessary to discover what he did and did not know through his own observation and experience as well as what adults had told him, in order to eventually reorient this patient.

When the psychiatrist saw this drawing, and heard about Nick's behavior and comments, she agreed that this picture was the patient's first approach to the deeper aspects of his personal problem. She, therefore, concurred in the writer's intention to work in the art sessions for the further release and outward expression of Nick's buried conflicts, and she also agreed that it would now be necessary to give adequate assistance in response to the patient's further questions in relation to the problems of love, marriage, birth and sex, whenever they appeared in either pictorial or verbal form. How these subjects did develop sequentially through an entire series of pictures and many conversations will now be described.

In the next art session, Nick, for the first time, expressed more interest in talking than in making pictures. "You won't be angry if I tell you a secret?" he whispered again. He needed urging and encouragement before he whispered, "I love you." With the satisfaction of an assurance of reciprocal response, there followed immediately the question that he had really wanted to ask. "What do people do when they marry?" Purposely the writer parried the question, asking Nick what he thought they did. "It begins with a k," suggested Nick. Urged to go further, he whispered, "A kiss. Will you kiss me?" Receiving it, he responded to this assurance by jumping up and flinging his arms about the writer.

With complete rejection by the mother and the continued absence of the father, this patient, with no adult to turn to at home, is constantly seeking assurance and affection on the ward. His pleas for a positive expression of affection ought to be met — through a sympathetic and open response that would free the patient, rather than an over-intense approach that might bind him to any adult.

At the beginning of the following art period, the writer reviewed with Nick what he had already expressed about love and marriage; reminding him of his previous hesitation, she assured him that he could ask whatever question he wished about marriage or other problems and receive a true answer. He need now have no fear of punishment for asking questions. But since he had been so afraid to speak of marriage before, it was suggested that someone must have forbidden him to do so. To this Nick answered in the affirmative but hesitated to identify the person. But when asked whether it might be his mother, he nodded assent. Parents, it was explained, who had been brought up without having their questions answered when they were young, often treated their children in the same way. Might there not be something else besides the matter of kissing that he would like to ask about marriage? Or did he perhaps know more himself?

"Yes," he replied immediately. "When a woman has a baby she goes to the hospital and the doctor operates and it takes a long time."

In the conversation that followed Nick was able to describe that the baby came out of the mother. To quiet any anxiety he was assured that it was a natural process, in which sometimes the doctor gave more help than others. He showed also that he was well informed about the way in which the baby came forth from the mother, explaining that the body and legs followed after the head. He had, it seems, obtained this information when his aunt had her child in a hospital. He now felt sufficiently at ease to ask, "Why don't animals have doctors when they have babies?"

This question demanded some explanation of the way the baby is attached to the mother by the umbilical cord and of how the doctor takes care of cutting that connection; it also required a description of the way that animals, such as a mother cat or mother dog would cut the cord with their teeth when their babies were born. This was as far as Nick's questions went on that day. He seemed relaxed and apparently satisfied with the answers given.

"I'd like to do a picture now," announced Nick, "of a wedding. But I can't make a bride. Will you help me draw the dress?"

He was encouraged to try it himself and soon produced the outline of a white bridal dress, to which he then attached a head and arms.

He was humming the wedding march happily as he drew the bride. How this wedding, "The Bride and the Steeple that 'Cracks'" developed is described beneath the illustration (Fig. 30). "What about the rest of that wedding?" enquired the writer. "Where are the bridegroom and the other people?"

FIG. 30. THE WEDDING: THE BRIDE AND THE STEEPLE THAT "CRACKS"

This picture was initiated by the patient, quite spontaneously, after some of his questions about the nature of birth and marriage had been answered. "I'd like to do a picture now," he announced, "of a wedding. But I can't make a bride. Will you help me draw the dress?" On the baseline in the center of this picture is the bride. With encouragement the patient succeeded in drawing it himself — first the dress and then the face and arm were added. The wedding scene began quite peacefully, with the bride in white, her blue automobile waiting, the Holy Father drawn in red; two soldiers are set to guard him as he stands by the church which is outlined in yellow with its high steeple and cross in red. A large American flag was flung from the belfry window. Only later, after the second wedding picture of the marriage (Fig. 31) taking place in the room below the church did the patient return to the preliminary wedding scene, set the bride's automobile on fire and introduce airplanes and bombs which blast the steeple, make flames burst from the belfry and cause the steeple to develop the large "crack," as in three previous war scenes. This time the church steeple was described as toppling over to the ground.

"Oh, they're downstairs. The bride will leave alone later in the automobile," Nick explains. Further questioning, as to why, brought the answer that the bridegroom would have to remain and fight the Japs. This led him to link the wedding with his return to the conflicts of war. When time had elapsed for some bombing, the writer asked, "Had you thought of adding another sheet of paper below the church picture to show that room downstairs where the wedding takes place?" Responding to this suggestion, Nick seized another paper

FIG. 31. THE WEDDING IN THE ROOM BELOW THE CHURCH

The wedding is actually taking place on the base line of this picture. The bride with her long train is considerably larger than the groom. The Holy Father is the figure nearest to the large cross. "There are four soldiers guarding the bride." The figure with his horse, in the upper space is "The spirit of George Washington and his horse. I'll make four soldiers with tommy guns to guard him." The two serrated lines, one to the right and the other to the left, represent means of descent and ascent to this lower room. The staircase to the right was the way the wedding party entered. The "secret" stairs to the left were a means of escape when the church on the other wedding picture was bombed Everything in this picture was drawn in red except the outline in blue of the spirit of Washington, his horse, his four guards, and the line of descent by means of which Washington's spirit came to the ground and was then transferred over to the cross where Jesus was drawn. All the people in the wedding scene escape safely by the secret stair.

and placing it below the first one made a connecting red staircase that descended to the floor below. He began to draw the steps hurriedly, but impatient to proceed he substituted straight lines for the rest of the descent, explaining, "They slide the rest of the way." The description of what takes place in "The Wedding in the Room Below the Church" is told below the illustration. (Fig. 31).

Again Nick breaks away from the actual wedding scene (Fig. 31) and returns to the battle in the air (Fig. 30) which is going on again

FIG. 32. THE RAINBOW AND THE CYCLE OF NATURE

This picture was drawn spontaneously, following the two wedding scenes. It expressed a serene and happy mood and deals with the forces of nature in an almost cosmic sense. The rainbow is drawn in purple, yellow, gray, brown and orange. Then a "banana-moon" followed by golden stars of assorted sizes, was added; a large branching tree with green foliage followed. "It's snowing," the patient then announced, and drew white snow across the rainbow. Red flowers with green leaves and a small green house completed the picture. This fusion of spring and winter, day and night, rainbow and moon within a single picture was no accident.

above the church. He dramatizes the struggle between the Japanese and American planes, describing it as he draws: "Bombs drop. A shot misses the church steeple. Flames break out at the two windows."

Again the split shown in so many war pictures reappears as a double jagged line; it is drawn by Nick at the base of the church steeple with "Crack" printed beside it.

"The steeple is going to fall down and the people in the room will not be able to escape through the door upstairs. But, downstairs, there is a secret door by which they can escape."

At the next art session, Nick refers to the wedding pictures and pulls them out of the portfolio. Examining them, he comments, "The planes spoil the picture. I shouldn't have made them." Asked why he had done so, he explained that the Japs were coming. This was Nick's first expression of awareness that plunging into war in the midst of another theme did not improve the picture.

When Nick again brought the conversation back to the subject of birth, the writer asked whether there were not still some things on his mind that he wanted to know about marriage.

"Yes, how were Adam and Eve made?" Asked whether he knew the story, he replied, "Yes, God made them." Questioned further as to whether he remembered how he had 'told the writer at a previous art period that God had made him, he said "Yes." When Nick showed that he was still puzzled as to how he had been born, he was asked whether he knew what mothers and fathers were for. To this he replied without hesitation: "Yes, a mother takes care of you when you are small and a father when you get big. And the baby comes out of the mother."

Asked then whether he knows where the baby comes out, he points to his own navel. It is explained how this only marks the spot where the baby was originally attached to the mother. Then Nick points to his open mouth and asks, "Does the baby come out here?" He is reminded that there exists a special opening for this purpose, between the legs of the mother. Further elucidation is postponed until the writer is able to obtain from the patient a more complete expression of what else he had observed or imagined. As this fear of speaking about sex decreases, he begins to describe quite clearly what he knows and has seen.

In order to assist the patient to release aspects of his repressed traumatic experience, and place what he knew and what he still wants to know about sex and birth in an ordered relation, the writer directed the talk to the differences between boys and girls. At first Nick evaded the subject with a comment that "girls have longer nails than boys." He was asked if he had ever noticed any other differences between boys and girls. Finally he said, " A boy had a 'pisser' and a girl had hair down there." Asked how he knew that, he explained: "I've seen it." When queried as to what else he had seen, he whispered: "A soldier f---." He does not say the forbidden word, so the writer, as she prepares the art materials, pronounces it quite casually, asking whether that is it? To this he nods assent, but seems afraid to continue the subject further at this time. So the writer continues the conversation about differences between the sexes, by asking whether he had ever seen his aunt's baby girl in her bath. Nick said that he had. The writer asked, pointing to the upper part of his body, whether he knew if there is any difference between a man and a woman up there.

"Yes, the woman is bigger."

"Do you know why?"

"Yes, she feeds the baby."

It is evident from these conversations that Nick had received a certain amount of correct information and had also applied his personal observation to the subject of sex, and had become gradually freer in his willingness to speak of such matters without acute anxiety.

In order to help the patient release more of his repressed traumatic experiences, the writer referred to the talk of the previous art session. Nick was reminded of what he had said about the soldier, and was asked whether he had seen such things happen. Quickly he answered, "Yes." To further questioning, he admitted that he had seen the soldier do it to his mother. He then added, quite spontaneously, "And when I was eight years old a man did it to me."

"So you saw the soldier with your mother?"

"Yes, I saw him put the 'pisser' in her."

Here at last was a genuine emotional release in words of some of these traumatic sexual experiences that the boy had not been permitted to mention. Now for the first time he was having the subject of sex treated as something natural that was neither bad nor taboo.

When the patient reached the stage where he was able to bring out a description of his observance of intercourse between his mother and one of her lovers and to tell of his seduction by one of these men as well, he was at a crucial point in the release of his anxiety. This occurred during the fourth month of hospitalization and the fifth week of his art work. Now that it had been possible to deal more openly with such experiences, it became important to bring to the patient a sense of the normality of sex as related to the birth of a child through the love and marriage relationship of the parents. With this in mind the writer asked: "Would you like to have me tell you more about marriage and how the mother and the father have their baby?"

"Yes," but as Nick answered, he looked anxiously toward the door. "Lock the door first."

To allay his anxiety, the writer did so, but assured him that no one would interrupt them.

"Can I come and sit near you?" Nick asked.

He drew his chair as close as possible to the writer. So anxious and immature did he seem, and in need of temporary physical security, that the writer allowed him to sit in her lap. Clinging tightly, he behaved, at first, like a very young and frightened child.

It becomes necessary to summarize briefly how the subject of sex and birth was presented to Nick, for this information was then related by him to his further questions and his drawings. As simply as possible, he was told how, when parents love each other and want a child, the seed is planted by the father and grows inside the mother in the same way that the seed of a plant grows within the earth. The wider significance of procreation as it takes place, not only in man but throughout nature, was suggested and examples were given of how various familiar animals, as well as birds and fish, gave birth to their young. Nick followed intently and now quite at ease, supplemented the story with examples of his own. When he was reminded that baby kittens came from their mother he added, "like baby porcupines and baby monkeys come from their mothers."

It was now evident from Nick's relaxed and natural behavior that the problem of birth and its relation to sexual functioning was being accepted in its universal and natural place in the growth of all life. When asked whether he knew how long a baby grows inside of the mother before it's ready to come out, Nick had replied nine years. When the time span had been corrected, he asked, "Did that happen to you, when your son was born?" When assured that it had, he flung his arms around the writer, saying, "I love you."

"I love you too," he was assured. "Now do you think you understand a little better how the baby is born?"

"Yes, now I'll make a picture of the mother and the baby and the doctor at the hospital." For the description and Nick's explanation see illustration (Fig. 33).

This hospital scene was evidently constructed from information previously obtained from the aunt when she had her child. Since emphasis on the doctor's large shears showed again Nick's anxiety over this operation as described by the aunt, efforts were made to remind him of the naturalness of the process of birth and that the doctor was only present to help. Again, the subject of the way the child was attached to the mother by a cord was discussed. This led Nick, who was now actively and happily engaged in making his picture, to stop and begin to phantasy, playfully. "Oh, when I was inside my mother I had such fun. Sometimes I would pull on the rope and stop breathing and then I would jump around inside."

When the birth scene was complete, Nick added "This only looks like a hospital, it isn't really." Following a transformation of the hospital into a fort with secret radios and hidden planes, he explained that "the mother, the baby and the doctor are real." When asked what happened to the mother and baby, he added another figure in green, saying, "She takes up the baby and puts it in his own bed." He draws the baby's bed as he speaks, then bending forward, with arms crossed, he rocks back and forth as though cradling a child and sings a lullaby.

When Nick finished drawing the hospital he volunteered suddenly, "Bobby and I did that together."

"Did what?"

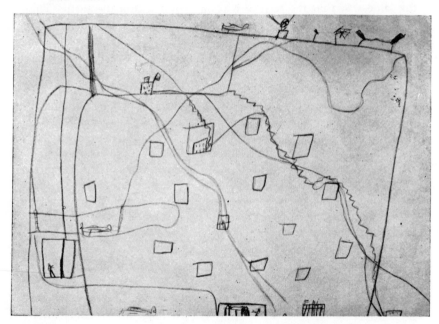

FIG. 33. THE BIRTH OF THE BABY AT THE HOSPITAL

"Now I'll make a picture of the mother and the baby and the doctor at the hospital," said the patient, spontaneously, after questions concerning birth and sex had been clarified. The hospital was drawn in red. To the left was placed an elevator moving down to deposit the doctor on the lowest floor. In the center of the base line is an oblong room containing the mother lying on a bed and the doctor standing to her right. The mother and the bed are drawn in brown; the doctor's head and shears are red, his body purple and the legs brown. A small green box was drawn beside the bed. "That's in case the baby should die. Little babies have lots of black hair, when they are born." When the birth scene was complete, the patient explained, "This only looks like a hospital, it isn't really." Then came a return to war as in the wedding scene. The hospital was described as camouflage, and secret radios and secret airplane passages and stairs were added. The airplanes were drawn in blue, the radio in green crayon. Nick was back again in the thick of war, "Planes drop from the sky and land on the ground. They hit a water hydrant and water shoots out and puts out the fire." But though the hospital was now only camouflage, "The baby and the mother and doctor are 'real'" the patient explains.

"F----"

There followed with the same directness an admission that he had been the active one in this sex play. "He lay down, I did it to him." To further questioning he said, "No one on the ward knows. I want to ask you something else."

"What is it?"

"About kissing." He then came close to ask whether the writer would kiss him. When she had done so, he waited, unable to find the right words to ask the question that was evidently on his mind. Asked whether he had been wondering whether kissing had something to do with marriage, he answered, "Yes."

"Well, a mother and father do often show their love for each other by kissing and so do other people who are fond of each other; a mother often kisses her child, and brothers and sisters kiss each other and so do good friends. Are you still puzzled, Nick, or do you think you understand about what happens in marriage, when a mother and father love each other and the father plants the seed in the mother?"

"Yes, I understand," he replies, "I could draw it."

And he jumps up and goes to the table to begin immediately. Without further talk Nick turned to his paper and in a few swift strokes made a diagram of the male and female sex organs (Fig. 34a). He drew it spontaneously, to illustrate what he knew concerning the role of the father in planting the seed. It was clearly based on his personal observation and included the addition of pubic hair to both the male and female forms. When the diagram was complete Nick added a line to show the path that the seed must take to enter the mother. Within five minutes he had completed the drawing without a vestige of embarrassment or concern. He then asked for more paper and immediately redrew the diagram (Fig. 34b). This time the male organ was drawn more realistically and its function emphasized by his comment: "See the slime coming out. That's where the seed comes from for the baby, isn't it?"

This second drawing seemed to be necessary so that Nick could elaborate the nature of the procreative process. There was now a third picture (Fig. 34c). Here interest shifted from the sexual parts of the male to the form of the female. Starting at the upper edge of the page, Nick drew rapidly the profile of a woman's breast, torso and leg in a single, sure and clear outline. To this figure, a red nipple, the vaginal opening and pubic hair were added, but no comments were made. The male organ was then drawn, but it was extremely small in proportion to the woman's form. Emphasis went to the woman's full breast and the man's smaller penis, suggesting identification by the

THREE DIAGRAMMATIC DRAWINGS OF SEX ORGANS
(FIGS. 34A, B AND C)

These three brown crayon drawings were made spontaneously in quick succession, by the patient, after he had completed the explanation of the preceding hospital picture about the birth of the baby. Various aspects of the patient's questions concerning love, marriage, birth and sex had been met in the talks that occurred during the art sessions. When asked whether he now understood the role of the father in relation to the birth of the child, the patient replied, quite naturally, "Yes, I understand. I could draw it." Asking for a sheet of paper, he made in swift succession, all three diagrammatic drawings with no sign of either hesitation or embarrassment. His purpose was evidently both to explain, by means of pictures, what he now understood as well as to describe what he had already witnessed (as confirmed by the clinical history) of his mother's promiscuity. How such art expression helped to liberate the patient from aspects of such traumatic experience is elaborated in the text.

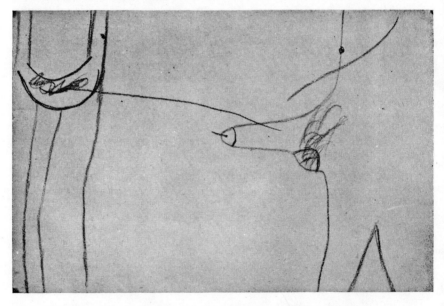

FIG. 34A. FIRST DIAGRAMMATIC DRAWING OF SEX ORGANS

This was drawn to illustrate the way the father plants the seed in the mother. When completed the patient added a line showing the path that the seed must take to enter the mother.

patient with the masculine role in this diagram. (Nick had previously drawn the groom in the wedding scene as smaller than the bride.)

It is evident from an examination of these sex drawings (Figs. 34a, 34b, 34c) that Nick like most children was confused as to the nature of the vaginal opening and identified it with the anus.[8] His admitted seduction undoubtedly reinforced this misconception. When the nature of the opening for the birth of the child occurs again in Nick's drawings, the subject is then clarified with the help of diagrams.

In this forthright dramatization of the sexual act, Nick was only stating what he knew to be true from his own observation. Such a candid portrayal of sexual knowledge by a child may still surprise some adults, for in our culture we are less able to allow pictorial than verbal expression of sex. It might, therefore, be well to recall how consistently in past civilizations these phallic symbols have been openly

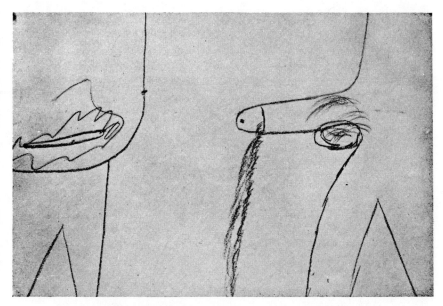

FIG. 34B. SECOND DIAGRAMMATIC DRAWING OF SEX ORGANS

The patient immediately began a second drawing in order to show more clearly and realistically the nature of the procreative process. Pointing to the male organ he said, "See the slime coming out? That's where the seed for the baby comes from, isn't it?"

used for religious, ritual or artistic expression. The child, if we permit him to return to this more immediate language of form and symbol, may more readily release valuable material buried in the unconscious.

While Nick had expressed in symbolic form much suppressed hostility and anxiety in pictures already described, these three sex diagrams are of a quite different order of expression. As designs, they are more diagrammatic and tell much that he had been previously forced to conceal because of threats from the adults in his environment. When all of Nick's suppressed sexual knowledge had fallen into its functional place in the story of the birth of the child, he then felt free to tell in pictures what else he knew on related matters. From the moment he had released this traumatic material in art expression, he developed a poise and liberation that helped him to speak more freely with both the psychiatrist and the writer about his resentment over rejection by the mother. Data on this subject are developed in

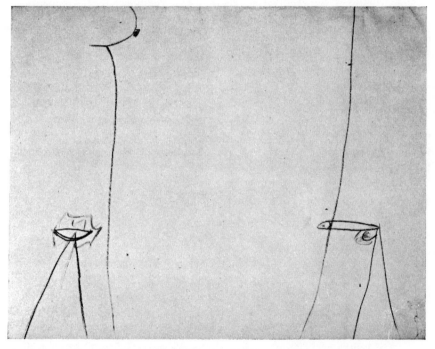

FIG. 34c. THIRD DIAGRAMMATIC DRAWING OF SEX ORGANS

In this third picture the interest shifted from the sexual parts of the male to the form of the female. Starting at the upper edge of the page, Nick drew rapidly the profile of a woman's breast, torso and leg in a single sure and clear outline. To this figure, a red nipple, the vaginal opening and pubic hair were added, but no comments were made. The male organ was then drawn, but it was extremely small in proportion to the woman's form. Emphasis went to the woman's full breast and the man's smaller penis, suggesting identification by the patient with the masculine role in this diagram. These three drawings were completed in no more than twenty minutes.

the next series of pictures which deals with the running away from home adventures.

Other behavior problem, as well as normal, children, when they have succeeded in releasing their sexual conflicts and questions through art work, have also shown similar decreases in anxiety and a growing freedom from a sense of guilt in matters pertaining to sex. Such corroboration has led this writer to regard parental attitudes and the cultural standards of our own society as primary factors in creating an unwarranted sense of guilt in children concerning their own sexuality. Confirmation of this viewpoint is to be found in the words of Karen Horney:[10] "In our culture the sexual sphere is the one in which guilt feelings are most frequently stimulated. — I do not see that sexuality as such is a specific source of anxiety. I do believe, however, that there is such a specific source in hostility or more accurately in repressed hostile impulses."

Release from such feelings of hostility was clearly indicated in Nick's drawings of war and his wish to destroy those specific "enemies" that represented his mother's lovers. Further intense hostility was released in the making of these love, marriage and sex drawings which also revealed, for the first time, the full import of his traumatic sexual experience to the patient.

The next pictures to be described, while an inherent part of the sex cycle drawings, deal with the forces of nature in an almost cosmic sense. The first of these is the large Rainbow (Fig. 32) which was drawn immediately following the pictures of the wedding. And the second is a picture of Spring (Fig. 35) which was drawn a little while after the diagrams of the sexual organs.

These nature pictures developed spontaneously and expressed a serene and happy mood for the patient, in which no threat of war or destruction entered to mar the scene. Until the drawing of this large rainbow, in the eighth art period, there had been but one previous design, apart from those which dealt with birth and sex, that did not deal, entirely, with war. Seizing four colored crayons, yellow, green, brown and orange, at random and holding them together as one, he made a sweeping arc of a rainbow across the breadth of his paper. This scene is described in the illustration of "The Rainbow and the Cycle of Nature" (Fig. 32).

This fusion of spring and winter, day and night, rainbow and moon within a single picture was no accident. Nor was it due to either impulsive or inaccurate observation. For on other occasions, Nick proved himself a keen and sensitive observer of the changing phases of nature. From that day, Nick became more relaxed and freer in his creative expression. While war pictures still continued to appear from time to time, they became less frequent and were not as explosive and violent in character.

The next picture, which developed into a scene of Spring was stimulated by flowers brought by the writer, in order to illustrate how pollen is carried from flower to flower, by bees and butterflies in the process of fertilization. Nick responded with delight to the flowers, and inhaling the faint odor of the pansies, said: "It smells like country and they look like butterflies." He began his picture with narcissus-like flowers and a golden sun. The rest of the design, including "The Major who Picks a Flower," the boy scout, and the baby in the carriage, which seem to indicate a symbolic representation of the patient's life, are described in more detail beneath the picture (Fig. 35).

FIG. 35. SPRING — "THE MAJOR PICKS A FLOWER"

This picture of spring was stimulated by flowers brought to the art session by the writer in order to illustrate how pollen is carried in the process of fertilization, from flower to flower. The patient drew the narcissi with his own inventive variations of red blossoms. The tree was then added with multi-colored leaves. When asked about this, he explained, "Oh, you know how it is in spring, the little leaves are pink and green and yellow and all colors." A wasp-like creature drawn from memory from an insect book is moving towards the flowers. The grotesque profile of a man, with the correct number of stripes on his arm, was described by the patient as "A major picking a flower." There are also drawn on the base-line, a tiny boy scout with a tent and a woman pushing a baby carriage. This series of figures, the baby with the mother, the boy and the major, seem to indicate a symbolic representation of the patient's own life. But no attempt was ever made with this or in any other drawing to interpret directly to the patient, the meaning of the picture. Why this was not done is explained in the paper.

While Nick was making these two landscapes of the Rainbow and Spring, he worked more quietly and spoke less. Both scenes gave the impression of serenity, combined with a sense of the joy and wonder of life.

When Nick examined a series of diagrams that showed the development of the human fetus and the differences in the structure of man and woman, he was much interested, asking many questions and commenting freely without the least embarrassment. He made apt use of these illustrations to verify his own knowledge and to check the correctness of the sex information he had received from the writer. On noting the diagram of the way the child was attached by the umbilical cord to the mother, he recalled the function of the cord and said, "The baby is fed and breathes that way through the mother." As Nick examined a picture showing the baby calf carried within its mother, he pointed to the cow's anus and commented, "That's where the baby comes out." Again, as Nick was told that this was not the opening, he ran through all the infantile birth theories, suggesting in quick succession first the navel and then the mouth, as possible openings through which the baby was born. By turning to the diagram, which showed the child carried within the mother's womb, it was possible to show him how it was ejected through the opening of the vagina. Nick was troubled and commented, "The baby's head is too big to come out through that opening in the mother." The process of the temporary expansion of the vagina was duly explained and accepted by him without further comment. He also found pictures of flowers and bees corroborating what the writer had already told him about the cross-fertilization of plants. When Nick had finished examining the pictures and had enquired directly and naturally, about each one in turn, he was asked whether he still wanted to know anything else. "No," he replied quietly, "now I understand."

With the completion of this series of pictures relating to love, marriage, birth and sex, several changes had taken place in Nick. He had succeeded in releasing the long-buried traumatic experiences concerning sex and had acquired, through a series of talks and the examination of diagrams, a clarification as to the nature and function of sex; anxiety and guilt feelings concerning such matters as sex, birth and marriage, were no longer in evidence and were now replaced by a natural and confident attitude in dealing with these subjects. As the result of a wider conception of the process of evolution through all forms of life, Nick's previously narrow and troubled concern over sex expanded to include a wide variety of subjects in new books. Whereas, at first, only those about tanks and planes and wars had interested him, he now began to bring to the art room, a series of illustrated volumes that told about mother animals and their babies, the life of undersea creatures and the "seeing eye" dog and its mate. This brought evidence of a spontaneous sublimation of the patient's newly acquired sexual understanding to a wider range of interests about plants, animals and man.

THE RUNNING AWAY ADVENTURES PICTURES

Nick had resisted all efforts at home, in school, or in the hospital to gain information about where he went or what happened to him when he ran away from home. He had been in the hospital five months and had attended art sessions for three, before the first picture on this subject was obtained. And it was only possible to overcome his intense resistance to the subject by suggesting that its more adventurous aspects would be worth recording in pictures.

The clinical history describes the patient's first brief and sporadic disappearances from home at four years of age when the mother left with a lover; it also traces how this grew into habitual truancy from school. While living at the hospital the patient found ways of escaping on various occasions when playing outdoors. At times he has returned by himself, voluntarily; on other occasions he was picked up by the police.

The patient, whenever asked, either at home, at the Bureau of Child Guidance or at the hospital why he had run away, always replied, "I don't know why." And it was evident, that he had so deeply repressed the painful reason for escaping that he really was unable to admit to anyone, least of all to himself, that he was running away from home because his rejection by the mother was intolerable to him. How the motive for these escapades was symbolically revealed in several drawings will be described before the corroborative comments of the patient to the psychiatrist are quoted.

When Nick came to an art session the day after one of these running away episodes, the writer decided to make an attempt to obtain, if possible, some pictorial expression of this experience. It was known that the Statue of Liberty was a location sometimes selected by Nick for these escapades. He had even suggested drawing it on one previous occasion. He therefore responded eagerly to the suggestion that he draw such a picture on that day. For the description of how he went to work and what he said, see the picture of "The Statue of Liberty" (Fig. 36).

Through the two drawings of the Statue of Liberty made by this patient, and his description and interpretation of these pictures, much light was thrown on the motivation of his attempts to run away. The

THREE RUNNING AWAY ADVENTURES (FIGS. 36, 37 AND 38)

After several months of art work it became possible to obtain some pictures from the patient about the places he visited when he ran away. He had, up to that time, refused to discuss these escapades and had always declared that he did not know why he ran away. And it was evident that he had so deeply repressed the painful reason for escaping that he was really unable to admit to anyone, least of all to himself, that he was running away from home because his rejection by his mother was intolerable to him.

FIG. 36. THE STATUE OF LIBERTY (First Drawing)

This first drawing of the Statue of Liberty was obtained on a day after he had again run away. It was known to be one of his favorite places. He drew the figure which is both comic and crude in appearance with great seriousness. He described the arm held aloft and the book in her other hand as he drew it. The statue was done in olive green, the crown and flag in orange; an oblong opening was placed at the base of the statue, as well as the interior spiral staircase mounting up within the woman's figure. He spent some time describing how strenuous it was to climb up inside the statue. The tall "buildings" in the foreground probably representing New York, were drawn in green and orange and the trees in their natural colors. "The flagpole," the patient explained, "is larger than the statue." (The sexual symbolism is evident.) That this statue symbolized the lost mother that he was searching for when he ran away was evidenced by a number of his comments of how he had his fare paid on buses by strangers in order "to go to Jersey to see my mother" and "to ride back to New York to see my mother."

text below these pictures should be read carefully (Figs. 36 and 37).

As Nick completed the picture, the writer asked whether he had often been to the Statue of Liberty.

"I went there with my mother," replied Nick. He admitted, when asked, that he had been there at other times also and that it was one of the places he liked to go to when he ran away. When questioned further as to whether he got there by subway, he said, "Yes." — "And then the ferry."

He resisted being questioned, giving only the briefest replies. After admitting that he had no money for this trip, he explained, when asked, how he had slipped through the subway stile. When the subject of whether he had not run away on the previous day was approached, he replied, "Yes, but I'd rather not talk about it." In spite of his usual attempt to evade this topic, certain facts were obtained; that he went to Jersey, out into the country by bus. Since he admitted having no money, he then told how he had asked a man to pay his fare. The reason he gave for his bus ride to the stranger is of special interest. "I said," Nick explained, *"I was going to meet my mother,* and when I wanted to come home I did the same thing. *I said I was going to see my mother in New York."*

It is evident, without going deeply into its symbolism, that this drawing of the Statue of Liberty signifies the mother — the lost mother that Nick is seeking to find again. He confirms this by describing how he saw this statue for the first time with his mother, and by his emphasis on climbing up inside the statue by means of the spiral staircase. The male symbol of the "flag pole that is larger" is set beside the woman's figure, expressing, in the language of the unconscious, another aspect of the patient's desire to return and possess the mother. Further corroboration, that in running away from home Nick is looking for a mother who will love him, is expressed in the way in which he obtained his bus fare from strangers by first saying that he was going to Jersey and then to New York to meet his mother.

Nick's reluctance about dealing with any of his running away experiences continued. When he was reminded of the plan to list all of these for pictures, his face quivered and he said: "Do I have to?" By joking with him and recalling those already planned, he was persuaded to help in drawing up the list for future pictures which included: subways, trolleys, ferries, automobiles — hitch-hiking and stealing rides on dashboards, going over Washington Bridge and the Statue of Liberty. Another day the subjects of trains, movies and Coney Island boat rides were added to the list. "Now I'll draw Washington Bridge," said Nick.

In order to draw Washington Bridge, he glanced out of the hospital window and said, "Let's see how it looks again." When he had received an impression of the bridge, he sat down with the colored chalks and said, "I'll do it at night." For a description of this completely imaginative picture, see the accompanying illustration (Fig. 38). This was one of the few times he was willing to speak, however reluctantly, of the subject of running away.

A month later, Nick again chose to draw the Statue of Liberty. He made no reference to his previous picture on that theme, but drew it with another color scheme and a different setting. This was in no sense a replica of his previous drawing; while set in a more imaginative background, it deals with realistic events based on his actual

FIG. 37. THE STATUE OF LIBERTY (Second Drawing)

A month later the patient again chose to draw the Statue of Liberty as a running away adventure. He made no reference to his previous drawing on this theme and drew it with a different color scheme and setting. The compelling power of this figure as a mother symbol, to this patient, is shown again by the way he creates an elaborate phantasy about the way "The Statue of Liberty who has been there for a thousand years turns purple," and "men in diving suits" have to "go under water to see if the Statue of Liberty is going to cave in." Clearly a phantasy to relieve anxiety about the loss of the mother. In this second picture the statue is outlined in bright blue and filled in with orange. The setting is more realistic than in the other drawing. The gulls and the "frank" stand and the boats in the harbor are described as they are drawn. The spiral staircase within the woman is again described, although not drawn.

observation of the Statue and its surroundings, including the gulls, the "frank" stand and the boats in the harbor. The chief interest of this picture is, however, focussed on saving the Statue from complete destruction by collapse into the sea; this is a phantasy clearly expressed to relieve anxiety about the loss of the mother. The description of how this picture was made and Nick's comments as he drew it, will again illustrate the compelling power of this figure of the Statue of Liberty as a symbol of his own mother whose impermanence and

FIG. 38. WASHINGTON BRIDGE AT NIGHT

This picture of an actual running away experience is, however, a completely imaginative drawing, showing the bridge in bright yellow, the water blue and green, one boat red and green and the other black. Great emphasis was placed on telling about the searchlights that shone from the bridge at night. These were drawn in purple, rose and yellow. The plane in the sky was also purple. Finally the hospital building, with its windows open, is placed on the right side of the picture. It is interesting to contrast this clear and decisive landscape towards the end of the art sessions with the turmoiled and explosive phantasies of war made in the earlier art periods.

instability are poignantly depicted in the eternal vigilance of the divers who prevent the Statue from sinking into the bay (Fig. 37).

From following the process of creation in these two pictures of the Statue of Liberty, it can be seen how much of the patient's anxiety concerning the mother was being released in both pictorial and verbal expression. This evident liberation through "free" expression may suggest how, with increased time allotted to such art work, more effective therapeutic results might be achieved.

A striking reaffirmation of the importance to Nick of this symbolic guarding and protection of the mother occurred when he later received, for Easter, a set of tiny baby chicks with a large mother hen. Pleased with the present, he took the mother hen out of the box, placed her on the table and said, "I'll put a baby chick on each side to guard her." He then set two more baby chicks, one behind and one in front of the hen as protection. After that he replaced the hen and chicks in their box. Other devices for guarding and protecting are to be found throughout the war pictures.

With the growing liberation of expression concerning his inner problems that had been achieved with the creation of these pictorial images accompanied by verbalized phantasy material, he had made clear, symbolically, why he was running away. It was then possible for him to become more articulate to the psychiatrist, concerning his long buried resentment against his mother. Such hostility he had previously been able to release only against the mother's "men friends" as his "enemies." But now, after his mother had failed to keep her appointment to visit him, he said to the psychiatrist, "The trouble is, I'm afraid my mother won't take me when I do get my week-ends. Maybe she won't come to see me tomorrow. I don't think she likes me anymore. She likes those other men a lot better than me."

When asked whom he meant, he described one of them as "Tommy B. She went away with him once and she promised me she was coming back the next morning, but she lied to me. She didn't come back for three or four months." The patient, by this time was sobbing hard and looking heart-broken. After a long silence, he said, "If it was just one or two men, then me and Bobby and the rest could beat them up, but what can you do with four or five?"

On another occasion after running away, when his mother was leaving him at the hospital, he told the psychiatrist on the following day, "I am sorry I ran away — I knew I shouldn't. I didn't want to leave my mother, but something said, 'Nick go. Go Nick,' and I just couldn't help it" — "I love my mother such a lot, but I am afraid my mother doesn't love me. Maybe she doesn't want me to come home ever — I used to think my mother really loved me, but now I think maybe she's turning on me." Asked why, he said: "Because she might love those men more than she loves me." Later he admitted: "Yes, I want my mother to love me more than those men."

It is evident that in the fifth month of his hospitalization, Nick was now able to articulate clearly his need of the love of the mother who kept on rejecting him for a series of lovers.

THE PATIENT'S RELATION TO THE FATHER AS EXPRESSED IN THE ART SESSIONS

The patient's attitude towards the mother has been followed in the series of drawings about "enemies" in the battle scenes, through the cycle of pictures about love, marriage, birth and sex, and in the running away adventure pictures. What concerns the patient's attitude toward the father appears less often and in more oblique fashion during the art sessions.

Soon after telling about his father's escape from a bombed oil tanker, he drew such a ship, the same boat that split apart with a "Crack" (Fig. 27); reporting his father's war exploits Nick exhibited a mixture of pride in his father and anxiety concerning his security.

In creating the wedding scene, he probably made his only pictorial allusion to the relation between the mother and the father; he drew the bridegroom smaller than the bride. His father, Nick stated some days later, was actually smaller than his mother. The figure of the groom in the wedding scene may, therefore, have stood for the insignificance of the father, both physically and spiritually, in the life of the family; and it may also have done double duty as a symbol of both father and son in relation to the bride-mother.

In the contradictory and unresolved relationship between mother and father, the patient was forced to undergo a constant strain; there was cause for anxiety in relation to both the mother and the father. As he grew more articulate, he was able to express to the psychiatrist, the nature of the anxiety caused by the anticipated return of the father from convoy duty. Besides his feelings of fear about his father's being lost at sea, he manifested equal fear about his father's homecoming to find his mother with another man, in which case he said he knew that his father would divorce his mother because he had heard him threaten to do so. He also feared that the mother would "tell the worst about him" to the father; meaning by "worst" the many times he had run away.

Receiving neither security nor sustained affection in his relation with either parent and recognizing his inability to compete successfully with the mother's succession of "men friends," it is not surprising to find a number of references in both play therapy and art sessions to some form of wish to escape from his intolerable home situation, through death or self-destruction.

When Nick was feeling quite depressed, after he had become involved in some sex play which was dominated by the ward bully, he began to model in both the art and play therapy sessions with the psychiatrist a series of battles between snakes and crocodiles. A medley of snakes and crocodiles, eagles and men, fought each other in life and death struggles and sucked each other's and their own blood; these episodes evidently symbolized the sex play that had occurred. At the end of one battle Nick announced: "This snake is glad he was killed, he wanted to be out of this world. He wouldn't live a long time. They shot at him with spears. He only had a little blood left."

When the patient had run away again from his Aunt's house in the country soon after the father, against the hospital's advice, had signed his release, he told the psychiatrist that, "If my father found me, he would send me to a reform school." It had been his hope that he would never be found. Asked what would have happened if he were not found, he replied, "I guess I would have died. That would be O.K. with me."

The father departed again on convoy duty, leaving the patient in charge of the mother. She continued her rejection of the patient, neglecting and ignoring him and then trying to make it up with perfunctory gifts and movie treats. Unwilling or unable to give him the maternal love he needed, she remained, to the end of Nick's hospitalization, unwilling to allow him to become emotionally independent of her, going so far as to complain that "Nick had been 'very platonic' in his attitude to me on Sunday."

Conclusion

In presenting this study of the psychodynamics of the art work of a nine-year-old behavior problem boy, the writer had a two-fold purpose in view: first to illustrate the way in which the projective technique of "free" art expression could be used to supplement the play therapy sessions of the psychiatrists and offer additional diagnostic material; and, secondly, to demonstrate how a child can be helped to release, in both realistic and symbolic art forms, what he could never express so frankly or completely in words thus using "free" art expression as a means of therapy.

A vital implication to be derived from this and other studies that have or are being made on children's art expression as an aid to diagnosis and therapy is that imaginative, creative expression is, in itself, a source of growth and sustenance as well as a language of communication in the life of every individual, whether he happens to be mentally disturbed or inwardly at peace with himself.

No clearer statement of the failure of our western civilization to accept such spontaneous expressions in all forms of art as a normal and necessary aspect of daily life is to be found than in Laurence Binyon's words: "At the present moment we in the West experience, and in experiencing resent, a consciousness of frustration. We have mastered and harnessed the forces of nature for our own uses, but something, after all our efforts, eludes us. We have divided life into separate compartments, each presided over by a science with a separate name; but the wholeness of life has somehow been obscured. What we seem to have lost is the art of living." [11]

Mr. Binyon continues by praising the positive and life-giving aspects of art as the lasting "record of human happiness, of human joy." In describing the work of the great Chinese artists, he says that: "It is an escape not from life, but into life. Therefore these paintings are mostly serene and exhilarating. Nor is there anything unreal about them; it is no dream world that they create."

In the East, unstinting recognition has always been accorded to art, as an expression of and not as an escape from reality; could the West bring itself to an acceptance of all forms of creative expression as a universal, normal and integrating experience that is neither effeminate nor neurotic, our culture might again find ways to restore harmony and balance to the disequilibrium of the modern psyche.

BIBLIOGRAPHY

[1] Frank, Lawrence K.: "Projective Methods for the Study of Personality," Journal of Psychology, Vol. 8; 389-413, 1939.

[2] Rapaport, D.: "Principles Underlying Projective Techniques," Character and Personality, Vol. X, No. 3, 213 March 1942.

[3] Prinzhorn, Hans: Bildnerei der Gefangenen Studie zur Bildnerischen Gestaltung Ungeübter, Berlin, Axel Juncker 1926.

[4] Lewis, Nolan D. C.: "Graphic Art Productions in Schizophrenia," Vol. V. Asso. for Research in Nervous and Mental Disease, pp. 344-368. Paul B. Hoeber, New York, 1928.

[5] Naumburg, Margaret: "Children's Art Expression and War," The Nervous Child, Vol. 2, No. 4, p. 360-373, 1943.

[6] —: "The Drawings of an Adolescent Girl Suffering from Conversion Hysteria with Amnesia," The Psychiatric Quarterly, Vol. 18, No. 2, p. 197-224, 1944.

[7] Freud, Sigmund: "New Introductory Lectures on Psychoanalysis," W. W. Norton and Co. New York, 1933.

[8] —: "Three Contributions to the Theory of Sex," Nervous and Mental Disease Publishing Co. New York, 1930.

[9] Jung, C. C.: "Collected Papers on Analytical Psychology," Second edition, London, Balliere, Tindall and Cox, 1917.

[10] Horney, Karen: "The Neurotic Personality of Our Time," W. W. Norton and Co. New York, 1937.

[11] Binyon, Laurence: "The Spirit of Man in Asian Art," Harvard University Press, Cambridge, Mass., 1936.

III

THE PSYCHODYNAMICS OF THE ART EXPRESSION OF A BOY PATIENT WITH TIC SYNDROME

INTRODUCTION

This paper will consider the art expression produced by an 11-year-old Jewish boy, while under treatment at the New York State Psychiatric Institute. His condition was diagnosed as maladie des tics, and his case has been described and discussed by Dr. Margaret Mahler and Dr. Leo Rangell in a paper published under the title of "A Psychosomatic Study of the Maladie des Tics (Gilles de la Tourette's Disease.")[4]

This particular study of the art work of a single patient is one of a series now being reported as aspects of a special research project at the New York State Psychiatric Institute and Hospital in order to investigate the possible use of creative art as an aid in diagnosis and therapy.[5-9] None of the patients in this study were chosen on the basis of special creative ability and several of them even expressed a dislike for art based on their formal training in the subject at school.

REPORT ON THE PATIENT'S ART EXPRESSION

Freddie had been hospitalized for seven months before he commenced art work with the writer. The patient continued these art sessions for six months: five months while hospitalized and one month more while under treatment in the outpatient clinic. After the summer holidays, when the patient returned to school, an attempt was made to continue the art periods. But he was unable to give sufficient time or attention to this effort for besides carrying a full time school program, he was now undertaking psychoanalytic treatment.

While the art sessions were in progress, written records were kept not only to include the manner in which the art work developed, but also to report on whatever significant conversations and other activities occurred during the art periods. In the case of this tiqueur the variations in the patient's involuntary movements were also noted.

Freddie had already been under psychotherapeutic treatment for over two years when the art work was begun. He had, by that time, reached that phase in the development of his disease described by Mahler and Rangell as the third stage when "the tics seemed fewer in number, but also seemed more isolated from awareness and demarcated from the rest of the personality."

In the first few months of art work Freddie was unable to maintain his interest for more than half-hour periods, but as he developed ability to express his experiences in original art forms he would ask for more time in order to complete his pictures. When this patient walked into the art room on the first day, he announced, "I know what I want to make." He chose the plastecine and modelled an airplane with experienced skill. But when the wide-winged plane was completed, the wings dropped off. Without making any effort to repair the damage, the patient sat staring at his broken plane, uttering his complaint that "the wings always fall off."

An attempt was made to show him how he could overcome this difficulty by inserting small wooden sticks as structural supports to brace the wings against the body of the plane. The success of this new technique encouraged and delighted the patient.

When this plane was satisfactorily completed Freddie was asked whether he wished to try painting. But he evaded the use of anything but plastecine by saying: "No, I do that pretty well. I'm not perfect." Only after several more periods of art was Freddie finally willing to try drawing for the first time. It then became evident that he had been disguising his inability to draw or paint by a pretense of expertness.

To do things "perfectly" was evidently a matter of deep concern to this patient; so also was his desire to please and be approved by both adults and children. His behavior on the ward and in school, as well as in the playroom with the psychiatrist, was motivated by this persistent desire to be approved. The ward nurse described his behavior as "too good" and the class teacher was critical of the patient's neglect in completing his school work while striving, nevertheless, to obtain gold star rewards. Similar behavior was evident at first in the patient's response to art work. How this inordinate need of approval was modified as he found himself in creative expression will be discussed as the various phases of the patient's art are described.

On all subjects that related to his own life and relationships he maintained a defensive and noncommittal attitude during the art sessions. Asked by the writer as to which school subjects he liked best, he replied, "Everything; I like arithmetic, reading, geography, everything." When he was questioned as to ·which he preferred of two movies, he answered "both."

On the first day, however, he went so far as to admit that he did like making "lots and lots of planes and sometimes boats and guns" at home. This corresponded to the aggressive war play described by the psychiatrist in the play therapy sessions.

In the final month of hospitalization, the patient voiced one criticism of his family during the six months of art work. As he was departing for a week-end visit, he was asked by the writer to describe the first thing he would probably do when he reached home. "Talk, I guess," he replied. Pressed further to tell what he liked to talk about with his sister, he explained, somewhat scornfully, "Oh, she talks a lot about her dolls and school." And then, evidently recalling a recent disagreement with her, he added, *"She contradicts me. And I'm afraid I'll be wrong."* In his own words Freddie had expressed, for the first time one of the motivations of his consistently noncommittal attitude on all subjects that related to his life. Having unintentionally revealed resentment against his sister, he immediately tried to disguise it by offering a brotherly expression of approval with the comment : "But my sister's all right."

It seemed possible that the patient was afraid of being wrong in a verbal quarrel with his sister because such an admission came too close to one of his central conflicts ; namely, that something was wrong with himself. It was later reported that this boy did show a constant fear of being a damaged person in the course of his psychoanalytic treatment.

This single episode suggests how persistently Freddie had succeeded in repressing vocalization of all hostile feelings against his family. It had been recognized that, as the youngest of three children, he was under the constant strain of competing with two older siblings. A dread of being wrong or of becoming a failure played a dominant part in his feeling of not being a complete person.

Freddie's original doubt of his own power to create in either crayons or water colors was also motivated by a sense of insecurity similar to his vocalized fear of-being wrong with the sister. In the first art session, he had attempted to disguise his dread of experimenting with such untried media as chalks and water colors by pretending that he used them so well that he would prefer to model in plastecine. In both situations — at home with his sister, and in the art room with the writer — the patient was making efforts to disguise his exceptional lack of independence to deal with new and unfamiliar situations and media. As in the case of many behavior problem boys, whose ego has remained undeveloped, Freddie strove to conceal his insecurity from others as well as himself ; in order to avoid facing new situations he invented devious and varied mechanisms of defense.

The patient began his art sessions by choosing to model bombing planes and other instruments of war. When he gained the confidence to draw his own pet cat in colored chalks, he was less afraid of further experiments. He then attempted to recapture some dreams in crayons and in plastecine. With water colors he was soon able to create landscapes of Riverside Drive. For his aggressive impulses he soon discovered a new release in making scenes of war in a series of crayon drawings. These were promptly followed by a more peaceful Easter Phantasy. In the concluding phases of his art work, Freddie invented a series of episodes to illustrate life in the Armed Services; and he also created many lively sketches showing the activities in modern Sports and Games. A certain male assertiveness was evident in the choice of subject in these final drawings, but they no longer expressed the extreme aggression of his earlier plastecine modelling of implements of war and destruction.

In relation to the modifications observed in Freddie's artistic expression it is interesting to quote a description of this patient's behavior from the Mahler, Luke, Daltroff study.[2]

"F. K. displayed, at the beginning of treatment, quite an active desire to join the children on the block in their group play — gradually the mother's and the big brother's ambivalent anxieties for his well-being were taken over by him, and he gave up the struggle for his freedom, but not before two little accidents, which quite obviously were induced by his inner conflict, 'convinced' him that the rough play 'is not good for me'."

This description of Freddie's withdrawal from active play throws interesting light on his many pictures of sports and games made in the last phase of his art expression. Such over-determined action drawings will then be understood to serve as a phantasy release from his motor neurosis.

The way in which this patient's aggressive impulses and involuntary movements related themselves to certain changing aspects of his creative expression will become evident as the art products are described.

Since this patient, whose art work is to be described, was under treatment for $2\frac{1}{2}$ years, first at Mt. Sinai Hospital and then at The Psychiatric Institute, a condensation of the clinical history as reported by Mahler and Rangell is reproduced.

CLINICAL HISTORY

Freddie, an 11-year-old Jewish boy, began at the age of 7 to display a series of increasing involuntary tic-like movements of various parts of the body. These were followed later by the uncontrollable emission of inarticulate animal-like noises. Echolalia and echopraxia then appeared but only on occasions of great excitement, as at the movies.

The patient is the youngest of three children, the son of Russian-born immigrants, there being an older brother of 19 and a sister of 13. The mother is a highly emotional, neurotic woman, definitely the dominant member of the family, and the father a passive sort, who is a poor provider, irritable and insecure. The home life is a hectic one, with constant quarrels, shouting, and emotional scenes, superimposed upon ever-present financial distress. There is no family history of nervous or mental disease.

Freddie was an unplanned, unwanted child, whose mother, during her pregnancy with him, did everything within her power to induce an abortion. After the birth of the child, the mother felt "he must surely be a cripple," and immediately set about compensating for her conscious as well as unconscious guilt feelings toward him by a markedly overprotective attitude and constant anxieties about his health. The patient was a normal infant, and developed normally in all respects. He was overindulged with food and was always over-weight. In the last few years, he has shown a voracious appetite and an unusual degree of insatiability, which have resulted in a marked obesity. An important event, which occurred when the patient was 3 months old, and which was probably not unconnected with the emotional and psychological environs of the patient's early life, was the fact that at that time the father, who until then had worked steadily as a taxi driver, suffered an automobile accident which resulted in a serious injury to his spine. This caused a permanent work incapacity which has been responsible for the dire financial straits of the family since that time.

The patient had whooping cough, measles, and chicken-pox during childhood, with uneventful courses. Most careful and repeated questioning of mother and father did not reveal illness to support suspicion of encephalitis in the patient's anamnesis. He had a tonsillectomy at four and otitis media at five years. His habits were normal; he was an average student in school, and mixed well with other children. He shared his parents' bedroom, sleeping part of the time with his mother, until the age of 2. From then until 8 years of age, he slept in a bed with his older brother. The mother states: "They could not get along. Freddie used to throw himself around in bed. That's how it all started."

The patient began at the age of 7 to blink his right eye. This seemed at first to be in imitation of a friend of the patient's brother, with whom the latter worked and played. The involuntary winking soon involved the left eye as well, and subsequently movements began to occur in other parts. There developed in succession "twitching movements of the head to the left," "shaking of the right hand and right arm," "puckering up of the lips, and protrusion of the tongue." When trying to fall asleep, "his whole body would shake" and he often would have to be taken out for a walk by the mother at 2 a. m. to relieve his restlessness. The patient then began to make involuntary noises imitating a cat or a dog, sounds which were distressing and resulted in much difficulty at school. During periods of great excitement, it was noted that the patient would imitate the words and actions of others in an uncontrollable manner, as for example when at the movies. The symptoms have progressed, although there have been variable periods of relative quiescence.

After a two-week hospitalization on the neurological service of the Mt. Sinai Hospital, diagnosis, psychogenic tic, the patient was referred to the Mental Hygiene Clinic of that hospital in August, 1940, at which time regular observation and psychotherapeutic visits were instituted. After an initial therapeutic success, aggravation of the symptoms occurred in November, 1940, following an accident in which the patient cut one of his fingers and the mother, in her haste to secure aid, fell down a flight of stairs, necessitating treatment for both of them. The patient was admitted to the Children's Service of the New York State Psychiatric Institute on June 2, 1941.

Physical examination showed the patient to be an obese white boy with the general appearance of the Fröhlich habitus.

In the neurological examination only the description of the involuntary movements of the patient will be quoted. These movements were more active and varied in the two years of treatment prior to those final months of hospitalization when the writer began the semiweekly art sessions with this patient.

There were many involuntary movements, occurring almost in spurts or paroxysms, varying considerably in their frequency and severity, and alternating with periods of relative quiescence. These movements included rapid, lightning-like successive turning movements of the head to the left, followed by forceful turning of the head back to the midline. There occurred lifting of the eyebrows, wrinkling of the forehead, and an occasional winking of the left eye. Often the lips were involuntarily puckered, with the lower lip thrust far forward. The tongue was sometimes forcefully protruded. More rarely, there was a forward thrusting movement of the right shoulder and arm and still less often of the left arm.

The electro-encephalogram was within normal limits, though there were many movement artefacts.

The revised Stanford Binet showed the patient to have an IQ of 118.

The patient was discharged from the Psychiatric Institute in June, 1942. Since that time, he has continued to be followed in the outpatient department of that institution and at present is under psychoanalytic treatment.

The Rorschach test, which was performed and interpreted by Dr. Z. Piotrowski, confirmed the patient's response during the art sessions. Only that paragraph which describes the patient's psychological responses as they relate to his phantasy life and inhibitions will be quoted. As Dr. Piotrowski states:

"The boy is of superior general intelligence but his intellectual effi- ciency, especially his conscious control over the thought processes, is inferior. The boy seems to be capable of a great variety of psycho- logical experiences. There is an intensive phantasy life; some tendency to, and even habit of some self-analysis. While there is an intense psychological life, the outward activities of the boy do not seem to be commensurate with his inner experiences because of marked inhibi- tion. The boy is cautious in his dealings with others. If he shows a genuine feeling from time to time, an impulsive emotion now and then, he does this in part because of his poor conscious control over his thoughts and at times also over his actions. He would like to keep himself under strict control but cannot always succeed in this desire. The prolonged voluntary attention is too poor."

The "marked inhibitions" mentioned by Dr. Piotrowski are over- come with difficulty by the patient in the art sessions and the "inten- sive phantasy life" for which "his outward activities do not seem com- mensurate" eventually finds new forms of expression as the art ses- sions proceed.

How New Themes Developed in the Patient's Art Work

During the first two art sessions Freddie preferred to model such familiar types of war planes and submarines as he had made at home. In the second period he remarked, "I suppose I ought to make a head of George Washington." When this idea was not too enthusiastically received, he proceeded to suggest the substitution of a head of Lin- coln or Harrison.

An attempt was made to interest the patient in modelling something with which he was familiar in his own life experience, instead of a head of an American president. Freddie's response was to suggest making a head of his mother.

The Patient Draws His Pet Cat

Since the chance of success with this difficult untried subject seemed doubtful, the conversation was shifted to pets. Freddie was eager to tell all about his cat Queenie. "We thought," he explained, "Queenie was a she when we named it. But the man who gave it to us told my father that Queenie was a he. But we kept the name just the same."

It was not difficult at this point to encourage the patient to try modelling his pet. "But I don't know how," he added. He was asked to decide, first, in what position he wished to model the cat. He re- plied, "Lying down."

Although Freddie had intended to make Queenie in plastecine, he became so interested in capturing his pet in crayon and chalk drawings that he never modelled his cat. The patient, persisting in his interest during two art sessions, made six drawings of his pet.

He was most critical of his first attempt. "That nose," he remarked, "looks more like a chicken's than a cat's." Freddie was asked, before making another picture of Queenie, to close his eyes and try to recall just how his pet would look. As a result of this imaginative projection, the second profile drawing had more resemblance to the form and quality of a cat (Fig. 39).

THE PATIENT'S PET CAT (FIGS. 39, 40, 41 AND 42)

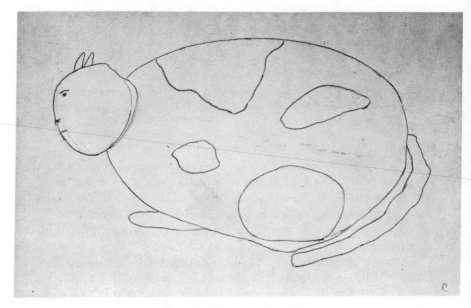

FIG. 39. SECOND ATTEMPT

This is the second of six drawings; the first was described as having "a nose that looks more like a chicken's than a cat's."

Since the patient was inclined to tense his entire body as well as his arm and hand whenever he attempted to draw, it was necessary to spend some time in showing him relaxing exercises. Release from misplaced body tension is needed, not only for the large swinging arm movements in good drawing, but it is also essential in directing the control of free brush strokes in painting.

Freddie, like most beginners, tried to set down too many remembered details in small constricted pencil lines. It was therefore necessary to make him aware of the larger rhythmic movements needed in drawing his cat upon the sheet of paper. He was asked to attempt to draw the entire curve of the cat's back in a single easy swing of the pencil across the paper. Then, instead of worrying about the details of the cat's features, he was shown how to sketch in the general position and balance of the head in relation to the rhythm of the body. When the rounded haunch on which the cat rested had also been drawn with a free, swinging stroke, the addition of the features presented less difficulty to the patient; whiskers, paws and tail were then added in order to complete the design.

So absorbed did the patient become in capturing a likeness of Queenie that he made four outline drawings on the first day. The

FIG. 40. THIRD ATTEMPT

This was done in brown crayon with white crayon used for the spots. To the patient the resulting realism elicited the comment, "This looks just like Queenie."

last one pleased him so well that he decided to fill it in with brown crayon (Fig. 40). Pink ears and large white spots were added. "It looks just like Queenie," he commented, as he laid down his crayon at the end of the hour. He then suggested drawing more pictures of his pet in the next art period.

In the following session, Freddie began by outlining his cat in purple chalk with a dish of milk beside him. This was the fifth drawing that the patient had made of Queenie (Fig. 41). Thus far he had tried for a realistic presentation of his cat. In the sixth picture (Fig. 42) a great change took place. Interest in a new box of colored chalks led, apparently, to a complete modification of his approach. He was attracted to a brilliant magenta chalk and decided to outline his cat in that color; he then proceeded to fill in the creature's form with a solid mass of this same shade. But instead of completing the rounded haunch of the cat in the same color, he covered it with emerald green. The background of this picture was then filled with deep blue and the floor on which the cat rested was done in solid purple. Unfortunately, the reproduction fails to suggest the unusually vivid and imaginative color relations that Freddie developed, for the first time, in this design.

Fig. 41. Fifth Attempt
This shows the cat with a dish of milk.

The patient, by overcoming some of his inhibitions had begun to express his affection for his pet cat in original crayon and chalk drawings. This made possible the initial release of that repressed phantasy life which Dr. Piotrowski had described in his interpretation of the Rorschach test. In the final picture of a magenta cat he was able to conceive a creature in unrealistic colors that satisfied his own taste.

The transformation of the patient's repetitive creation of model planes and boats into this varied series of cat pictures now made him able to carry out his own ideas more easily in the following art sessions.

The way in which these cat forms came into existence may serve to suggest how the process of liberation into "free" expression in art cannot take place by merely urging a patient to make whatever he wishes. For, in order to prepare a patient to pour his own experience and imagination into forms of creative expression, he must first gain confidence and discover his ability to do so.

Fig. 42. Sixth Attempt

This shows a magenta cat with green haunch, a purple background and a blue floor; a completely imaginative design has been substituted for the previous more realistic conception. See also color plate II.

In such an approach, technique is not ignored but is introduced in an incidental manner *after* the patient has begun to express himself. In this, it differs from the traditional method of teaching art; for the formalist tends to introduce rules of technique before the patient has attempted to give shape to his own conceptions.

The Patient's Cat and the Problem of Birth and Sex

As soon as the patient had described his cat Queenie with the explanation that "She was a he," it was evident that some aspects of the problems of sex and birth remained to be explored. That Freddie was misinformed on the subject was corroborated by the psychiatrist's notes that were recorded several months before Freddie began the art sessions. "The patient speaks of his cat with a great deal of affection and likes to play with it. He derives some security and satisfaction from the cat that is denied by the family. — The patient was sure Queenie is a boy simply 'because it didn't have babies. If it were a girl,' he said, 'it would have babies when it was nine months.' He believes that baby cats and baby dogs come from inside of the mother's stomach and are born through the mouth. He believes that only females can have babies and that there does not necessarily have to be a father. Asked by the psychiatrist as to what part the father played, the patient replied, 'Oh, he reads the paper'."

The psychiatrist reported nothing more, in the progress notes, concerning the patient's remarks on sex or birth. Had this patient not been destined for psychoanalytic treatment in a few months after leaving the hospital, the writer would have pursued further the unresolved problems concerning birth and sex in this 11-year-old boy. How such matters were approached when they appeared as aspects of other patient's conflicts, may be found in several of the other studies of art expression in this series.[5-10]

THE MODELLING AND DRAWING OF DREAMS

The patient attempted to reveal two of his dreams during the art sessions. In the second period he modelled a coiled cobra with flattened head. This was made in response to a query about frightening dreams: "Yes, I saw some cobras and ran away," he explained. Besides being afraid of snakes, Freddie declared, "The other thing I'm afraid of is that I can't go home to my family." When assured that, as he improved, he would return home, he responded, "Yes, I'm better. I don't move so much or make noises."

This was one of the rare references that the patient made to his disease in the art room. His comment about the reduction of his involuntary movements and noises corresponds to an analysis of the patient's inner struggle as reported by Mahler and Rangell:

> The patient's conscious desire to ward off outward expression of his inner impulses is extreme. Thus, in discussing his tics, he states, "I can always feel where I am going to have to move. I get a funny feeling in that part first. It gets worse and worse and I try with all my might to fight against it, but I can't, and finally it moves and I can't stop it." The same inner struggle is carried on within the personality of the child in respect to all his impulses, so that often the outer appearance is deceptive and belies the inner turmoil. The inhibitions and control, however, are inadequate. The symptoms break

through and thus involuntary expression is given to the impulses which cannot be successfully retained.

With the development of the intrapsychic struggle, another tendency was established, namely that of increased self-observation. This increased narcissistic attention to his own body was a secondary effect, and was responsible for the hypochondriacal traits which the patient displayed and which have been described. It also accounts in part for the rapid defensive actions on the part of the patient at the slightest increase in tension due to perception of somatic stimuli (from within the body).

The tic movement is a disguised gratification of an impulse which cannot be controlled. The very same disposition to tic formation serves in these patients to ward off the gratification and the defense against it, set up a vicious circle. More and more groups of expressional muscles become involved, more and more gestures are used, and soon there are added to these automatisms primitive vocal expressions, as well as vasomotor symptoms and hypochondriacal self-observation.

During the first year of observation, each tic corresponded with and could be traced to a specific emotional situation and represented a specific affective expression. The violent denying gesture of his head and neck, the defiant sticking out of the tongue, the pushing movement of the arm, as if shoving away an imaginary threatening person or thing, are only some of the examples. The tics were interchangeable in that, for example, when he was forced by his new teacher to suppress those tics which disturbed the class most, namely 'the noises,' another channel for expression had to be used, and the patient, to his own dismay, forcefully stuck out his tongue.

The changes which have taken place in the patient's disease during the course of the writers' observation have been described. Whereas originally, at the age of 9, the tics were diffuse and widespread, increasing promptly with excitement to paroxysms of generalized movements, accompanied by vocal utterances, echo phenomena and vivid mimicry, at the present time, at the age of 11, the tics are more isolated phenomena, fewer in number, more automatic in character, and more fully demarcated from the total personality. The vocal sounds are minimal, and the echo phenomena have disappeared. Mimicry has diminished markedly, the facial expression having actually become flattened out and at times even somewhat masklike from restraint. The patient is apparently in the stage before the appearance of coprolalia, in which he is defending himself against the existence of "mental coprolalia."

The significance of this analysis of the inner conflict of the patient, as expressed in the production of involuntary movements and sounds, is reinforced by the cycle of development in his art work. When the last phase of Freddie's drawings has been described, it will become evident that the patient here succeeded in projecting into his art expression some of the symbolic significance of his suppressed involuntary movements.

MOUNTAIN AND AIRPLANE DREAM

Before describing the mountain and airplane dream that the patient used in the fifth art session, it is necessary to state that Freddie's ambition in life was to become a pilot. In this dream he was flying his own plane. But after narrating the events of the dream, he made it in a

A DREAM: THE PATIENT PILOTING A PLANE (FIGS. 43, 44, 45 AND 46)

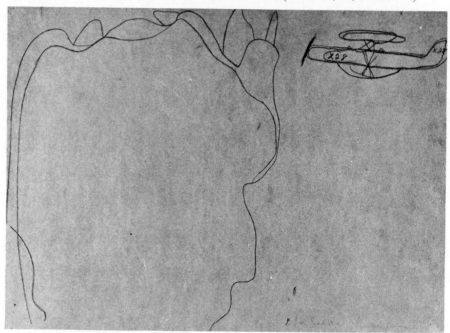

FIG. 43. FIRST VERSION

The patient's plane is flying towards the mountain with what may be phallic symbols. There is no catastrophe, because the patient asserts: "I always wake up before anything happens in a dream."

series of drawings with two different conclusions. In the first report, the patient was flying head-on toward a high mountain, upon which he saw "a kind of house with a chimney, but still it wasn't like a real house." It took some persuasion to get Freddie to draw this house with its pointed protrusion, posed on the right of the plateau-like mountain (Fig. 43).

As he described how his plane was flying toward impact with the mountain, he was asked what happened next. His reply was: *"I always wake up before anything happens in a dream."* Here is evidence of profound anxiety which the patient attempts to ward off by waking himself before the catastrophe is upon him.

When he undertook to draw this dream he constructed it so that one ending held the catastrophe in suspense and in the other the plane crashed to destruction. In the original version (Fig. 43) the patient was flying in his plane toward the mountain with the peculiar pro-

FIG. 44. SECOND VERSION IN THREE DRAWINGS. First Episode.

Several planes mounting skywards from their hangars. The patient's plane is described as nearest to the sun.

tuberance. He drew this scene over twice before it satisfied him. He said that he would then draw the introductory picture of the dream. In this picture he had a number of other fliers mount into the air with him, and their hangars were drawn in the lower section of the scene (Fig. 44).

The third and fourth drawings that Freddie now made illustrated the second ending to the dream. In this conclusion, the catastrophe, which the patient had first insisted never took place in a dream because he always woke himself up, was now permitted expression in two pictures. This time Freddie drew a golden rayed sun in the sky to the left of the plane (Fig. 45) ; he then explained: "The sun is so hot it explodes the gas in the engine of the plane." The resulting disaster was drawn in the fourth sketch (Fig. 46), in which Freddie and his plane are falling downward to destruction beside the steep mountain.

Interest in this dream carried over into the next art session when Freddie proposed to repeat it again in plastecine. He spent the entire period modelling carefully only the plane in which he flew.

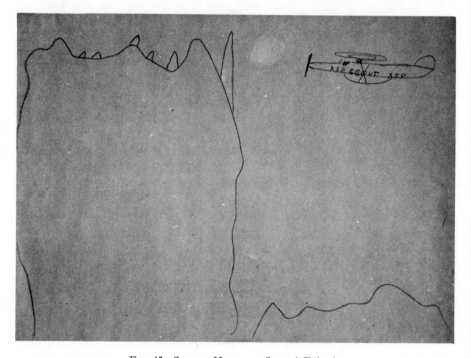

Fig. 45. Second Version. Second Episode.

The patient, as pilot, approaches the sun and its heat explodes the engine of the plane.

Absorption in this dream still dominated the three succeeding art sessions in which the large dream mountain was modelled in relief. Not only was the peculiar pointed projection on the house reproduced, but several other pointed peaks were added. When placing a final, tiny peak, he commented: "See here's a little one. Doesn't that look far away?" Asked whether these other projections had appeared in the original dream he replied: "No, I just put some more in because

they look nice." The same reply was given to modelling of the cave
that he had chosen to add in the side of the mountain.

No attempt was made to deal further with the unconscious significance of the protrusions on the mountain which may be phallic symbols; or with the birth phantasy symbolism of the cave within the
mountain because of the planned psychoanalytic treatment of this
patient.

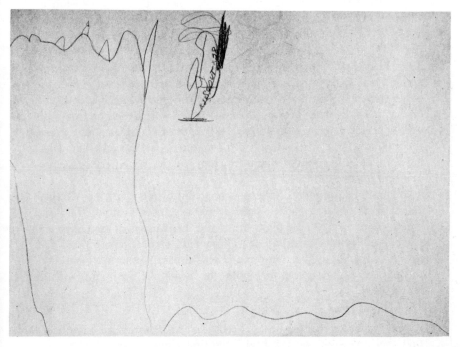

Fig. 46. Second Version. Third Episode.
The patient and his plane crash to destruction.

In this patient's dreams as reported by Mahler and Rangell: "The
patient's earlier phantasies and dreams usually contained a mean older
brother, a spy or traitor, sometimes even a robber, and as a counterpart, a young boy or brother. There was usually a happy ending,
either a reconciliation between the two, or a punishment of the evil
one."

Only after completing the analysis of Freddie did Dr. Mahler review the data obtained during the art sessions. She noted a number
of confirmations of her own findings concerning this tiqueur's attitude toward his family, himself and his sexual conflicts.

Of special interest is her comment on the symbolic significance of

the series of drawings just described. Dr. Mahler pointed out the
exact correspondence in time between the dates of Freddie's dream
drawings, in which he depicted himself as pilot, with the period in
which his older brother was in training as an army air pilot. But the
brother was soon found unfit for such combat duty and was then reduced to ground crew status. In the art expression, as in the analytic
treatment, the same ambivalent attitudes of the patient toward his
older brother are evident; this was combined in an expression of
admiration and aggressive envy. "While Freddie pretended to be 'so
happy' that his brother was less exposed to danger in ground crew
training he showed," says Dr. Mahler, "that he was actually disappointed by his brother's reduced status from pilot to ground crew
man. In his analysis several phantasies were produced concerning the
patient's relation to his big brother. Freddie had shared a bed with
his brother for some time and his phantasies were concerned with his
own superior manliness as compared to that of his big brother. Since
the brother's male attribute played a prominent part in such phantasies,
it is probable that these dream drawings, of the same period, are expressing the same theme."

In the later periods of the psychoanalytic treatment, Dr. Mahler
also reports that the patient used deeply disguised symbolic material
which centered upon the big brother and the dangers of sexuality and
more specifically masturbation. This would seem to correspond also
to the symbolic subject matter of these dream pictures which show
the patient as pilot colliding with the penis-like formation of the
mountain.

WAR IN PICTURES

Before describing a series of Freddie's war pictures, it is significant
that their creation coincides with the first training period of the big
brother as a combat pilot, before he had been reduced to noncombat
service in the ground force.

The patient had long found release for his aggressive impulses in
war games and modelling of bomber planes, warships and weapons of
destruction. But in the tenth art session he made his first picture of a
battleship. He was stimulated to this attempt by the successful chalk
drawing of another patient which showed the burning of the Normandie. To compete with this achievement, Freddie announced:
"I'll make a picture of the British Ark Royal" (Fig. 47). The sinking
of this airplane carrier had been recently reported.

The patient had chosen to draw a plane-carrying warship. But,
ignoring the realistic, gray garb of a ship prepared for battle, he gave
his imagination free rein and drew the outline of the Ark Royal in
bright red; the planes resting on the deck were blue green; the port-

War and the Sublimation of Aggression Figs. 47, 48, 49 and 50)

These three drawings of war done in colored chalk or crayon were drawn within a couple of weeks of each other, Appropriate sounds of battle were introduced to dramatize each episode. The tempo of violence and hostility increased until, in the third design, "War on the Ground," chaos and destruction are achieved. A joyous Easter picture sublimated the aggression in the next art session.

Fig. 47. The Ark Royal

This was an unrealistic drawing of the recently sunk British airplane carrier. The outline is in red, the planes on the deck blue green, the port-holes olive green and the funnels bright orange. The only realistic touches were the gray guns, the black smoke and the blue sea.

holes were done in olive green and the funnels in bright orange. The only realistic touches in this design were the gray guns, the black smoke and the blue sea.

Before planning the next war picture, Freddie asked, "Shall I make a fight?" When the decision was left to him he decided to do so. A red cruiser stood by as a series of red and green planes battled in the sky; the red planes belonged to the Allies and the green to Hitler. He called it "War in the Air" (Fig. 48). The scene was dramatized with all the sounds of bomb explosions and whizzing bullets furnished by Freddie as he completed the design.

Three weeks later he came to the art session, announcing: "I want to do a great battle picture with tanks and barbed wire." As the scene developed, Freddie called it "War on the Ground" (Fig. 49). Five or six tanks of various sizes in the foreground move across the scene of carnage. Tangled barbed wires are stretched in every direction across the deep trenches. "I must have dead men," he announced, as his face lighted up with a smile.

As he filled in the battle scene he explained, "The ground is brown. There are gun shot explosions. There are hidden machine gun nests." He spent much time filling the air with a series of star-like explosions in white, yellow and blue. "I must have dead Japs," and he strewed a series of them sprawling in yellow crayon across the battlefield. "They're stinking Japs," he explained. As the tanks were drawn emitting shots and the machine guns fired in reply, Freddie made all

FIG. 48. WAR IN THE AIR

"Shall I make a fight?" the patient asked before beginning this picture which depicts a battle between a red cruiser and red planes of the Allies and green planes belonging to Hitler.

the whirring and explosive sounds and acted out all the movements of the troops. Asked how the battle would end, he replied, "I don't know. I hope the Allies win." Then he asked, with great intensity in his voice: "Isn't war terrible?" He was excited, and the dead men, both Jap and Allied, and the noise of battle, produced enormous satisfaction and release in the patient. For the first time after several months of art work, Freddie was here giving vent to his inhibited feelings of aggression in a veritable orgy of destruction. He was rather proud of his picture of "War on the Ground." It was indeed a stark representation of the chaos and destruction of war.

Dr. Mahler notes that this design of "War on the Ground" corresponds in time with the assignment of the big brother to ground crew instead of pilot training. Freddie here created the violence of ground warfare, making this as dangerous as possible, whereas previously, when the brother was training as a pilot, the dangers of war as depicted in air combat were emphasized.

FIG. 49. WAR ON THE GROUND

This scene was begun as "a battle picture with tanks and barbed wire." The trench to the left is filled with tangled wire. "Dead men — stinking Japs" lie about the ground. A series of large star-like explosions in white, yellow and blue fill the air. The patient, in the midst of his delight in battle, asked, "Isn't war terrible?"

In these two aspects of the patient's art expression of war in the air and on the ground, there are exact time correspondences with the periods when the big brother was training, first as air pilot and then as a ground crewman in the armed services.

As soon as this design of "War on the Ground" was completed, the patient announced, "Next time I'll do an Easter picture."

ASPECTS OF PATIENT'S SUBLIMATION THROUGH IMAGINATIVE EXPRESSION

Freddie had not forgotten about the proposed Easter scene when he entered the room for the next art session. "I know exactly what I want to make today," he announced with a certain satisfaction. "I see

it all very clearly: a house and a garden on the right and over there,"
pointing to the left side of the paper, "woods with big trees." As he
completed the drawing of these forms (Fig. 50) he explained further:
'I'm going to put bright colored curtains in this house." After drawing the first pair in yellow, he asked, "Do they look like curtains?"
And at each window he varied their color.

FIG. 50. EASTER PHANTASY

As he completed "War on the Ground," the patient said, "Next time I'll do an
Easter scene." A row of crudely drawn trees is silhouetted against the blue sky.
The sun is shining and flowers bloom in the garden. A rabbit is running away
after ringing the doorbell of the house.

In the previous scene of "War on the Ground," Freddie had dared,
for the first time, to make human figures, even though they lay dead on
the ground. Now, envisaging a happy Easter scene, he undertook, for
the first time, to draw trees, a house and garden and an Easter rabbit.

The trees were crudely drawn with great brown block-like trunks
and fuzzy green added hurriedly as foliage. "There are sometimes
brown leaves, too, on the trees. You know, when life is dead." So
brown and orange leaves were included in the treetops.

Here Freddie's courage began to waver. "Now I must make a
rabbit, but I don't know how." He no longer repeated his earlier re-
frain of "I can't"; he readily responded to the suggestion that he draw

a rabbit first on practice paper. On his fifth attempt he was satisfied with the results. He then placed a copy of this brown bunny in his Easter scene. The rabbit was drawn carrying a basket of Easter eggs and running away after ringing the doorbell of the house.

When trees, grass and house were complete, the patient exclaimed: "It's a lovely day. I'll put in the sun and the blue sky." When asked about the kind of house he had placed in the picture, he answered, "Just a home."

As he worked, he would smile happily and describe what he would draw next. "Haven't I good ideas?" he would ask. When praised for his execution of this new picture, he replied: "I'm going to do lots more. I think next time, maybe, I'll do knights on horseback."

He showed greater relaxation and serenity during the development of this Easter scene than at any previous art session. In the weeks preceding the creation of the Easter phantasy his movements had increased. He was now happier and more self-confident and it was noticeable that he was free of involuntary movements for almost half an hour.

From the time that Freddie had succeeded in sublimating his aggressive impulses into this gay and imaginative Easter scene, he became more confident of his own ability to express himself. He was now less afraid to try out his own ideas; landscapes and animals and people were drawn without hesitation whenever he needed them to complete a picture.

The rest of his art work divides into three phases: some water colors of Riverside Drive, pictures illustrating the armed services and finally a series of dynamic drawings of Sports and Games.

RIVERSIDE DRIVE PAINTINGS

In the third month of his art work Freddie began to use poster paints. His earliest attempts were extremely simple and quite crude in execution. But they were based on his personal observation of Riverside Drive and they led him to experiment with the possibilities of water colors for expressing his own ideas. He made three views that were intended to be joined together when completed; they showed sections of the Drive where Freddie and his friends played baseball and other games.

Before attempting these water colors he made a small crayon drawing of Riverside Drive. He had chosen a familiar scene for his picture, which seemed to allow free range to his imagination. When clouds, sky and grass had been drawn in their true colors, he turned his attention to the rocky eminence where he liked to climb. As in the previous Easter scene he gave special attention to the leaves, scattering green and yellow ones upon the ground. In order to express the quality of the mottled rocks he drew them in brown and spotted them with large black dots.

When the rocks in this sketch were done, he filled in a space at the top of the hill with a heavy layer of black crayon. "This is mud, lots of mud," he declared. This emphasis on mud corresponds to the anal sadistic component common to tic syndrome patients in the study by Mahler, Luke and Daltroff.[2]

"We find in these children not only anal sadistic, but strong oral and genital habits and symptoms. More specific, however, are fixations in the affectomotor sphere. It is probably this very factor which accounts for the marked lack of ego synthesis despite superior endowment."

At the next art session, Freddie said he would like to paint but was unable to decide on a subject for his picture. As he was inexperienced in the use of water colors, it was necessary to show him how to obtain easy brush strokes and control the free-flowing water colors. (With less repressed patients it would have been unnecessary to give so much preliminary assistance on technique.)

The attempt to use new art materials immediately made the patient drop back into his previous hesitation. He stood before his paper unable to decide what he should make. The writer therefore suggested the possibility of continuing the subject from his last drawing of Riverside Drive. This appealed to Freddie and left him free to give his attention to learning to manipulate the water colors.

When asked to decide what colors he would need for his picture, he answered, "Oh, the same as last time." In order to prevent the patient from making a slavish reproduction of his previous sketch, he was asked to close his eyes and envisage the entire scene as he wished to paint it. Following this suggestion, he immediately called out, "Oh, I could make the rocks with all different colors: silver, gold, yellow, red, brown and white. And I need blue for the sky and brown for the trees."

Freddie was then ready to outline the rocks and bare trees in black (Fig. 51). When he repeated his request for both silver and gold he was told that metallic paints were not available. This seemed the moment to show him how colors could be modified and combined. Those which he had selected for rocks were then diluted, and one at a time they were combined with some of the white paint. As Freddie observed the creation of these new shades of bluish gray, yellowish tan, and violet, he exclaimed with delight, "Why, you've made colors

that look just like rock." Under the stimulus of this demonstration
Freddie was now ready to experiment on his own. He spent the rest
of the art period in making multicolored rocks.

RIVERSIDE DRIVE PAINTINGS (FIGS. 51 AND 52)

FIG. 51. A HILL WITH TREES AND MULTICOLORED ROCKS

Two additional pictures of Riverside Drive were then painted.
Both designs represented adjoining sections of the Drive where he
liked to play games with his friends. As he worked he explained how
there should be a ball field in the right hand scene and on the left a
place for other games.

It is interesting to note that this theme of games and sports was
destined to reappear later as the basis of many imaginative drawings
in the final phase of this patient's art expression. Freddie overemphasized his interest in athletics by means of his sports pictures
while remaining inactive and clumsy in relation to participation in
games. This corresponds to the report of Mahler, Luke and Daltroff
in their study of tic syndrome children.[2]

"Another puzzling discrepancy (in tic syndrome children) is that
of ambition and its realization through performance and achievement

in the motor area. Most children spontaneously stated or implied a preference for outdoor activity. But none of them, at the peak of their motor neurosis or before, were poised enough to be outstanding or even good in gymnastic or athletic achievement."

The third of the Riverside Drive paintings (Fig. 52) developed into a remarkably balanced, though simple composition. It shows a strip of blue river across the centre of the page; the semicircular black arch in the centre was described by Freddie as a "look-out over the Hudson." After painting in blue streaks for sky, he said, "Now

FIG. 52. THE HUDSON WITH A VIEW OF JERSEY IN THE DISTANCE

The semicircular arch represents a "look-out." Two benches face a gravel path.

I'll make Jersey over there," pointing to the area above the river. He then painted a brown strip to represent the shore line. Jumping up he looked out of the window. "Let's see," he said, "if Jersey looks like that." He seemed satisfied and went back to complete his painting.

In the foreground he placed a broad swath of grass; against this green background two black benches were set, one to the extreme right and the other to the left of the scene. Along the base line of this painting a gravel path of spotted pebbles was placed below the two black benches.

This design, although crude and stark in execution, illustrates how, when creative imagination is fused with personal experience, the patient's inherent sense of rhythm and balance comes into play quite spontaneously.

This painting of Riverside Drive shows a rather stiff and exactly balanced pattern; but as Freddie was now ready to use more of his own ideas, he soon began to create some rather unusual and daring space arrangements in his later drawings.

Even in the case of this poorly coordinated boy who was unable to master his involuntary movements, a sense of rhythmic and balanced composition evolved as he gained in confidence and ability to express himself.

DRAWINGS OF THE ARMED SERVICES

When the patient returned to the hospital after the Easter holidays, he suggested making the Coast Artillery. Fearful that his attempt might not succeed, he said that he had changed his mind. Only after some persuasion did he return to the subject and produce a scene in which two cannons emitted black smoke and fire across some water. Later Freddie transformed the picture into a camouflage scene with green foliage added to disguise the form of the cannons. This picture changed and grew spontaneously as he worked. He had, by now, forgotten those days when he depended on the subject of a president's head to copy.

Coast Artillery was the first of this series of eight drawings that Freddie made to illustrate the activities of the armed services. He had found them listed in his school reader but the composition of the drawings was entirely his own; the rest of these designs consisted of Tank Corps, Engineer Corps, Infantry, Air Corps, Signal Corps, Coast Guard and Cavalry.

The patient's growing interest in drawing war scenes was related to the placing of the big brother in the Air Force as has already been suggested. The development of these armed services pictures continues to follow the same pattern of interest in all aspects of war training.

The third drawing of this series was the Engineer Corps (Fig. 53). On that day Freddie came into the room saying, "I'll start right to work." He had apparently thought out in advance the entire idea for this picture. The air of assurance with which he divided his paper in an original composition, by running the river diagonally across the page and then placing trees on the opposing banks of the stream, was striking. "The bridge is being built by the engineers," he explained, as he drew its span across the river. "But I'm not going to finish it."

THE ARMED SERVICES (FIGS. 53, 54 AND 55)

A series of eight drawings to illustrate the activities of the armed services was made by the patient; they included Tank Corps, Engineer Corps, Infantry, Air Corps, Signal Corps, Coast Guard and Cavalry. The list of these services was found in a reader by the patient, but all the pictures were original. These were his first designs with figures of people in lively action.

FIG. 53. ENGINEERS: BUILDING A BRIDGE

Three men were then placed at work on each side of the incomplete bridge, while an officer in charge of the operation stood on the shore with arm aloft in the act of giving orders to the others. "Gee, wouldn't these guys get cold if they fell in the river?" Asked why he did not picture some that way, he replied, "Gee, that would be too cruel." When reminded that he had already made war pictures that were cruel, he replied, "Yes, but I don't feel that way now. That's different."

On the same day Freddie drew two other armed services, the Infantry and the Air Corps. In the Infantry design (Fig. 54) he also introduced a group of human figures. He had been relatively free of involuntary movements as he became interested in doing this picture. After drawing six of the soldiers, he glanced at the men with satisfaction, commenting, "It's coming out all right. I thought," smiling,

"I could never do it." As he made this remark, his previous sense of insecurity was recalled as his tics again increased.

When he continued to add the other soldiers to the scene, the tics subsided. But when he stopped drawing in order to weigh his accomplishment, the tics increased. "The men are done," he said, "but the picture isn't finished yet. I have to make the sky and trees." Again, as he worked, the tics subsided. Pointing to the third tree he had just drawn, he commented critically, "It's too skinny." His mouth again began to twitch involuntarily in response to this negation of his achievement.

FIG. 54. INFANTRY ON THE MARCH

As Freddie prepared to draw the concluding picture of this series (Fig. 55) he said, "I'm going to do the Cavalry today. I've never made horses; I would have been afraid to try before. But I'm going to now." He sat down and went to work immediately. After sketching the first two animals he was critical. "They don't look much like horses, do they?" But the third horse, the one in the lead, satisfied him completely. These three lively figures of horses and riders, although drawn naively, are full of action and give evidence of the patient's growing confidence in himself. Such pictures of the armed services and also those of sports which followed allowed the patient to gain a release by thus expressing his preoccupation with the themes of military and athletic exploits.

In the development of these illustrations of the armed services, Freddie showed a new confidence in his ability to improvise designs and carry them out successfully. He spoke more freely, commenting on the purpose of his drawings and expressing his own awareness that he could now make men and animals in action.

FIG. 55. CAVALRY

Only the horse in the lead met with the patient's approval.

The involuntary movements decreased whenever the patient was absorbed in creating an original design and they increased whenever he became hypercritical or doubtful of his success.

Freddie made several other sketches before he was ready to undertake what soon developed into a sequence of seventeen sports pictures. The Roof Playground design was one of these drawings (Fig. 56). This was made on a day when the patient had been unable to originate any idea of his own and the writer had asked whether he might like to draw this roof where he played. The idea appealed to Freddie and he immediately blocked in its square surface in black crayon. He stopped short in the midst of his work and exclaimed, in a tone of surprise, "But this is your idea!" It had just dawned upon this insecure boy that since he could now originate his own designs he should no longer depend on others for any suggestion.

Freddie was assured that if he were temporarily unable to find a new topic for his next design, he could justifiably use a theme pro-

posed by someone else and yet produce a picture that was authentic-
ally his own. This explanation made it possible for the patient to
return to his playground drawing with renewed interest.

After enclosing the square rooftop with a protective railing, he
added a glimpse of the green park below; to either side of the playground he placed adjacent hospital wings in flattened sideview. One
of these he called "an open air gym," the other "a school for doctors."
The entire design was drawn, as viewed from above, with absence of
perspective.

Fig. 56. This Roof Playground Is Drawn As Seen from Above

The green park and trees are far away and the adjoining hospital wings are
drawn to the sides of the playground without perspective.

That Freddie had hesitated for the first time to accept a suggestion
for a picture was evidence of a significant change in this patient; a
clear sign of growing confidence in the new strength of his still immature ego.

In some of the sports designs Freddie also used this same naive de-
vice of drawing without perspective; in several sketches he laid such
upright constructions as goal posts and umpire's stands lengthwise
upon the ground. Such a direct and untutored way of drawing objects
without pretense of perspective is akin to the stylization in certain
forms of primitive art.

DRAWINGS OF SPORTS AND GAMES (FIGS. 57-68)

This series of seventeen pictures began with the four team games of Baseball, Football, Basketball and Hockey. As background to the human action of these games, the stage was carefully set; playing fields were laid out with goal posts, yard lines and bleachers; often audiences were symbolized by black dots or colored ovals. In this series of action drawings, the patient began to develop a distinctly personalized style of expression, most completely expressed in the varied rhythms and lively action of the Hockey Game. In the individualized sports as well as the team games, the action of participants is underscored by lines of movement. The implements of sports, such as balls or pucks are also emphasized by directional lines of displacement. The compensatory significance of this tic patient's over-determined action drawings is discussed in the text.

FIG. 57. BASEBALL

Note the directional lines of the ball thrown by the pitcher and struck by the batter. Also the lively figure of the outfielder left, rear, prepared to catch the ball. The bleachers in the rear seat an audience.

ACTION DRAWINGS OF SPORTS AND GAMES

Freddie was prepared to draw a baseball game (Fig. 57) when he had completed the pictures of the armed services and his first sports drawing led to another. Soon an entire series of team games had been drawn in colored crayons. These included Football (Fig. 58), Basketball (Fig. 59) and Hockey (Fig. 60).

As background to the human action in these games, the stage was always carefully set; playing fields were laid out complete with goal posts, yard lines and bleachers; each sport was also given its appropriate physical setting and audiences, symbolized by black dots or colored ovals, were sometimes included in these designs.

It was noticeable that in these sports drawings the patient had overcome his fear of attempting to draw people. He began to use them

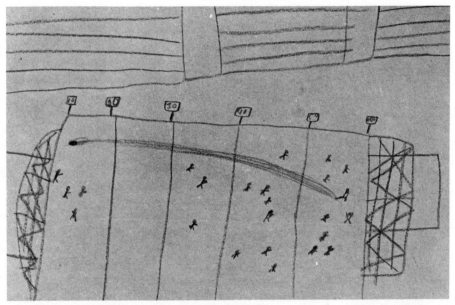

FIG. 58. FOOTBALL

Note the line of movement of the football being kicked across the field and goal posts drawn sideways without perspective.

either singly or in groups. In the team games, each side was mobilized in correct positions while engaged in the active play of striking a home run or making a goal. Opposing teams were drawn in contrasting colors; red and blue or black and yellow were used for this purpose. In some of these designs people run and jump, in others they kick balls or they fence; sometimes they swim in water or slip on the ice. In other pictures men play golf or engage in boxing matches.

In this consecutive series of action drawings the patient began to develop a distinctly personalized style of expression. This is perhaps most completely expressed in the varied rhythms and the lively action of the Hockey Game (Fig. 60). Here, the swiftly moving figures in black and yellow are silhouetted against white ice; their rhythmic action is broken by the gyrating movements of a falling skater. The sides of the rink serve as a dark frame to complete this design. Apart from its psychological significance, the picture is probably the patient's most complete artistic achievement.

Already in the team games the action of the participants was underscored by lines of movement from an old to a new position in the game. But in the implements of sport, as well as in the figures who played the games, action lines accent all movement. In the ball games illustrated, the directional displacement of ball or puck is thus emphasized. In relation to the struggle of this patient to inhibit his involuntary movements, such an exaggerated emphasis on controlled action becomes extremely significant.

FIG. 59. BASKETBALL

The tension of team action and movement improves as the patient becomes more skillful. Here the lines of directional displacement of players as well as ball are clearly emphasized.

Tennis (Fig. (61) and Ping-pong (Fig. 62) followed the team games. Then other sports such as Swimming (Fig. 65), Fencing (Fig. 67), Boxing (Fig. 68), Shooting (Fig. 64), and Clock Golf (Fig. 63) were drawn. Racing events were also included; these ranged from Horse and Auto Speed (Fig 66) to Sailboat and Running Races.

Points of special interest in the sports designs that are reproduced will be briefly noted.

Instead of drawing the usual oblong form of a tennis court with its four divisions, Freddie produced a peculiar six-sided court, subdivided into triangular, instead of oblong, sections. Questioned about the reason for this form, Freddie explained that he had never seen a game of tennis in real life. "I've only seen it in the movies," he explained.

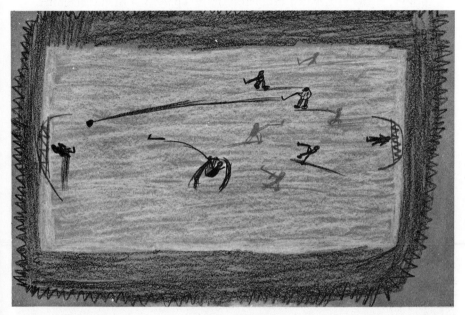

FIG. 60. HOCKEY

The lively action of swiftly moving figures in black and yellow is silhouetted against white ice; their rhythmic action is intensified by the tumbling skater with hockey stick flying through the air. The sides of the rink frame the picture.

In the Ping-pong game other peculiarities in this composition demand an explanation. The Ping-pong players and the table are drawn, quite small, on the right of the empty space which is surrounded by an audience on three sides of the design. When this game was drawn, Freddie drew to the left of it a large triangular pattern. Asked what this meant, he said, "Oh, just a design." This is mentioned simply to illustrate how a need to fill in this empty space led the patient to add, quite spontaneously, an abstract form beside the Ping-pong table.

In the more individualized action of a game of Clock Golf (Fig. 63) and the Gun Target Shooting Scene (Fig. 64), emphasis is again placed on the line of movement of the golf ball toward the hole and the gunshots toward their targets.

In both these drawings the compositions contain unusual groupings of human figures. In the golf scene a fat man moves toward his ball and the caddy is also in action. On the edge of the green a group of spectators stand in a row, while the five flags of the clock golf holes are beautifully balanced in relation to the figures in this design.

Again in the target-shooting sketch, while the picture is naively drawn, it shows decided originality in its opposition of the diagonal lines to those that parallel the base line of the paper. It is somewhat reminiscent of the use of the diagonal design in the picture of the Engineers (Fig. 53).

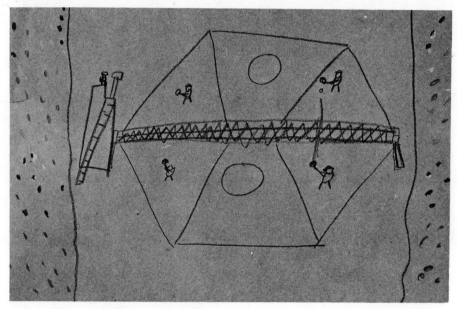

FIG. 61. TENNIS

This strangely designed hexagonal tennis court was the result of the patient's inaccurate observation at the movies. He had never seen a real game of tennis.

Two of the races are reproduced. One is of five swimmers moving rhythmically through the water while two excited onlookers wave their arms (Fig. 65) ; the other shows a series of racing cars swinging around a track, with an audience drawn to the left and the judges' stand to the right (Fig. 66). Action lines again emphasize the speed of the moving cars.

In the final sports drawings of Fencing (Fig. 67) and Boxing (Fig. 68) figures in action are accompanied by the expression of sounds. The fencers as well as the umpire and the onlookers all have words that they speak printed above their heads. In the Boxing Scene, the movement of the boxers is dramatically interrupted by the sound of the bell. The word "bong" is printed in large letters at the top of the design and below it are drawn lines that are meant to show the reverberation of the sound of the gong. Again, in this design the audience forms four squares of black dots surrounding the boxing ring.

In reviewing the development of these action drawings, it is of psychological importance to note the way in which audiences to these various sports were gradually introduced into these scenes by the patient. They were drawn in the first Baseball picture; in the Tennis and Ping-pong matches, in the Clock Golf game and the Swimming and Auto Race as well as in the Boxing Contest. The grouping of these audiences was varied with the composition of each design; sometimes they were set at the back of a scene or to both sides or surrounding the sport.

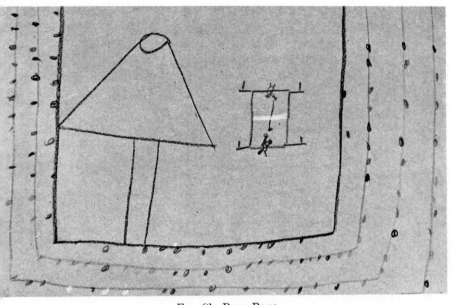

FIG. 62. PING PONG

The small Ping Pong game to the right surrounded by an audience on three sides, showed an empty space to the left that the patient felt the need to fill in with what he called a "design."

Audience participation has appeared, in similar fashion, in the drawings of several other behavior problem patients. In all cases it followed the liberation of a form of personal creative expression and suggests a symbolic attempt of these somewhat withdrawn and isolated patients to bring themselves into more active contact with the outer world.

FIG. 63. CLOCK GOLF

Shows a stout gentleman sending his ball toward the hole. The caddy moves toward him and the audience stands on the side lines.

FIG. 64. GUN TARGET SHOOTING

Again the lines of movement from the muzzle of the gun to the target are emphasized. The diagonal composition is interesting and resembles that of the engineers.

FIG. 65. SWIMMING RACE

Black figures swim rhythmically in a blue pool with two excited onlookers waving their arms.

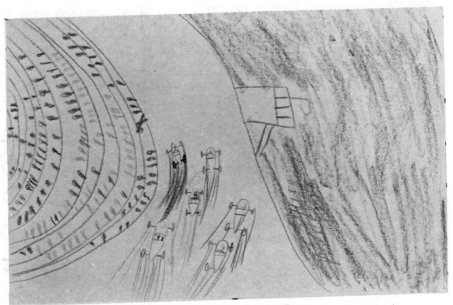

FIG. 66. AUTOMOBILE SPEED RACE

The swiftly moving cars are shown leaving trailing action lines behind them. The audience sits in rows to the left and the umpire's stand is drawn sideways without perspective.

FIG. 67. FENCING

Here the figures of umpire and onlookers as well as the fencers in action, are accompanied by speeches, the words printed above their heads.

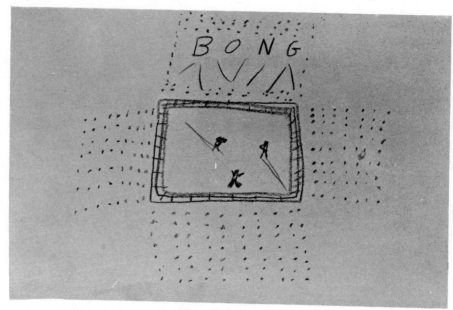

FIG. 68. BOXING

Here again the accented movement of the boxers is accompanied by the "bong" sound of the bell, which is also emphasized by special lines of reverberation.

Conclusion

The failure of the patient to gain mastery over his own involuntary movements found a substitute satisfaction in his ability to create coordinated and rhythmic movements in the figures that he invented for his pictures. In these sports sketches his crayon controlled not only the perfectly timed action of the athletes, but it also emphasized the directional lines that each implement of sport might follow. Thus the movement of a ball through space, a gunshot toward its target, and an auto along its race track were all carefully underscored. The subject of this entire series of Sports Drawings might well be termed "Variations on the Theme of Controlled Movement."

But the patient revealed, neither by comment nor by overt act, that he was aware of the apparent symbolic significance of this work. When the art periods came to an end, after the completion of these sports drawings, Freddie had not gained sufficient insight to recognize the compensatory significance of his overdetermined action pictures.

The modification that took place in Freddie's art expression released many of his inhibitions and made him gain sufficient confidence to express his affection for his cat, the anxiety of his dreams, the horror and excitement of war or the fun of sports in a series of original pictures. The range of emotions expressed by the patient broadened, and his aggressive impulses were translated into imaginative designs.

The pendulum-like swing in the patient's art expression from extreme aggression to increasing passivity corresponds to the development of similar behavior in other tic syndrome patients. In the summary of the Mahler, Luke, Daltroff study, it is stated:

"Temper tantrums found in 63 percent of our cases indicated that the clash between the child's active aggressive impulse to expand and the restrictive environment, formerly essentially external, had started to become an internal conflict between active and passive tendencies."

The patient's final mastery of controlled and rhythmic movement in his sports pictures suggests, therefore, the importance of continuing this investigation of the inhibitions and conflicts of tic syndrome patients through the use of "free" art expression.[3]

Bibliography

[1] Mahler, Margaret S.: Tics and impulsions in children: a study of motility. Psychoanalyt. Quart., vol. 13, no. 4, 1944.

[2] Mahler, Margaret S., Luke, Jean A. and Daltroff, Wilburta: Clinical and follow-up study of the tic syndrome in children. Am. J. Orthopsychiat., vol. 15, pp. 631-47, Oct. 1945.

[3] Mahler, Margaret S. and Luke, Jean 3.: Outcome of the tic syndrome. J. Nerv. & Ment. Dis., vol. 153, no. 5, May, 1946.

[4] Mahler, Margaret S. and Rangell, Leo: A psychosomatic study of maladie des tics (Gilles de la Tourette's disease). Psychiatric Quart., vol. 17, pp. 579-604, 1943.

[5] Naumburg, Margaret: Children's art expression and war. Nervous Child, vol. 2, no. 4, pp. 360-73, July, 1943.

[6] Idem · The drawings of an adolescent girl suffering from conversion hysteria with amnesia. Psychiatric Quart., vol. 18, pp. 197-224, April 1944.

[7] Idem: A study of the art expression of a behavior problem boy as an aid in diagnosis and therapy. Nervous Child, vol. 3, no. 4, pp. 277-319, July 1944.

[8] Idem: A study of the psychodynamics of the art work of a nine year old behavior problem boy. J. Nerv. & Ment. Dis., vol. 101, no. 1, pp. 28-64, Jan. 1945.

[9] Idem: Phantasy and reality in the art expression of behavior problem children. Paper in vol. Modern Trends in Child Psychiatry, New York: Int. Univ. Press, 1945.

[10] Idem: A study of the art work of a behavior problem boy as it relates to ego development and sexual enlightenment. Psychiatric Quart. vol. 20, pp. 74-112, Jan. 1946.

IV

PHANTASY AND REALITY
IN THE
ART EXPRESSION OF BEHAVIOR PROBLEM CHILDREN

INTRODUCTION

Before presenting the development of the art work of a behavior problem child, it seems advisable to review the varying role that art has played in relation to both classification and treatment of mental disorders; its function has ranged from the formal limitations of test requirements to the spontaneous release through "free" expression.

Art has also contributed to the construction of standardized norms in the development of the Goodenough Test, whereby the maturity of a patient is measured by his drawing of a man.[1, 2]

In the rapidly expanding area of projective techniques as a means of exploring and reintegrating human personality, patients have been subjected to a wide range of experiences.[3, 4] Those that include visual or creative responses are of special concern to the subject of this paper. Projective techniques might be divided into two groups: those that, like the Rorschach and Thematic Apperception Tests,[5, 6] focus the patient's responses on specially prepared visual material — and other more fluid and spontaneous projective techniques that are to be found in variants of play therapy [7] and in such methods of registering personality development as handwriting analysis and gesture.[8] The use of such creative arts as music, drama, dance, sculpture and painting for the purpose of diagnosis and therapy, belongs also in this second category of more flexible projective techniques. Some of these approaches which lend themselves to direct expression of feeling and action without recourse to words are of special value with young children.[9, 10, 11, 12]

This brief review of the development of art in the treatment of mental patients must also include mention of methods devised by Occupational Therapy in its manipulation of both arts and crafts. The trend of Occupational Therapy has been towards group or class instruction rather than to an individualized psychotherapy. Its emphasis has been on the mastering of the special technique and practice of a craft related to an ordered sequence of models and designs. Achievement of technical proficiency in the handling of craft material, rather than the goal of original creative expression, has largely motivated the activities of this branch of therapy.

Graded training in the process of making specific products has also been regarded by·such therapists as an important means of controlling, as well as disciplining, the wayward impulses of disturbed patients.[13, 14] The theory and practice of Occupational Therapy is directed to handling the conscious level of the patient's performance. Its avowed purpose, therefore, differs from those projective techniques that seek to probe the unconscious depths of personality, by encouraging the development of forms of "free" expression.

An elaboration of this contrast between the approach of Occupational Therapy and the various projective techniques can be found in one of the previously published studies of behavior problem children in this research project.* The following is quoted from that paper:

> "While full credit must be given to Occupational Therapy for what it has accomplished with mental patients, there remains an important area in the development of spontaneous creativity as a means of diagnosis and therapy which it has not entered. This field includes original work in the practical as well as the fine arts. For when emphasis is placed on the expression of the patient's personality through his art, and not on any technical proficiency attained, it serves a different therapeutic purpose. For the patient, it helps to release unexpected capacities which bring confidence and provide satisfaction; and to the psychiatrist, it offers a revealing projective technique for both diagnosis and therapy. When the patient has been helped to overcome his inhibitions and is able to express his deepest fears, wishes and phantasies on paper or in clay, he is tapping the unconscious in the symbolic language of images, which will often bring to the surface what he dare not or can not say in words.
>
> "This method of supplementing the psychiatric interview with the use of 'free' art expression as a projective technique, demands some reconsideration of the role of imagination and phantasy in the course of treatment. As soon as original art work is encouraged, instead of dependence on models and specific techniques, the focus of a patient's art activity is modified. He will begin to draw on his own inner resources and this will inevitably lead to some expression of the conflicts within the personality, which may reveal aspects of the pattern of his mental disease as well as the specific insecurities or traumatic experiences within the patient. Such release, drawn from both the conscious and unconscious levels, may in itself have a distinctly therapeutic effect on the patient, while it offers to the psychiatrist another avenue of approach in the treatment.
>
> "When such a patient is encouraged to express imaginatively and freely whatever interests him, the themes chosen are likely to range over many subjects; such work may deal with the actual happenings

*A Study of the Psychodynamics of the Art Work of a Nine Year Old Behavior Problem Boy, "Journal of Nervous and Mental Disease," Jan. 1945.

of the personal life, treated as either inner or outer events; or it may recreate either factual or phantasy experiences of childhood; or dramatize wishes and daydreams about the present or the future. Dreams also are likely to be included in some of these spontaneous art forms.

"Since the language of images is the speech of the unconscious, it serves as a more primitive and direct mode of personal expression than words. Such personality patterns as are revealed through spontaneous art, have been more thoroughly studied with psychotic than neurotic patients.[15, 16] Further cultivation of 'free' expression as a projective technique may become increasingly useful as a supplement to the psychiatric interview. Research in this field will probably develop more rapidly in the future as an aspect of the psychosomatic study of personality."

Recent developments in modern psychiatry seem to favor the further expansion of individualized projective techniques as supplementary means of dealing with mental maladjustments.

In the use of art as such a projective technique with behavior problem children, there are certain obstructions which may interfere with the fulfillment of expression that is genuinely "free." Conventional standards of behavior imposed by home and school act as an early barrier. But it is far more difficult to obtain spontaneous art expression from a child already conditioned by formal school requirements than from one of pre-school age. When behavior problem children are subjected to formal school recitations and conventional art lessons their natural responses to life are more severely affected than those of normal children. Early symptoms of childhood maladjustment can disguise themselves behind formal school procedures. A dangerously recessive child can easily pass unnoticed beneath the passive obedience of what the teacher regards as a "good" pupil. Another child with tendencies to compulsive behavior may all too easily conform to those stereotyped responses that satisfy school requirements but limit the child's more balanced development. Tendencies to hyperkinetic or predelinquent behavior are likely to increase under the requirements of silence and immobility in classroom procedure. Evidence of obstructive responses are more easily detected by the teacher than any of the less obvious, but equally serious, compulsive or recessive types of behavior.

Because such maladjusted children are often unaware of the cause of their neurotic or delinquent behavior, the approach of play therapy and other projective techniques becomes valuable in revealing unconscious motivation. Forms of play therapy that range from those which limit the child's choices within a controlled environment to such as allow complete latitude in preferred activities, have, each in their own terms, contributed to a deeper understanding of behavior problem children. Art as well as dramatics and puppet shows and music, are sometimes included as adjuncts to this type of psychotherapy.[17, 18, 19, 20]

The significance of art in the life of the individual, with special emphasis on the nature of phantasy as opposed to reality, is given considerable attention throughout Freud's writings. Elaboration of the Freudian concept of art as it concerns both the creator and the audience is to be found in the papers of Sachs,[21] Levey [22] and Kris.[23]

There are two ways in which any art or play expression can be used in psychotherapy; either as a passive experience with the patient as spectator or as an active experience with the patient as creator. A recreative and cathartic experience can take place when a group shares a dramatic or musical event as audience. But a deeper therapeutic response is obtainable when any of the arts is used actively by a patient as a means of releasing his own unconscious conflicts in some form of individual and original expression. This report proposes to deal primarily with the spontaneous use of art as such a channel of release.

This paper will describe and consider examples of the art work of a behavior problem boy who has been studied in a special research project at the New York State Psychiatric Institute and Hospital in order to investigate the possible use of creative art as an aid in diagnosis and therapy.

The patients to be included have been selected on the basis of behavior difficulties without consideration of evident artistic ability. Some of the patients even expressed distaste for art owing to their previous experience in school art classes.

The manner in which such art sessions with behavior problem patients proceed can best be described by quoting from another previously published study in this series :*

> "The art periods occurred either once or twice a week. How long each patient might be able to spend in such sessions would depend on the opinion of the psychiatrist, the requirements of the educational program and the type of response the patient was capable of making to such activity. But whatever experimental work in art is being carried out in this research project, with a limited number of behavior problem children and adolescents, is not related to the group activities of the regular school or occupational therapy program. The length of the art periods depends on both the age and condition of the patient. This does not mean that the art sessions are entirely con-

*A Study of the Art Expression of a Behavior Problem Boy as an Aid in Diagnosis and Therapy, "The Nervous Child," Vol. 3, No. 4, 1944.

cerned with art expression. Much time, especially during the early weeks of adjustment to this new creative approach, may be spent in getting acquainted with the patient by encouraging various types of personal experiences in games, play or conversation that develop spontaneously.

"All the patients in this study, whatever their individual maladjustments, have held in common the idea that art stems from an ability to trace or copy pictures. This misconception about art and the nature of the creative process is derived from the kind of teaching still offered in many public schools. While it obviously limits the growth of normal children and constricts the development of their potentialities, it does more harm to such children as enter school life without a sound personal orientation. For when art teaching is dealt with as a routine process it discourages efforts at spontaneous and creative expression and forces pupils into a degree of stereotyped reproduction of known models that encourages regression and evasion of creative effort, even in normal children.

"In attempting to get behavior problem patients to express their innermost thoughts and feelings in creative expression as a substitute for the routine of tracing and copying, they need to be convinced that their own responses to life are worth while recording. Such children tend to undervalue what they make; they will explain that their pictures are not good because they do not trace from a book or copy them from a chromo on the wall. In order to release such a patient's spontaneous expression, it is essential, whether it takes weeks or months, to convince him that his own emotions and experience, both pleasant and unpleasant, are the stuff from which creative art is made. As soon as such recordings of his inner or outer world begin to appear and win the response of those around him, he gains confidence and usually moves ahead more easily into unexplored areas of creative experiment. Joy and wonder grow as the patient begins to discover his own original ways of expressing such buried conflicts and repressions. Hidden doubts and fears, unvocalized hates and anxieties begin to be liberated in both imaginative and objective form through such work."

The youngest child studied in this research project was 5 years of age. A report on his case follows.

CLINICAL HISTORY

When Jimmy, a 5-year-old Jewish boy was brought to the hospital for treatment, it was stated that his behavior at home and in nursery school had been extremely provocative; that it was characterized by disobedience, destructiveness and boastfulness. From the school report he was described as over-excitable and over-sensitive; his interest span was said to be short and his mental activity unfocussed. He was further depicted as irritable, unruly and bold; with changing

moods that varied from extreme indifference to violent displays of
emotion. His eating habits had become poor. But the chief com-
plaints of the parents against their child concerned his increasing use
of obscene language and his uncontrollable masturbation. The diagnosis was primary behavior disorder, conduct type, with some evidence of neurotic traits. The behavior disorder was evident in the
patient's "acting out" against the family; this included many forms of
aggressive and obstructive behavior, ranging from such acts as delight in creating noise and other unwanted disturbances, to the punc-
turing of an auto tire with a pin and the incessant use of profanity.
Neurotic traits were shown in expressions of hypersensitivity and a
rich phantasy life.

Jimmy was an only child, born after six years of marriage, to a
forty year old mother and a forty-two year old father. The parents
had been married five years before they planned to have a child. The
neurotic difficulties of the parents was increased by financial insecurity. Although Jimmy was said, by the mother, to be a wanted
child, he seemed to have been rejected by both parents. She complained of his constitutional restlessness since infancy. The patient
had, from early childhood, been subjected to three conflicting types
of authority in the home. The grandmother seems to have been the
one source of real affection for the child whom she spoiled and
petted. Violent scenes took place in which mother, father and grandmother disagreed in the child's presence as to how to handle his misbehavior. While the grandmother would condone it, the father would
whip him for it. To punish the patient for uttering obscene words,
his mouth would often be washed out with soap. It is reported that he
made the suggestion that he would prefer to have it done with white,
instead of yellow, soap as this tasted better.

The mother admitted that the patient had been subject at home to
too much shouting and loss of temper with sudden changes from
affection to rejection by his parents, so that he probably did not know
whether he was loved or hated. It was also evident from the mother's
statements that both parents had been unreasonable in their demands
on a five year old boy, expecting him to show an intellectual understanding and control that was far beyond his years.

That the mother's seductive treatment of the patient had over-
stimulated him was made clear by her description of how she had
cured him of thumb sucking at the age of two. She was in the habit,
she said, of lying down with the patient when he went to bed for the
night and she would continue to stroke his hand as a preventative
against thumb sucking until he finally fell asleep. This was often
delayed for as long as two hours. The father, losing patience with
this procedure, finally insisted one night that the child be left alone to
cry until he went to sleep.

As an example of the mother's attitude towards the patient's childish eagerness and curiosity, she reported "Jimmy is never willing to

take anyone else's word. He has always insisted on learning things by his own experience. For instance he insisted on touching hot things." Disregarding the child's healthy impulse and wish to do things for himself, the mother still continues to dress him completely.

She described an imaginary playmate that the patient has now had for over a year; Jimmy appeared to both see and hear this boy whom he called Jerry. He seemed to be real and always present to the patient. (More about several imaginary playmates who appeared in the art sessions will be described later.)

The grandmother's sudden death undoubtedly acted as a severe traumatic experience to the boy. Additional traumatic experiences between the ages of 3 and 4 were related to a series of severe illnesses. Pyelitis, purulent otitis media, and a tonsillectomy came close together. It was then that his eating habits became progressively worse.

Since this patient's hostility against his parents was emphasized in the oral aggression of forbidden language, it seems important to relate it to the history of his feeding problem. While the child is reported to have had no feeding difficulties in infancy, it is stated that he vomited intermittently from birth to nine months without apparent reason. This has continued up to the present time with similar lack of physical cause.

This brief summary of significant aspects of the patient's history shows conditions of excessive frustration and overstimulation, of rejection and affection to which this five year old boy of superior intelligence was subjected by the conflicting authority of the three adults. At one moment he was spoiled and treated like a baby and the next instant he was expected to behave reasonably as an adult. A home environment that contributed to the patient's present behavior disorder is therefore clearly indicated.

Patient's Response During Art Sessions

During the first few art sessions Jimmy's gestures were sudden and spasmodic. Several tic-like movements were observed during his early attempts to make pictures. The right eye twitched intermittently and both eyebrows contracted suddenly from time to time; now and then the left side of the mouth remained open and the tongue could be seen moving stiffly from side to side as the patient worked. But such tic-like movements subsided within a few weeks and did not reappear. In contrast to the patient's tense and hyperkinetic body movements, his left hand and arm were over-relaxed, so that they failed to hold the paper in a firm position as he drew with his right hand.

Masturbatory activity was manifest, on several occasions, in rhythmic leg movements as the patient sat absorbed in his art work.

He never seemed conscious of going through such motions and they soon ceased.

Jimmy, the youngest of the behavior problem children studied in this research, was the only patient who had not yet come under the formal restrictions of grade school requirements. He had, however, been prematurely frustrated by the constant prohibitions and punishments meted out by both mother and father. While the patient expressed some of his hostility to parents and nursery school teachers by means of physical disobedience, his chief mode of aggression was oral. By using obscene and blasphemous language, he was able to disturb and dominate. Another aspect of this boy's oral release came through the incessant narration of his phantasies.

Fig. 69. Head of Hitler

It was soon evident that creative expression, developed by using his hands in the art sessions to exteriorize his feelings, had not, previously, been emphasized as a channel of release. Jimmy's first attempts to use crayons and plastecine as a means of expression showed the same episodic and erratic responses as were reported in home and school behavior. But he soon became interested and able to express his real and imagined experiences in art forms.

In the first art period he covered seven sheets of paper with a conglomeration of subjects. On a single page four or five different objects were sometimes intermingled with the printing of the alphabet (Figs.

71 and 72). A large head of Hitler, drawn in purple chalk, made its appearance on the first day (Fig. 69). This was followed by another huge round head of a man drawn in the same color (Fig. 70). Asked what this second face represented, he replied, "My Daddy." He then drew a smaller figure in yellow-green to the right of the large head. Questioned, he explained, "That's me." Asked to tell about his father, he said, "He's away on a boat. He's fighting to help save the poor children who haven't any food." This was only one of the many imaginary roles that he attributed to his father in both play therapy and art sessions.

FIG. 70. "DADDY AND ME"

In the next art period, besides several sheets of practice letters, he filled two pages with combinations of printed A's, houses, balls, swastikas and so forth (Figs. 71 and 72). In the first of these pictures the letters as well as the house, which he said was his own, are posed at extremely irregular angles. In the second picture, balls, A's and a swastika are evident; the A to the right of this page stimulated Jimmy to create a phantasy by adding cross bars as ladder steps to the letter A. "A man climbed up, and then he fell down and killed himself." This man was the patient's first mention of death as self destruction.

In the next art session Jimmy wished to model. His first attempts to use plastecine consisted of pushing broken bits of it around and calling them boats and airplanes. It took a number of art periods before he had really developed sufficient interest to soften the plastecine and use his finger tips in modelling the desired form. But once he had really become conscious of the effectiveness of such methods, he constantly drew the writer's attention to how he had improved in smoothing the surfaces of the forms he made. His modelling soon

FIG. 71. "MY HOUSE AND PRACTICE LETTER A's

became less fragmentary and he gained the ability to carry out elaborate phantasies without hesitating to produce rocks, oceans, boats, life preservers, animals, people and whatever else was needed to complete the play. The writer was always expected to share in his activities; but he set the limits to the role she played. Proposing a game of dominoes with a handful of crude and irregular oblong blocks that he had made out of plastecine, he manipulated the imagined game so that he won the first round; but he saw to it that the writer was victor in the second one. In a race between two plastecine PT boats, Jimmy's ship generally won; but the writer was also allowed, in a single race, to tie Jimmy's boat.

For his first attempt at modelling, Jimmy made a round flat head; requesting a stick, he then gouged out the eyes, nose and mouth. When asked who it was, he said, "It's me. But I don't know how to make the body. You make it." A constant resort to "You do it," or "You make it," showed his habitual dependence on adults and his unwillingness to attempt anything new by himself. With encouragement and a little assistance, he succeeded, eventually, in attaching a body and legs to the head. Then bombs, he declared, crashed down from a plane overhead and the figure that represented Jimmy was completely destroyed.

FIG. 72. A BALL, PRACTICE LETTER A'S, A SWASTIKA
("A man falling off a ladder killed himself")

Death and destruction appear in many forms of bombs and explosions and fires in his art work and play. Men died in his phantasies either by bombing, shooting, falling or drowning. When he made models of boats, planes and trains, he used them for games which came to a conclusion in ship wrecks, train collisions or explosions. A maimed and a one legged man, as well as a two legged lion and a two legged cat appeared in the models that he used in imaginative play.

The psychologist's report on the patient's response to the Thematic Apperception Test corroborated certain play and phantasy tendencies which were said to show "concern over death and signs of depression."

The meaning of Jimmy's drawing of his father and himself, (Fig. 70) made after the portrait of Hitler (Fig. 69), took on added significance as a series of phantasies evolved, which dealt with how he (Jimmy) would get the better of Hitler when he went over to Germany. That the image of Hitler and the head of the father, drawn in quick succession, were one and the same all powerful father, was reinforced by the patient's later phantasy about his blood relation to Hitler. "I'm German," he announced, at one art session. "Yes, I'm

Hitler's little boy. But I don't like him any more." It was impossible
to get any further explanation of this statement at that time. On several occasions he told how he would outwit Hitler when he went over
to Germany. "I'll be very sweet to Hitler so he won't hurt me," he
would explain. "Then when Hitler isn't looking I'll get behind him
and hit him." Again several weeks later, after drawing a picture of
Hitler and Mussolini, and drowning Mussolini, he repeated the same
story of how he would treat Hitler when he went over to visit him.

A similar pattern of response towards those who are more powerful
appears in Jimmy's boast, in an art session, that he was going to knock
out Harry. The writer, aware that the boy referred to was the ward
bully, asked the patient how he proposed to deal with him. "Oh, when
he isn't looking, I'll trip him up."

Jimmy's phantasies about hitting Hitler from behind or tripping up
Harry when he wasn't looking contain the same mechanism of response. The immature ego of the patient can overcome the threat of
the overwhelming force of the father or Hitler or the ward bully only
by means of a sneak attack. Here clearly is evidence of the initial set
of an ego response to the threat of paternal domination that could
easily become the fundamental character pattern of this five year old
boy. Release of his pent up hostility into creative forms of satisfying
expression offers one way of helping to modify the crystallization of
such behavior into a lasting pattern.

Twice during the art sessions, the wish to destroy the father was
expressed in phantasy. One day, while he was playing with some
balls of plastecine and calling them bombs that the Japs were sending
at him, he asked, "Do grenades kill when they explode?" He was told
that they were likely to, if well aimed. He then began to play that the
Japs were hitting his father with a grenade which he had modelled
out of plastecine. "But," he explained, "it's filled with tooth powder
instead of gun powder, and so it didn't kill him." (It is interesting to
note that tooth powder acts as a substitute symbol of oral aggression
in place of the obscene words with which he usually attacks his
father.)

While much more attention was given to the father than to the
mother in this patient's art sessions, there were pictures in which the
mother played her role; in one drawing "a baby cat and a mummy
cat" and in another, "a baby fish and mother fish" were closely associated.

The second wish to destroy the father came in an art session some
weeks later. An elaborate phantasy about a large whale and a baby
fish and a mother fish developed in a series of three pictures. These
drawings were made the day after he had returned from a mid-term

vacation. So they were certainly expressive of the recent home experience. First he drew an ocean of wavy blue and green lines. In the ocean he placed the picture of a large fish and called it a "whale." To "make it beautiful," he added stripes of green-blue, lavender and yellow. He then drew a boat with a gun on it, "which is going to shoot the whale." But to make the whale something that ought to be destroyed he placed a swastika on it. As the gun, just made for that purpose, blasts the whale the creature falls to pieces. To represent its complete destruction, Jimmy obliterates the last vestiges of its form with a purple crayon. "Where," he then asks, "is a horrid color?" He seizes an orange crayon, overlays the purple patch with orange and then covers that with black crayon strokes. The whale is not only dead but reduced to blackness. The father, symbolized as the whale, has again been totally eliminated.

In the next drawing that follows immediately he makes a small fish in the sea. "It's a baby fish with an American cross on it." (Note here the American cross for safety for himself and the German cross on the whale for destruction of the father.) Asked whether there are any other fish in the sea, he replies, "A mother fish. She is larger and more beautiful." He then places red and violet and gray lines across the larger mother fish. "She guards the baby fish."

A third drawing follows which includes again a jumble of things; there are stars, swastikas and red circles and suddenly he adds what he calls a "Christmas tree." He then turns his attention back to "the mother and baby fish." He sets them spitting at the stars, swastikas and circles in the sky of the third picture.

First, the patient released his long buried hostility against the father in destroying the whale with the swastika; he then reemphasized his tendency to oral aggression by having the baby fish and its mother spitting skyward at the universe. He showed intense satisfaction at the completion of this phantasy.

Jimmy's other family relationships concerned imaginary brothers and one sister. He also phantasied about a pet dog and a kitten. These will be described after his use of obscene language is discussed.

Release of Obscene and Blasphemous Language

In the stories which Jimmy invented to accompany his pictures of his father or himself, he would frequently scatter such words as "piss," "shit" and "ass." Each time he did so he would watch out of the corner of his eye for an expected reprimand. When none was forthcoming the patient was nonplussed. At successive art periods he still continued his provocative use of obscene language. No emotional reaction or comment was ever made by the writer.

In the second art period, when a torrent of such language had been released, the patient was asked, rather casually, whether, since he kept repeating such words, he would like to use them in a picture. This was a new idea and Jimmy stopped work to consider it for a moment. Since it appealed to him he took a new sheet of paper and covered it with violet crayon scratches that represent "shit" and "piss." A second picture followed; it was filled with haphazard lines of black and yellow-green. He then looked up, laughed self-consciously at what he had drawn and said, "No more shit for today. Now I'll make something nice." But the day's release was not yet complete, for his final drawing as he described it was "A picture of shit of many colors" (Fig. 73). Black and yellow-green lines are dominant in this drawing, but scrawls of orange and red color are included. It was less chaotic than the previous pictures.

Fig. 73. *"Shit of Many Colors"* See also color plate III.

Jimmy was in the habit of withholding spontaneous comment as to what took place during his week-ends at home. When asked, during the first art session, he said, "Play, of course." But it is not surprising that only the aftermath of the boy's conflicts and frustrations with his parents should have carried over to the art sessions; here it was released in the form of oral aggression and phantasies about his real and imagined family in relation to himself.

In the fourth art period, after spending some time on the practice of printing letters, he asked to see his "pictures in the black cover." This was the first time he had referred to anything that he had drawn previously. "I want to throw all those shit pictures I made into the garbage pail," he announced suddenly. As they were not in the room, he was told he could do so next time. But he never referred to them again.

It was not difficult to understand such reversal of behavior. Jimmy had just returned from a week-end with his parents and had, at home, undoubtedly met with further physical punishment for his continued use of obscene language. It is even possible that following the art session practice, he had also begun at home to make pictures to illustrate these words. Under such circumstances he would certainly have been ordered by irate parents to dispose of them promptly. As Jimmy grew more at ease during the art sessions, he was soon able to admit that whenever he used forbidden language at home he was severely punished by his parents.

DEVELOPMENT OF TRANSFERENCE

From the day on which Jimmy had been encouraged to release his oral hostility in the making of "shit" pictures, he showed signs of becoming more friendly. As he met the writer in the hall, he would slip his hand in hers to walk towards the art room. Then, in episodes already described, he allowed her to win a game or tie him in a boat race. But it was not until the end of the fourth month that a more positive sign of transference appeared. "What are your initials?" he asked. When told, he printed them beside his own on the picture of a "piss box," that he had just completed. "Now," said Jimmy, "the picture belongs to us both together." This, as a gesture from a child who had remained aloof and unable to make satisfactory contacts with either children or adults on the ward, was an advance. Jimmy was apparently ready now to accept the writer as he realized that she had accepted him, by offering to share with her his picture. That it dealt with a phantasy about a "piss box" among presents beneath a Christmas tree added significance to this suggestion. For now the patient had found an adult whom he could apparently trust since she did not reject him or any of his behavior.

Soon after this episode there was a distinct improvement in the patient's health and attitude on the ward. This carried over to the art periods and the writer commented to Jimmy that he was looking better and seemed happier now in the hospital. Was he having more fun on the ward? "Yes," he replied, "but I would like to go home." Asked if he had some good friends at home that he wanted to play with, he gave this answer: *"When I play with the boys on the street,*

I have to say 'shit' and 'piss' or they won't let me play." Here the patient showed his need of justifying his use of obscene words to the writer, although she had never criticized or punished him for using them.

"Is that so," was the writer's only comment as she still maintained an uncensuring attitude. "You know that it makes no difference to me, whether you use such words or not. You can say anything you like here in the art room. I do not feel like those boys on the block or your family at home. Tell me why, then, you need to use those words with me?"

This posed a new question for Jimmy. He had no ready answer. He thought a moment and then explained, "I do it just for a copy for you."

This reply showed the patient's fumbling attempt to discover why, when not frustrated by the writer, he missed his usual satisfaction in oral aggression.

In the next art session, the writer decided that she might now be able to speak more directly with Jimmy about the use of these forbidden words. While painting some red and green boats, he began again to narrate phantasies that included the words "piss" and "shit."

"Jimmy, you've noticed, haven't you, that I don't care whether you use those words or not?" said the writer.

"Yes," answered Jimmy, as he smiled responsively.

"Why do you think I don't object when you say them?"

"Because," Jimmy suggested, tentatively, "you like those words?"

"Not particularly."

"Then you like me?" he hazarded.

He was assured that he was liked, but that was not sufficient reason for listening to his many repetitions of these words. He was told that since he said these words so often, he was probably too full of them to be able to stop. So the writer was just going to let him go ahead until they all came out. She was not interested in these words but she did not intend to bother about them if he still needed to say them. Perhaps, some day, he would get through with repeating them. Jimmy listened quietly and attentively while this was being explained to him. He showed no impulse to return to his defiant use of obscene words in speech or pictures during the rest of that art period. His quiet and self-contained attitude suggested that Jimmy was beginning to be convinced that he no longer needed to use those words against the writer.

IMAGINARY PLAYMATES

In the fourth art period Jimmy first mentioned an imaginary companion. He said that he had a brother Jack who was five years old.

But "Jack can't make letters the way I do." In the play therapy sessions, Jack had also appeared a few weeks earlier. To the psychiatrist, the patient explained, "My brother thinks that hospital schools are stinking, but I'm trying to teach him they're not. Ever since I was a little baby, I've been trying to teach Jack to be nice." In both phantasies the brother, who is just his own age, plays the role of the babyish and unconforming aspect of Jimmy.

There were many references to games and play with this brother when he went home for week-ends. On one occasion he described playing with "My brother and my dog. He's a bull terrier. I hid in a trunk in the attic and my dog looked everywhere and couldn't find me. He knew I was in the trunk, but he couldn't get in." Asked whether the brother played with them, "No, he was in another part of the house." Then followed an elaborate phantasy about how his dog had a sword and swastika on his arm and fought the pilgrims.

When Jimmy introduced this imaginary dog at the hospital, in his first play therapy session, he told the psychiatrist: "There's a big dog in the cellar where I live; a collie goes in the cellar because I put his lunch in the cellar. I don't want anyone to know, 'cause I put his lunch in the cellar. I don't want anyone to know I have a dog. My brother's dog is a big collie like mine."

The brother image is clearly a replica of certain aspects of the patient; he is the same age and also owns a pet collie. But the imaginary brother, as Jimmy's immature self, wishes to avoid growing up and fitting into school routine. Jimmy is therefore able to play the part of training him to conform to what he does not like to do.

At the end of the second month, Jimmy made a picture of a "Tree, House and Garden" (Fig. 74). He first announced, "I'll make a tree." He began by drawing a huge brown oblong block in the centre of the page. At the top of this tree-trunk, he placed some green crayon marks which he called "leaves." The brown oblong was filled in solidly with crayon strokes. Pointing at the tree trunk, he said: "It looks like shit." Asked if he could add anything more to his picture, he suggested "a garden." He then drew irregular green marks to the left of the tree. "Carrots grow there," he announced, adding a patch of green to the right of the tree. He balanced this with similar crayon strokes to the left. "That's beets," he explained. "If there's a garden, there has to be a house," he reasoned. A narrow pointed house was placed beside the tree. Then a green door and window were added. To the question as to who lived in the house, he replied: "My mother and father and my dog." Later he supplemented with: "My sister Alice and two brothers live there too." These imaginary brothers were described as twins who were younger than himself.

Fig. 74. A Tree, House and Garden

Concerning his brother Jack and the other phantasy children, there appeared to be paucity of elaboration as to how his life with them was filled. His phantasies, however, about his play and adventures with the imagined pet dog were far more varied and complex.

When Jimmy first considered attempting a picture of this dog, he said he would make it "If you'll buy me a picture of a dog in the store. Then I'll trace it." But in a few more weeks he was ready, quite spontaneously, to paint a picture of "A little brown dog and a boy." The result was crude and left unfinished because a new idea intervened. The boy was left minus a leg and arm as Jimmy painted a boat on the same paper, then he returned to the dog and painted a house around him; he then added Christmas toys.

On another occasion he phantasied about a kitten. "I went to my brother's house and had a little black kitten with a pink tongue. And when it was dark you couldn't see the kitten, because it was black too —only its little pink tongue. And it said, 'Meeow, meeow.'"

Here again, with the purpose of releasing as many of the patient's oral phantasies as possible, whether they happened to be related to forbidden words or imaginary playmates, the writer would encourage attempts to project such ideas into forms of creative expression. Following this procedure, Jimmy created a picture of "the kitten with a pink tongue." (Fig. 75).

THE CLIMAX OF RELEASE IN BLASPHEMY

In the twelfth art session came Jimmy's major release in the form of blaspheming. After drawing the dog and boy just described, he asked, "How do you make a red cross? Will you make it for me?" Encouraged to try, he succeeded by himself. When the cross was done, he said, "There's a figure on it," and he then drew a head on the cross. That it was meant to represent Christ was evident when he announced "Cursing makes the cross black and God dies." He then proceeded to mumble under his breath "fuck," "bitch" and "son of a bitch." Now the cross grows black," he explained, as he blackened the red cross with his pencil, "and God dies." Again Jimmy reproduced this entire scene by drawing another red cross; this time he repeated the curses with the addition of "hell." When the second cross was blackened, Jimmy said: "Two Gods die." He seemed to derive great satisfaction and release from this.

FIG. 75. A BLACK KITTEN WITH A PINK TONGUE

Asked whether his parents got angry when he cursed at home, he said, "Yes." He nodded agreement, when the writer suggested that he probably enjoyed cursing like that until they got angry. "Then they hit me with a belt." This was the first time the patient had spoken of being whipped for his use of obscene and blasphemous language.

ANAL AND URETHRAL PHANTASIES

As the art periods proceeded, there were a number of anal and urethral phantasies released spontaneously into pictures. Seizing a yellow-green crayon, he tried the color on paper, saying: "This is mustard." Then he drew what he called "a big lump of mustard," followed by the placing of a large black frankfurter in the centre of the mustard. In a phantasy which followed, he also drew yellow-green mustard falling upon some goats that were chased by ghosts.

FIG. 76. "THE FLAMING TORCH MAKES BOO-BOO POPS"

The picture of the "Flaming Torch" (Fig. 76) followed the outbreak of cursing with the consequent death of the two Gods. This figure of a man he painted in bright red with emphasis on his "peep." While making it, Jimmy looked up with a knowing smile. Then followed a series of the man's "boo-boo pops" falling into a toilet. The figure also proceeded to "sissy from his peep." Continuing to use the red paint, Jimmy then made swirls of flame to the accompaniment of crackling sounds. "The flames," he announced, "go through the wall." With the picture consumed in fire the earlier part of the phantasy is partially obliterated as the patient's interest now centers on the flames.

A single dream picture was spontaneously produced in the ninth art session. The patient drew it twice in succession. The first time he made a house in the lower section and placed himself, as an orange

figure, high up in the sky. Jimmy is shown descending into the house
from the left and coming out on the right side in order to return again
to the sky. A moon and clouds are also drawn. But since it is night,
Jimmy blacks out everything except the orange figure of himself in
the sky.

FIG. 77. A DREAM: "JIMMY GOES UP TO THE SKY, COMES INTO THE HOUSE
AGAIN AND BACK INTO THE SKY"

In the second picture, he now calls the repetition of this episode
"a dream," and here speaks of himself as "a boy who goes up to the
sky and then comes to the house again. Blackness is night. There's
a daddy cloud and a baby cloud" (Fig. 77).

This phantasy, of a different order than the others that the patient
produced, may have been related to what adults had told him about
birth. The entire problem of the patient's infantile birth theories and
phantasies would have been dealt with, a little later, in the second
phase of his art work, had he not left the hospital quite suddenly.

The patient was interviewed by the consultant psychiatrist at a
staff conference two months after his admission to the hospital.
When the subject of the patient's brother was introduced, Jimmy was
told by the psychiatrist that the brother was not real and had been
invented by the patient because he was lonely. To this Jimmy objected
and continued to insist on the reality of his brother.[28]

Following this staff conference, the patient no longer produced any phantasies about his brother during the art sessions. Two months later, however, he began to speak again to the writer of this imagined brother. In describing his previous week-end at home, he made his first reference to the brother since his existence had been challenged. When asked if this brother had been with him on his outdoor explorations at home, he replied, "When I go out in the woods with my gun for a fox, I go alone. I can do it better alone." He then proceeded to paint a figure with huge blue-green boots which he said was his brother (Fig. 78). Unfortunately, the further investigation of the

FIG. 78. "MY BROTHER WITH BOOTS ON"

symbolic significance of this imaginary brother-figure in the life of this only child of middle-aged parents was suddenly interrupted by his unexpected departure from the hospital. But the final art session had supplied the evidence of what the writer had always suspected, namely that the disappearance of this phantasy brother had been but a temporary means of screening it from adult investigation.

More research concerning the significance of such phantasy expressions is needed in order to determine the role that such imagined companions play in the life of different types of behavior problem children. Are such pets and children created primarily as a means of escape from a too painful reality or are they sometimes used as symbols to help bridge the gap between the image world of childhood and the outer world of adult reality? Whatever the therapist ultimately concludes will have an influence on the methods of treating such behavior problem children.

From the data gathered in this paper concerning the art work of this five-year-old behavior problem boy, as well as supplementary material previously collected in relation to older behavior problem children in the course of this research project, it appears that such art products as are derived through phantasy release may aid adjustment to daily life; and that creative response to outer events also tends to stimulate the growth of imaginative art. When both phantasy and reality images are thus projected by behavior problem children into original art forms, it seems possible to develop them simultaneously as corroborative aspects of life experience.

BIBLIOGRAPHY

[1] Goodenough, F.: Measurement of Intelligence by Drawings. Yonkers, N. Y.: World Book Co., 1926.

[2] Idem: Children's Drawings. From Handbook of Child Psychology, edited by Carl Murchison, Clark Univ. Press, pp. 480-514, 1931.

[3] Rapaport, D : Principles Underlying Projective Techniques. Character & Personality, Vol. X, No. 3, 213, March 1942.

[4] Frank, L. K.: Projective Methods for the Study of Personality. Jl. of Psych. Vol. 8; 389-415, 1939.

[5] Rorschach, H.: Psychodiagnostics. Bern, Switzerland, B. Huber Verlag, 1943.

[6] Murray, H. A.: Thematic Apperception Manual, Harvard University Press, Cambridge, Mass., 1943.

[7] Section on Play Therapy, American Jour. Orthopsychiatry, 8:499, 1938.

[8] Saudek, R.: Experiments in Handwriting, Wm. Morrow & Co., New York, 1929.

[9] Despert, J. L.: Emotional Problems in Children: State Hospitals Press Utica, N. Y., 1938.

[10] Levy, J.: The use of art techniques in treatment of children's behavior problems. From American Assoc. on Mental Deficiency, pamphlet, Proc. and Addresses of the 58th Annual Session. Edited by G. B. Smith, New York, pp. 258-260, 1934.

[11] Harms, E.: Child Art as Aid in the Diagnosis of Juvenile Neurosis. Am. Jl. of Orthopsychiatry, Vol. XI, No. 2, Apr. 1941.

[12] Horowitz, R. and Murphy, L. B.: Projective Methods in the Psychological Study of Children. Jl. of Experimental Education, VII, 133-140, 1938.

[13] Haas, L. J.: Occupational Therapy for the Mentally and Nervously Ill: Bruce Publish. Co., Milwaukee, 1925.

[14] Haworth, N. A. and MacDonald, E. M.: Theory of Occupational Therapy for Students and Nurses: Williams & Wilkins Co., Baltimore, 1941.

[15] Prinzhorn, H.: Bildnerei der Geisteskranken: Ein Beitrag zur Psychologie und Psychopathologie der Gestaltung. Verlag Julius Springer, Berlin, 1922.

156 ART EXPRESSION OF CHILDREN

16 Lewis, N. D. C.: Graphic Art Productions in Schizophrenia, from *Schizophrenia* (Dementia Praecox). New York: Assoc. for Research in Nerv. and Men. Dis. Paul B. Hoeber, Vol. V, pp. 334-368, 1928.

17 Bender, L. and Woltmann, A.: The Use of Puppet Shows as a Psychotherapeutic Method for Behavior Problems in Children, Am. Jl. Orthopsychiatry, VI, 341-354, 1936.

18 Idem: The Use of Plastic Material as a Psychiatric Approach to Emotional Problems in Children. Amer. Jl. Orthopsychiatry, VII, 283-300, 1937.

19 Curran, F. J.: The Drama as a Therapeutic Measure in Adolescents. Amer. Jl. Orthopsychiatry, IX, No. 1, Jan. 1939.

20 Moreno, J. L.: Creativity and Cultural Conserves — with Special Reference to Musical Expression. Beacon House, New York, 1939.

21 Sachs, H.: The Creative Unconscious. Sci.-Art, Cambridge, Mass., 1942.

22 Levey, H. B.: A Theory Concerning Free Creation in the Inventive Arts. Psychiatry, III, pp. 229-293, May 1940.

23 Kris, E.: Approaches to Art. *Psychoanalysis Today*. International University Press, New York, 1944.

24 Naumburg, M.: Children's Art Expression and War. Nervous Child, Vol. 2, No. 4, pp. 360-373, 1943.

25 Idem: The Drawings of an Adolescent Girl Suffering from Conversion Hysteria with Amnesia. The Psychiatric Quarterly, XVIII, No. 2, pp. 197-224, 1944.

26 Idem: A Study of the Art Expression of a Behavior Problem Boy as an Aid in Diagnosis and Therapy. Nervous Child, Vol. 3, No. 4, pp. 277-318, 1944.

27 Idem: A Study of the Psychodynamics of the Art Work of a Nine Year Old Behavior Problem Boy. Jl. Nervous and Mental Disease. Jan., 1945.

28 Bender, L., and Vogel, F.: Imaginary Companions of Children. American Journal Orthopsychiatry, Vol. IX, No. 1, Jan. 1941.

V

A STUDY OF THE ART WORK OF A BEHAVIOR PROBLEM BOY AS IT RELATES TO EGO DEVELOPMENT AND SEXUAL ENLIGHTENMENT

INTRODUCTION

This paper will consider the art work of a 10-year-old boy, whose mother was Colombian and whose father was of German-Russian descent. He was brought to the New York State Psychiatric Institute and Hospital at the request of the school authorities because he was a severe behavior problem. He was considered almost impossible to teach as he lacked concentration, was inattentive and showed a tendency to annoy other children. He had a severe reading disability and played truant a number of times.

The patient's condition was diagnosed as primary behavior disorder, neurotic type, with obesity.

John was hospitalized for a period of eight months. From the second to the seventh month he attended art sessions. In the first phase of his work, half-hour periods twice a week were sufficient. But as his ability to express himself developed, he would ask for more time and was soon able to make satisfactory use of full hour sessions.

The development of John's art work can be divided into several phases. His earliest pictures were so immature as to suggest the work of a much younger child and he depended at first on copying ideas from other patients. As he found means of expressing himself in the drawing of animals, he began to reveal, through these designs, the basis of his anxiety and conflicts. While producing a group of pictures and modelled forms, he was able to acquire sexual enlightenment. After that, the patient showed an increased ability to express himself spontaneously in creative art forms and to improvise freely in both verbal and pictorial phantasies.

CLINICAL HISTORY

John, a 10-year-old Catholic boy, had difficulty in home as well as school adjustments. The mother complained that he was a disciplinary problem, manifesting infantile behavior, over-dependency and disobedience towards both parents.

The patient is the youngest of three children, having two older half-sisters of 18 and 13 years, who are of normal intelligence and without any outstanding personality difficulties. The mother is Colombian, apparently of dull normal intelligence. The father, of mixed German-Russian descent, is of borderline intelligence and said

157

to be very unstable. His earnings are marginal, and he is shiftless, stubborn, seclusive and quick-tempered. He is overweight, of short stature, has a round, pink face.

The mother asserts she married the father a year after the death of her first husband, primarily in order to have a provider for the home. She ended marital relations with him three months after the birth of the boy because of incompatibility. Since that time he has stayed on as a boarder and there has been no legal separation. The mother is a devout Catholic and is worried about her husband's irreligious tendencies and is shocked by his blasphemy. She is nervous and anxious about the patient's difficulties and worries about her household.

The father is said to be extremely fond of the patient and has completely spoiled him. He has insisted that the boy sleep with him; although the father retires early, his irregular habits have influenced John, who became afraid to sleep in a room alone, became fearful of the dark and developed night terrors. The father shows his affection for the boy by giving him additional food at irregular hours between meals; and he constantly gives the patient spending money which the boy often loses.

There is a continuous conflict between the parents about John's habit training and religious education; the mother has brought up the patient as a believing Catholic and the father, claiming to be an agnostic, scoffs to the boy about all religion. The mother is in constant dread that the father's irreligion and the patient's growing indifference to religion will bring disaster on the family in the form of divine punishment.

This boy was an unwanted child. The mother, during pregnancy, attempted abortion through the use of drugs. John was a "blue" baby with marked resuscitation difficulties; he was breast fed for six months; he was very slow in sitting up. At birth, he had gonorrheal ophthalmitis for which he was treated for three months. There were no residuals of this infection and the patient had no difficulty with his vision. The mother had contracted gonorrhea from her husband at the sixth month of pregnancy.

The baby had otitis media in the first year, which recurred annually until he was four. At 18 months he had pneumonia and at 8 years a tonsillectomy. The boy acquired no food idiosyncrasies and his toilet habits remained normal.

Both parents declared that the patient had shown no interest in sexual matters, and masturbation was emphatically denied. The child was described as rather shy about bathing and undressing in the presence of his family and was especially anxious that none of his body be exposed before his half-sisters. The mother says he uses vulgar and obscene language and she blames the father for it. The father described the boy's behavior in relation to his half-sisters as prudish.

John was shy and seclusive at school and had very few playmates. He preferred to associate with children several years younger than himself, with whom he could assume leadership. With those of his own age he failed to adjust, either as follower or leader.

He entered kindergarten at the age of 6 and began to annoy the other children by talking and keeping them from their activities. In the first grade he did not get along well, was unable to concentrate, follow the teacher's instructions or leave the other children alone. After spending one and a half years in the first grade, the public school asked to have him removed. He was then placed in a parochial school where, after one term, his removal was again requested. Throughout his constant changes from one school to another, he showed the same inability to learn or concentrate and always annoyed the other children. At the age of 7½ he began to play truant from school. Asked by the psychiatrist why he had run away from school, John answered that the teacher knew she was giving him things more difficult than he could do.

At the age of 10, John had not completed the third grade. His school reading was on the 1A level. For the past few years he has grown increasingly nervous, saying that he hated school and his teacher. He seemed self-conscious about his obesity and the teasing that it incurred. He has been increasingly subject to crying spells from anger and frustration. They now occur several times a day. He cries until he gets what he wants. Although he has dressed himself since he was 6 years old, he still cries and fusses until someone ties his shoe laces for him. He has grown increasingly irresponsible and inattentive to his parents, wandering about aimlessly.

On psychological examination John was found to be of dull normal intelligence, with an IQ of 90. He is retarded mentally about one year. The psychologist reports that he is severely retarded in reading and arithmetic and showed some insight into his former behavior at school and was eager for help with his scholastic difficulties, particularly in an individual situation (where it seemed easy to hold his attention). In the psychometric tests he also showed considerable use of the left hand, although he wrote with the right.

On physical examination, no abnormality was found except accumulation of fat tissue. There were no neurological findings which could support the diagnosis of Fröhlich syndrome, although some examiners express the suspicion on so-called typical fat distribution. The boy was of prepubital age and sexually undeveloped.

BEHAVIOR AND PERSONALITY DEVELOPMENT

The behavior and personality development of this patient showed many similarities to those described by Bruch as typical of obese children.[1, 2, 3, 4] There are also striking similarities in the background and personal development of John's parents to those observed by

Bruch in the parents of a large group of obese children. Many fathers of such children were found to be weak, unaggressive and without either drive or ambition; they played an insignificant role in the life of the family. With few exceptions, the mothers were domineering in the households and expressed open contempt for their husbands. Disharmony and fighting between the parents was common and frequently centered around the rearing of the child. Most mothers of obese children showed marked ambivalence in their attitude, displaying excessive anxiety and concern for the physical and spiritual safety of the child and compensating for fundamental rejection by overprotective measures and excessive feeding. Some fathers seemed to be able to give more warmth and affection to their children, but their positions in the families were so weak and insecure that they could not serve as images of masculine behavior and thereby give security to these obese children.

The problem of the patient's obesity as well as his interest in food was projected in symbolic form in several of his drawings. The constant disagreement between the parents, and the boy's inability to meet minimum school requirements, were crucial factors in blocking the development of John's immature ego. Only after some weeks of art work did the extent of the patient's anxiety concerning his sexual conflicts become apparent.

How the Patient Responded to the Art Sessions

John, during the introductory period of art work, gave the impression of being dull and clumsy in dealing with crayons, paints and plastecine. He showed no initiative as to what to make and waited to begin until he could copy an idea from some other patient. When he finally began a picture, his work was hasty and careless. In contact with other boys whom he met in the art room, he was either sulky or irritable. He showed no interest or sympathy with the activity of other boys and was given to complaining constantly about them.

He asserted his superiority over companions on the ward by maintaining that the sphere of the world which he had modelled in the first art session was better than the work of other boys because, "The world has everything on it, so it's best."

In his approach to modelling, he showed extreme awkwardness; it took several weeks of repeated demonstrations before John grasped the most elementary procedures in handling plastic material. But when, in spite of flabby hands and clumsy use of his fingers, he had succeeded in producing more recognizable objects, he began to grow rather enthusiastic. After the eighth session, he asked whether he could not come again the following day.

At the next art period the boy entered the room smiling happily for the first time. His mood was friendly and he was eager to begin work. Combined with this first genuine enthusiasm for the art expression, the writer noted an improvement in his physical appearance; his eyes seemed brighter and his skin more alive.

As John's first attempt to originate something of his own, he proposed modelling a mountain out of plastecine. In low relief, he built a steep and narrow form and called it an "Alp." When questioned, he explained that the subject was derived from the movies. As he worked, he looked up and commented with a smile, "You see, I haven't forgotten what you told me about how to smooth the clay with my thumb and the ends of my fingers. It has to be smooth, not a crack anywhere," he explained. John's new interest in flattening the surface of the mountain to perfect smoothness was turned into a rather childish game. The writer, whenever the patient asked, was to decide whether the surface of the mountain was growing smoother. Each time, as he received assurance that the mountain had improved, he would laughingly point to some mark or imperfection that had not yet been eliminated by the touch of his fingers. Finally, when he was satisfied with the slick surface of his spatulate-shaped mountain, he invited the writer to "touch it."

This request, to "touch it," combined with the penis-like formation of the mountain, narrow with steep parallel sides and flattened tip, left little doubt of the masturbatory significance of its symbolic form. This was confirmed some time later when, with the release of sexual conflicts, the patient admitted masturbatory practices, for the first time.

The Correlation of War Pictures to Emotional Disturbance

John's first war picture was drawn in the second art session. He had seemed dull and was extremely irritable before he began work. But his lethargy vanished when he prepared to make a picture of an air-battle between Nazi and British planes (Fig. 79). He became completely absorbed in his work and identified with each plane as it drove through space to attack. Accompanying sounds of bullets, explosions and crashing planes were introduced as the air battle grew in fury. "This war," he commented, "will never end. Wait and see, the next battle picture will be like a volcano or tornado."

The boy's comment about unending war was an accurate and appropriate description of the incessant conflict between his parents.

As John finished his battle scene, he became more friendly and said that he wished that he could show the writer his book on the First World War that his father had given him, but that he had mislaid it.

"My father," explained the patient, "was in that war; he used to run a bayonet through the throat of men." John's gleeful satisfaction in reporting this violence was also evident in his later sadistic treatment of cats and dogs. But when he was asked whether his father had enjoyed bayoneting men, he shrugged and said "He had to do it."

WAR PICTURES (FIGS. 79, 80 AND 81)

FIG. 79. AIR BATTLE BETWEEN NAZIS AND BRITISH

The patient was extremely reserved about what went on in the home, so that this mention of the father and his exploits in the previous war was one of his rare references to his family during the five months of art work.

In the next art session, John drew a second air war picture but his interest and enthusiasm for the subject had diminished. For the next three and a half months, the patient drew no more battle scenes, but he began to develop a greater fluency and originality of expression. His previous dependence on the movies and comics for subject matter decreased and he began to use his own observation of both animals and people in his designs. How his art expression continued to grow and develop into more original forms will become evident as the menagerie drawings and the birth cycle figures are introduced.

Some weeks after drawing these air battle pictures, John proposed making a Japanese bombing plane. This subject had been suggested by the attack on Pearl Harbor a few days before. While this actual bellicose event was the source of the boy's design, war and its violence were soon forgotten when John began to experiment with the vivid colors of his new crayon box. In this picture (Fig. 80) a Japanese pilot sits at the controls of a peaceful-looking multicolored plane. Its form is outlined in violet; the front section is turquoise blue, the part beneath the pilot is yellow, the next piece is red. The tail is gray and is bisected with an orange line. The lower section of the plane is green, and the light spot in its centre represents the Japanese sun symbol.

FIG. 80. A JAP BOMBER

(Drawn a few days after Pearl Harbor.) The theme is war, but the release of aggression is replaced by the patient's development of esthetic interest in using an unrealistic color scheme of violet, turquoise, yellow, green, gray and orange in the design of the airplane. See also color plate IV.

John worked with more care and control than ever before in filling in these colored sections of his design. The mosaic-like effect on the surface of the plane was most unwarlike and seemed reminiscent of the work of a much younger child. It had significance, however, as the boy's first, genuine expression of esthetic response in both form and color.

The patient continued to reveal his immaturity in his many childish pictures of stereotyped houses, farms and railroad trains. In his first attempt to use water colors, he made the traditional box-like house with pointed roof, doorway and chimney that young children produce. (Fig. 81). He painted his house red and chose blue for the door, grass, trees and clouds. When he had painted a red chimney, he remarked, "Fire is red, so I'll make the smoke red," and proceeded to do so. John was immensely pleased with this picture and what he felt was a real accomplishment in his first water color. "It's lucky," he remarked for the second time, "that I remembered how to paint from kindergarten."

While John was now beginning to gain satisfaction from the result of his efforts, he showed little control over his brush strokes and had no conception of how to prepare or mix the colors. But his new interest and enthusiasm in the use of paints was of value in developing his self-confidence, however crude such efforts might seem.

Fig. 81. A Red House with Red Smoke and Blue Trees
The patient's first attempt at painting

When the patient had obtained the praise he sought for this first water color, he remarked, "My doctor told me you said I was good." The eagerness in John's voice, as he referred to this comment by the psychiatrist, showed how much he was in need of appreciation and approval.

The Patient Draws Animals in a Zoo

On the day that John drew the Japanese bomber, he also proposed pictures of animals in a zoo. Asked which he would make first, he replied, "A great big animal with a thing in front." Pressed to be more specific he called it a hippopotamus. "It'll be black — in a cage.

It's big and fat." John then drew his large creature in black crayon
(Fig. 82). Its head is rather narrow and inconspicuous and the "thing
in front" projects from its head. As he was making this picture, the
patient drew the writer's attention to how fat the animal was. John
explained that the hippopotamus was in the water. Behind this creature he drew irregular upright black lines that he described as "the
bars of the cage."

FIG. 82. A FAT, BLACK HIPPOPOTAMUS "WITH A THING IN FRONT" BEHIND BARS
A symbolic picture of the patient and his conflicts

While this fat animal shows little resemblance to a hippopotamus,
it clearly symbolized the patient's estimate of his own size and dis-
closed the subject of his sexual conflict; for "the thing in front" of
the large creature suggested a symbolic substitute for the boy's own
penis; thus the patient's conflict over masturbation was presented in
pictorial form long before he dared to verbalize his anxiety over this
problem. The barred cage within which the animal is enclosed clearly
suggests the patient's own dilemma; he is trapped within the confines
of a quarrelling home and can discover no means of escape. The
entire drawing is done in a heavy black crayon that seems appropriate
to the irritable and unhappy moods of this boy.

When the hippopotamus was finished, John was so moved by his
own achievement that he begged for the first time to be allowed to

stay longer than his usual half hour in order to complete two other pictures of the zoo.

Pleading to remain beyond his allotted time, and promising to work quietly while the writer called for the next patient, John made an unexpected move; he raised his arms above his head and kissed their point of junction. Asked whether this represented swearing by the cross, he replied, "Yes, I'm a good Catholic, and it would be a sin to do that if I wasn't going to do what I say." John kept his word and was hard at work on his next drawing when the writer returned.

FIG. 83. THREE COBRAS WITH A GLASS CASE
Represents the patient's family pattern and his concern about food.

In this second design, the boy drew a sequence of coiled snakes which he called cobras (Fig. 83); the diminishing size of the three serpents suggest the family pattern of mother, child and father. (Although John had two older half-sisters, he was the only child of his mother's second marriage.) Later developments in the conversations which ensued, concerning birth and sex, showed the patient as still naively unaware in his conscious attitude of the sexual differences between the male and female form.

The three cobras are contained within an irregular oblong enclosure. The uneven, upright lines to the rear of the snakes show where John suddenly changed his plan. "Oh no," he exclaimed, "not bars. The cobras are inside of glass."

The third drawing shows the exterior of the zoo (Fig. 84). Each
of the seven doorways is supposed to lead to a different kind of animal. The lower left entrance is marked for snakes, spelled "snoks."
Lions, alligators and turtles were also mentioned as occupants of
some of the other houses. A place for food in a trough-like construction beside the snakehouse was not forgotten. The cobras in the
previous drawing had also been adequately fed from a bowl that John
supplied. In the centre of the menagerie, he then placed a tall pole
carrying an American flag. "They sometimes have a flag in a zoo,"
he explained, as he made it.

FIG. 84. MENAGERIE WITH SEVEN ENTRANCES TO ANIMAL HOUSES

The irregular position of the gateways suggests the unstable condition of the
patient.

The irregular forms of the hastily drawn doorways to the animal
houses suggest that the boy was still considerably disoriented. The
peculiar angles of these doorways are reminiscent of the work of some
organic patients. John's later designs showed no such pattern of disequilibrium.

PAINTING AND MODELLING AS RELATED TO THE BIRTH
AND SEX CYCLE

The Brown Dog Painting

During the third month of art work, John announced that he
wished to paint a brown dog. He had never made one before and was
unused to water colors. He was therefore shown how to outline his
imagined animal with a dry brush before using his paints. This preliminary exercise gave the patient confidence to proceed with his
painting (Fig. 85). As the form of the dog was placed in the upper
half of his paper, John remarked, "Artists sometimes just paint a dog
like this, and it doesn't have to go way down."

FIG. 85. PAINTING OF A BROWN DOG

The creation of this picture was the screen behind which the patient's concern
over the problem of birth and sex were hidden. His description of the way his
own dog gave birth to puppies followed immediately.

The dog's body was painted in profile, with its tail pointing upward
to the left, while the head done from a front view, showed a pair of
sharp ears, not unlike the tail in appearance. Beneath the head and tail
two uneven legs threatened the animal with uncertain balance. As a
final touch, the dog received a pair of blue eyes.

With considerable effort, but with undimmed enthusiasm, John
stuck to his work until he had done a painting of the dog in brown
wash for a second time; the result satisfied him completely. When

asked whether anything else was needed in this picture, he answered, "No, that's all. I've seen paintings like that — just a dog."

In the course of originating this second water color, the patient had begun to gain a new confidence in himself. His comment about "Artists just painting a dog, like this," showed a developing sense of identification with those whom he considered as genuine painters in the great world. He now seemed ready, for the first time, to take his own creative work seriously; he too was a painter. In spite of the naiveté of the design and the crudity of its execution, this picture had become extremely important to him. He became aware of having something to express in his own terms and he had also lost his habit of deprecating his own efforts. Such a complete shift from torpor and irritability to activity and enthusiasm denoted decisive changes in the growth and expansion of his personality.

As soon as John had finished his painting, he began to describe his own pet dog, Daisy. "He's a playful dog. I like playful dogs, don't you? Not dogs that fight."— "My dog's black. He's got white here," said John, pointing to his own forehead. "He had six babies and one was black and white like him, four were white and one was all black." When his attention was drawn to the fact that he called his dog a "he," even though it had babies, he replied, "Yes, it's a mother dog." He was then asked whether he knew how the puppies were born. He said "No," and then became silent. It was evident that this brief and negative reply was the patient's defensive response against what he expected to hear from any adult on the subject of birth or sex. It was therefore essential to uncover, as soon as possible, what the patient really did or did not know of these matters. For, until any misinformation and misconceptions that he had derived from home, school or street talk had been released, it would not be possible to clarify the boy's buried conflicts.

When John was told that the baby dogs were carried within their mother before birth, he commented promptly that "They must have been smelly when they came out." The patient's presentation of the cloacal birth theory [5, 6, 8] was met with an explanation that besides the opening for elimination, of which he was already aware, there existed still another opening in the mother, through which a child was born. The patient's first reaction to this information was to counter with, "I thought a kind of bird brought babies from heaven." But, showing how little stock he took in this myth, he did not wait for any reply, but pressed immediately for further enlightenment by asking, "Where is this hole?" He was told that this second opening was located underneath, between the mother's legs. John thought over this newly acquired information for a few moments and then showed his skepti-

cism when he suggested, "Then you'd have to cut the baby's head off
to get it out?" To reassure him of the truth of this statement, he was
given some further information about the process of birth. When
John commented that he thought the baby would "choke inside the
mother," he was told how nature helps to propel it through the opening when it is ready to be born.

"Gee," commented John, who was alertly following what he was
told, "I should think the baby might get stuck coming out. Doesn't
the doctor help?" He was told that the doctor did help in the birth of
children, but that like all animals, his pet dog, Daisy, was able to help
herself. To meet John's last question about the risks of birth to the
child, he was given an explanation of the way in which the vaginal
opening of the mother expanded, temporarily, to allow the release of
the baby. "Gee," John commented, "I'd like to see that. I'd like to
stick a knife or fork up a dog to see."

This was not the only occasion in which John referred to such a
manner of investigating the mysterious openings of cats as well as
dogs. The recurrence of similar stories suggested the patient's consistent desire to obtain, for himself, some first hand information on
the puzzling and forbidden topic of birth. John told of several such
episodes but always attributed them to other boys and not to himself.
A distinctly sadistic trend was evident in one of these tales, when
John with intense gusto described "a boy I know who was cruel to a
cat; he hung it up, killed it and then burned it." But then, the patient
explained self-righteously, "I would never do such a thing, because I
love animals." The suspicion that if the patient had not shared actively in the abuse of the cat he had at least enjoyed the affair as an
onlooker was confirmed some weeks later by John's comment about
his own dog. As he came to feel more at ease with the writer, he was
able to admit his sadistic enjoyment of being cruel to his own dog.

After the boy had been able to voice his wish to investigate the
nature of a dog's structure, he remarked suddenly, "I saw blood
when my dog's babies were born. Why was that?"

Here began the patient's first recall of observations about what he
had seen at the birth of the puppies; other repressed memories concerning birth and sex soon followed. John's direct question about the
blood made it possible to proceed with an explanation of how the baby
is formed from the substance of its mother. The patient then wanted
to know whether the writer had children. When he heard that she
had a grown son this seemed to increase his confidence in her statements. At this point the boy began to recall more that he had noticed,
after the birth of the puppies. "When my dog's babies were born, she
picked them up and carried them into a closet where it was all nice

and clean." Asked whether that had occurred recently, he answered, "No, a long time ago. But if she lays any more babies, I'll give you one."

This spontaneous offer was satisfactory evidence that the patient had now accepted, as correct, the information given him about birth.

Some striking modifications in the boy's behavior and attitude became apparent in the course of this conversation. Whereas he had previously been rather vague and inaccurate in his speech and un-focussed in his attention, he now became keenly alert, precise and logical. He followed the explanations given and challenged what was said with intelligent questions. And when he had begun to weigh the truth of the new information, he suddenly recalled his own observations concerning the birth of his dog's puppies; such memories had remained suppressed until additional data helped him to set the fragments of his own observations within an adequate frame of reference.

At this juncture John again repeated the crucial question, "Where does the baby come out?" But without waiting for an answer, he proceeded to attempt to explain it himself as though he had not been told about the vagina; first he pointed to his chest and then to his mouth in order to suggest that the baby might have come from such openings. "Oh," he then asked, without waiting for any reply, "Is it on the side that it comes out?" At the age of 10 John was briefly recapitulating all the typical infantile theories of birth.[5, 6, 8] Again, it was now necessary, for a second time, to explain how the baby was born through the vaginal opening in the mother.

John's next question was "Why don't fathers have such a hole?" Since this enquiry about fathers involved the broader subject of physiological differentiation between the sexes, the conversation was shifted to this more inclusive question. The patient was asked what differences he had noticed between men and women. "That ladies have finger polish," and "that ladies use lipstick," were his immediate replies. As the art period was then coming to a close, he was left to consider whether there were not some other differences that he could tell about next time.

John's primary concern at the following art session was to check his newly-acquired information about birth with some diagrams that the writer had promised to show him. He was now in urgent need of objective confirmation of her statements about the process of birth. "Have you got the cow picture with the baby calf to show me?" he asked immediately. "Somebody," he stated in an accusing voice, "is lying." Just what he meant by this remark was only explained at the end of the art session. Then, John volunteered, that a boy on the ward had told him that the writer's explanation about birth was untrue.

"But, I told Harry," said John, after this second hour's talk, "I didn't care what he said, I believed what you told me."

Much ground was covered in this second meeting. John needed to clarify what he had been told about birth, and he hoped, apparently, to verify his own observations on the sex life of his pet dog. The diagrams and pictures which the writer showed him helped to convince the boy that he was now being told the truth. The boy examined, with special interest, the diagrams showing the transformation and growth of the fetus and saw now for himself how the baby grew inside the mother. When he observed the umbilical cord in one of the diagrams, he was told how it sustained the child's growth within the womb. "And the baby," commented John, recalling what he had learned previously, "is made out of the mother's blood."

As John now became more relaxed and friendly, he described a wonderful mail order ring that he had acquired; as he told of its beauty, he pulled it from his pocket and demonstrated how its central stone could sparkle in the dark. The writer admired this precious possession and John wanted to give it to her immediately as a gift. It was difficult to persuade him to replace his treasured ring in his pocket. Again the boy's generous response to his need of enlightenment was a gratifying sign of his spontaneous appreciation.

As various aspects of the process of birth were clarified, John began to release more of his own long-suppressed observations concerning birth and sex; he then seemed eager to return to the creative work which he had abandoned for talk during three art sessions.

To help the patient understand the universality of the creative process, he was told something of the way in which plants, as well as animals, propagate themselves. In the course of this conversation, John said that he had never seen a plant grow up from a seed, so the story had to be begun at that point. (The ignorance of the processes of growth and propagation in a plant, and in animal life, as shown by all the children dealt with in this study, suggests that our city schools have underestimated the importance of including a simple course in nature study in the elementary grades.)

As John was reviewing for a second time, at his own request, the pictures which showed the birth of the calf and the human child, he was asked whether he had ever been to the country. "Yes," he answered, "it's so peaceful there." As he told of how he had actually seen a cow being milked, he pantomimed the procedure of manipulating the udder of a cow with his own hands. "That," announced John, "is how we get our milk. It's the grass the cow eats that makes the milk, isn't it?" A reply to this question emphasized that the cow produced milk in order to feed her own young, just as the human mother, after the birth of the baby, produces milk with which to feed her child. John resisted this statement and repeated that cows only gave milk for human babies. He was told, again, why a mother's milk was better for her infant than the milk from a cow; he was then shown the picture of a mother in the act of nursing her own child. John examined it with considerable interest. His next question dealt with the masculine lack of this function. "Men don't have milk?" he queried.

In an effort to check the validity of this newly acquired knowledge, about which he still had certain doubts, John now questioned the writer about her own child. "Did you feed your son that way when he was a baby, too?" Assured that all mothers did so if they could, he promptly shifted his ground and announced, so as not to be excluded from those infants who had been well cared for, "My mother fed me that way too."

When John's resistance to acknowledging that a mother did nourish her child with milk from her own breast had been overcome another repressed memory broke through. With a look of utter astonishment, the patient explained, "Oh I remember now, seeing a mother with a tiny baby at the American centre; and she was holding it up to her close to feed it milk." When the boy was reminded that only a few moments before he had denied emphatically knowing anything about the feeding of a baby with the mother's milk, he explained, "I didn't remember then. I just remembered now. And I remember too," he added, "that I was going to ask the doctor to take the baby away from the mother when she held it." This was John's second recall of forgotten memories in relation to the birth cycle.

The boy was ready with another question at the beginning of the next art session. "Does it take long for babies to come out of their mothers?" he asked. When the nine months period for the development and growth of the child within its mother was described, he exclaimed, "Isn't nature crazy!" In attempting to present the cycle of procreation as normal and natural throughout the development of both plant and animal life, John was told that if he had lived in the country he would have been able to observe many of these facts for himself. He would probably, it was suggested, have been able to watch baby chickens hatch from their eggs and have noted for himself how the mother cows or mother horses grew in size while carrying their babies.

John, who was still struggling to verify all this recently acquired information, confronted the writer with a new question, "Did all this happen to you, too, when your son was born?" Assured of this, he immediately exclaimed, "Oh, now I see. That's why my dog was so fat before the baby dogs were born!" Laughing aloud at the absurdity of his previous ignorance, he went on to explain, "I told my mother, then, not to feed Daisy so much because she was getting fat." Here came John's third recall of forgotten memories concerning what he had observed when the puppies were born. There was more to follow immediately.

"And I remember how, when the little dogs were small they all fought each other; they all fought to get to the mother at once to suck the milk." Again he was reminded that he had only recently doubted the truth of the writer's description of the way baby calves and human babies were fed milk from their mothers, and yet he was now describing in his own words how he had seen his puppies drinking their mother's milk. "Yes," John continued, quite excited by his further recollection, "the little black and white one was the strongest and he was always fighting the others. I pulled him away to give the others a chance." In telling this episode, John dramatized his recollection by imitating the sucking sound of the greedy pup as he snatched more than his share of milk from the mother dog.

"My dog can have more babies, can't she?" was the patient's next question. When such a possibility was affirmed he said, "Well, when she does, I'm going to pick the nicest one for you. I'll bring it here for you. But I mustn't take it from the mother too soon. Not until it's so high," and he illustrated the measure with his hand.

The Patient Creates the Process of Birth in Plastecine

In the next art session, the patient showed that he had reached a satisfying degree of clarification as to the birth cycle. He was temporarily, at least, ready to set aside asking questions. He now proposed to do some modelling. "I'll make a mother with a baby inside of her. First time, I'll make it (the baby) smaller and then later bigger when it starts to come out of her (the mother). Could I do that?"

John had originally planned to make these two modelled figures of the mother. His emphasis was, at first, on the growth and development of the unborn child with the mother as background to his theme. While softening the plastecine, he explained, "I'll make the stomach (of the mother) open so that you can see the baby inside. Then I'll make the mother with the baby coming out." He began, therefore, by modelling, with great interest, the tiny form of the fetus. The baby was crudely made with legs but no arms, although these were added later before the child was placed within the mother's body.

John then became absorbed in creating the torso of the woman. "I won't put on a head," he explained. "I'll just make the stomach with the baby." But as he struggled to bring out the sexual characteristics of the woman's form, his previous interest in the baby was temporarily forgotten. He became absorbed in trying to model the woman's breast. "A woman is bigger up here," he remarked, pointing to his chest, "and smaller down here," he continued, pointing to the waistline of the woman that he was modelling.

The patient was now making use of plastic expression as a means of reviewing and verifying his recently acquired information concerning the process of birth. Since the female form was now his major concern, he was asked whether he might not prefer to postpone the figure of the mother with the baby until later. This suggestion pleased him.

In modelling the first female form (Fig. 86a) John emphasized the breasts and the curved abdomen; he also located the vaginal opening correctly. "The woman is different, down here, from the man," he commented as he worked.

As the patient was occupied with enlarging the woman's breast to more adequate proportions, he held a bit of plastecine in his fingers and said, "I'll put this where she feeds her baby." As he hesitated over the term needed, the word "breasts" was offered to John. He replied, "We call them 'tits.'" He looked rather guilty in producing, for the first time, the vulgar word for this aspect of the female anatomy. Uncertain as to how this forbidden word would be received, John seemed relieved when it was accepted quite casually, by the writer, as just another term for breasts. Gradually he began to use his own sex vocabulary, even venturing to produce the slang terms of street talk as the art sessions continued.

As John's previous hesitation about dealing with the subjects of birth and sex was rapidly disappearing, he was now able to express his thoughts and pose his questions in a natural and spontaneous manner. While completing the first female form he inquired, "Do you like being a woman?" Asked what made him raise this question, he replied, "Well, girls have to wear skirts and boys wear trousers when they run and play. And girls have to play sissy games and play with dolls."

This was John's first formulation of male superiority. It offered the opportunity for continuing the discussion about the differences in the structure of man and woman.

By mistake in ward administration, John's new physician had an appointment to see the boy at a time which interrupted the art session. The patient, who was absorbed at that moment in modelling the female torso, did not want to leave his work. He was, however, promised an additional art period to complete the modelling after he had seen his new doctor.

That the boy should be forced to interrupt his art work at this crucial phase of clarifying his sexual questions was unfortunate. But the unexpected contact with the new psychiatrist produced some important responses in John. The boy's comments were reported by the physician shortly after.the first interview.

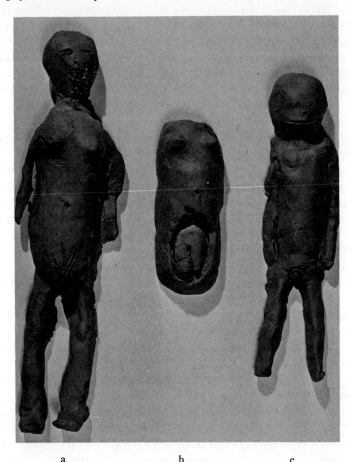

a   b   c

FIG. 86. These three modelled figures were produced by the patient as a means of showing the process of birth. a. THE PREGNANT MOTHER. b. THE MOTHER WITH THE UNBORN CHILD. c. THE FATHER. The patient's questions about birth and sex which led to the production of these figures are reported in the accompanying text.

John, who had been absorbed in modelling the mother, immediately explained to his new doctor, "We are making a woman so as to see how she is made and how the baby grows inside." He also explained how "the opening in the woman will stretch like elastic to let the baby come out." The doctor reported that John had also said that he had found out, from the writer, how the baby grows inside the mother. "At first," John declared, "I didn't believe her, but when I saw the pictures in the book, I knew that it was all true."

The young doctor had been surprised at John's friendly and easy approach, for it did not correspond to the sullen and irritable boy as described in the clinical history. This gave an objective proof of personality modifications that had begun to take place. John could accept a new adult with trust, and he told him, without hesitation, about his newly acquired sexual knowledge.

The psychiatrist asked, "How did the baby get inside the mother?" This was beyond the point where the boy's own inquiries had yet led him. But John's reply, as reported by the doctor, was, "I don't know, but Miss N. is going to tell me all about it." This was encouraging evidence that the boy had now established a secure relationship with the writer.

John returned eagerly to the interrupted art class. As he entered the room he commented, "That hat you have on is Egypt-like, isn't it? It's different. I like things that are different." Such quickened observation of what was an Egyptian style hat, and active approval of the writer's apparel, showed further awareness in the boy's responses.

As the patient returned to modelling the woman, he asked the writer to make the head for him, as he did not know how. He was offered assistance in getting started, but was told that he must really try to model the head himself. "Could you," John asked, "make it? Do you know how?" Apparently the boy was thinking that a teacher who did not either give pupils things to copy, or do the work for them, did not know her job. When John was assured, by the writer, that she could have modelled the head, but that she wanted to help him learn how to do it for himself, he then asked, "And you can paint too?" Satisfied with the replies, he then concluded, "So, that's why you come to help us paint and model."

At the next art session John suddenly said, "I don't want ever to marry." He later explained by saying that he did not wish to give his seed to a woman. When asked why he should now be worrying about marriage, he said, "But if you don't use the seed and don't have a child, you destroy life. I don't want to do that." He also asked, "Wouldn't I kill a child, if I have seed in me and don't give it to a woman?"

When John began to speak of his fear of destroying life by the release of semen he seemed to be expressing thoughts that were not primarily his own. Whether he had been threatened in this manner at

home about the dangers of his masturbatory practices or had over-
heard some religious discussion it was not possible to discover. After
some weeks John was able to describe and even admit, to the writer, his
own satisfaction in masturbating.

While modelling the female breasts of the second figure, of a
woman, John spoke of the "tits" again and remarked, "That's a funny
word, isn't it? And there's another name for tits — headlines." When
he was asked to explain the meaning of that word, he said "Headlines
is a clean word. It means they are in a straight line." As John worked,
he explained, "A woman's tits are long and thin and stick way out,
pointed and hard, don't they?" It took some time to convince him
that the mother's breasts were soft and flexible when the baby sucked
on them.

John's next question dealt more openly with the sexual differences
between boys and girls. "Say," he asked, "with a girl, the number
one and number two comes out of the ass, doesn't it?" This was the
second time that John had used the lingo in which boys exchange
sexual information with each other. Behind his last question evidently lay the thought "If a girl has no penis, how can she urinate."
He was therefore asked how he, as a boy, would do number one. He
answered, "With a pisser." (This was the first time that he had
mentioned his penis.) He was then told that a girl also had an opening in front, which, though not visible, served her when she urinated.

Since John had not begun, as yet, to ask about the role of the
father in procreation, he did not receive an explanation of the dual
function of the penis as being both a sexual and an excretory organ;
this information was postponed until his later questions pointed to
such a need.*

John had now reached a more conscious awareness on the subject
of birth. He had been able to gain a clear picture of the way the child
grows within the mother before it is born and he had chosen to model
the form of the woman in order to dramatize and clarify this newly
acquired knowledge. Just when his resistance against accepting the
facts about the child's birth and its feeding by the mother grew

*In Freud's well-known study, "A Phobia in a Five-Year Old Child" (Ref. 7)
he had advised the father, after little Hans had asked to see his mother's widdler
(penis) "to take away this aim by informing him that his mother and all females
lack widdlers, as he could see from Hanna (his baby sister) who had no widdler."
But the interest of little Hans as of the boy John, was, for the time being, on the
female manner of urinating, and not on the female sexual organs.

Melanie Klein, following Freud's technique, also allows a small boy in "The
Development of a Child" (Ref. 9) to identify both the excretory and sexual function of the penis as wi-wi, without clarifying the distinctions between the dual
mechanisms of the penis.

strongest, he would suddenly recall forgotten memories that related to the sexual life of his own dog or to his observation of a child being nursed at its mother's breast; such recaptured memories helped to strengthen this patient's confidence in the truth of what he had been told. More questions were now asked by John in quick succession, concerning other sexual characteristics of girls and women. He began by asking, "Doesn't a woman have a cut in front?" This was followed by "Why don't little girls have hair down there and women do? Is that so?" When these questions, covering what he had evidently heard other boys tell, had been answered, John finally came out with his most important question. "Say, is it true that a man has to fuck a woman to get a baby?" "That's piggy isn't it?" and John relapsed into his previous embarrassed manner after mentioning what he had been made to believe was both dirty and forbidden. It was quickly established that the boy had no real knowledge of what "fuck" meant. A simple explanation was now introduced describing more specifically the role of the father in producing the child. First the patient was reminded of what he already knew about the growth of the child within the mother; when he was told that the father's help was also needed to produce the child, he immediately asked, "Is it true that he sticks his pisser in her cut?" When his slang term "cut" had been linked to the vaginal opening with which he was already familiar, it was then necessary to describe the way in which the father planted the seed in the mother in order to help in the creation of the child. "Then," asked John, "if they wanted two babies, they do it twice?"

As soon as all of John's questions as to the nature of the sexual act had been answered, he again released another repressed memory concerning the sexual activity of his pet dog. "Oh yes," he exclaimed, as his face brightened, "I remember now, how I saw the father dog jump on my dog to have the baby dogs. She was sort of making a noise." To illustrate, John whimpered like his dog, and then continued, "And the next day the baby dogs were born."

There followed a discussion of the actual time that must elapse before the birth of puppies as well as human infants could be expected.

Again John wished to verify his newly acquired information by checking it against the writer's actual experience. So he asked, "You are married and have a husband?" When this question had been answered, he continued, "When you had a baby, did you do like that too, with your husband?" In reply to these questions, an attempt was made to establish the universality of the process of creation in the realm of animal as well as man. John was assured that each father helped the mother whom he loved to have a child in the way that had been described to him. It was suggested to the patient that the information he was receiving in these talks about birth be kept to himself. John responded readily to this suggestion and said, "If I told the little boys, they'd go and kill a cat to see how it is. I wouldn't tell them." And then he added, "I wouldn't tell Harry, (a boy his own age) because he'd tell Dick and they'd both say it's 'pig.' It isn't 'pig' is it?" The patient was assured that far from being "pig," the unceasing process of creation which continues throughout the universe in the realm of plant, animal and human life was a lasting source of wonder and beauty.

John was told that he was old enough, since he wanted to know, to be told the truth about how children were born and the differences between boys and girls. Apparently pleased at the idea of sharing such knowledge with the writer, he continued, "I won't tell Dick, he'd just make fun and tell others," and John mimicked Dick's expression and self-conscious laughter whenever he talked of forbidden sex matters to the other boys. With an air of superiority, John continued, "Dick doesn't understand these things. You don't tell him the way you do me?" he asked as an afterthought.

As John continued to work at the woman's figure, he looked up and said, "I'm so glad that you've told me about this." He was reminded that whenever he had other questions to ask about birth or sex, that they would also be answered.

Several times during the art session, the patient repeated that his figure of the mother and child should be put carefully away in the closet so that none of the other boys would see it. Each time the writer assured him that this would be carried out, and that no one would be informed. "All right," he said, satisfied at last at the end of the art period, "it's a secret."

Three times during the hour, as he modelled the form of the woman, John would question, "It isn't 'pig' is it?" And each time he would receive the assurance that it wasn't "pig."

Another thought concerning the forms of men and women was also voiced by John on the same day, when he asked, "An artist makes them both?" (He was apparently recalling the figures of Greek statues that he had seen in a book at the previous art session.) To this he received an affirmative reply.

An attempt was made to re-establish John's security as to the normality of the creative process; when the prodigality of nature in producing millions of seeds and eggs that never matured had been explained, he returned to the question of human fecundity. "What happens to the seeds in the man and woman if they don't meet and make a baby?" He was reminded of how many eggs were laid by fish or birds that never hatched, and that this same thing occurred with people. Pressing the subject further, John asked, "But what happens to these seeds then?" When he was told that they passed out of the bodies of both men and women if unused, he wanted to know how. The patient was reminded that he already knew how the penis of the male carried the seed germ which is placed within the woman. This brought John's next question, "It comes then in the same place as piss?" At this moment the patient was specifically asking for an explanation of the dual role of the penis. He was, therefore, told, in his own type of vocabulary, that it was both an excretory and a sexual organ, but that these functions were not simultaneous. "With the woman," continued John, "what happens to the seed if it isn't made into a baby?" It was explained that such unfertilized seed left the woman's body through the vaginal opening. He now remembered that this was the "hole" through which the baby was born.

Suddenly John announced, "I hate all women, don't you?" He was asked whether he meant *all* women. "Yes," he replied immediately. When questioned as to whether he included his mother, he answered emphatically, "Oh no." The boy was silent and thoughtful for a few moments and then added, "I like you. I know you. But I hate Miss X. Why doesn't she marry and have a baby?" Miss X was one of the patient's teachers in the hospital. But in naming her, John was emphasizing his unhappy experience with a long line of women teachers during his unsuccessful school career.

In his next question the patient returned to his investigation of coition. "Does a man put his 'paloma' into a woman in the house? — I'd like to see that. Sometime I'm going to look in a window and see them do it." (*Paloma*, John had explained, was a Spanish word for "pisser.")

MODELLING OF SECOND TORSO OF WOMAN WITH THE CHILD

John was not sure that he could make the torso of the woman with the child inside of her as he had planned, but he was willing to try. "I'll just make the body of the woman this time; not the arms and legs, and no head (Fig. 86b). None of that's important, is it? Just the baby inside the mother is important." He still had on hand the previously modelled form of the unborn infant that he had proposed to place within the mother.

It took much time for John to model this second crude torso of a woman and gouge out a hollow within her in which to place the infant. But when it was finished, the patient was extremely happy. He asked for the box in which he had already placed the other form of the pregnant woman. Before setting his newly modelled figure beside it, he asked for a piece of cotton on which to lay the mother and the child. After arranging the soft white cotton within the box, he laid the torso of woman and child gently upon it. Then, without speaking, he gazed with joy and satisfaction at his new creation. Glancing up at the writer with a glowing smile, he said, "You didn't think I could do them as good as that, did you?" Then, turning his eyes back to wonder at his unexpected achievement, he murmured as he gazed at the two figures, "I'm so proud! I'm so proud!" The profound emotion expressed, so spontaneously, by this boy as he began to discover his own creative power, was in marked contrast to his former dull, disgruntled and irritable self.

He stood some minutes longer contemplating what he had made and then he commented quietly, pointing to the child within the mother, "That's me." In a previous conversation, when he had been told how the father impregnated the mother, he had also identified himself with the procreative process by saying, "I must have been a pretty big seed." And then, as an afterthought John added, with a humorous smile, "And think of me now eating hash and spaghetti!"

Such playful phantasy and spontaneous gaiety was something new in the patient's behavior. Other noticeable changes were evident in the now clear and resonant quality of his voice and the direct and logical expression of his own ideas.

As John had taken stock of what he had achieved in modelling the two figures of mother and child, he announced how he now proposed to expand into more imaginative form his recently acquired understanding of the cycle of birth. In a tone of voice that mingled excitement with a sense of awe, John said, "Why now I could make human life and beast life!" With a steady flow of direct and concise words, he began to describe how he would create the story of the generation of life. First he would make a mother and father and they would have a child, a girl; then he would create another set of parents and their child, a boy, would marry the girl of the other family. Nothing less than a vast cycle of generation, both human and animal, was what John now proposed to create. His own pet dog was to be the starting point for the production of parallel generations of "beast life" from two dog families.

But his chief attention went to the human generation which he envisaged in considerable detail. Besides the birth of the child, he proposed to include all the phases of childhood and growing up; he spoke of the parents who would grow old and die and then other families would replace them.

The boy's description of his vision of the growth of generations of "human and beast life," in starkly simple words, was hauntingly

reminiscent of passages in the Bible which describe the endless sequence of successive generations.

As the patient released his plan for the creation of a new universe,
he was momentarily exalted by the sweep of his vision and the
sense of his power of playing God to the world that he proposed to

By permission of tne Brummer Gallery, New York City

FIG. 87. THE GODDESS OF CHILDBIRTH

This reproduction of an ancient Mexican-Aztec figure of the Goddess of
Childbirth is introduced because the patient also planned to model the figure of
a woman in the act of giving birth to her child, but was unable to execute it. It
suggests the kinship in feeling and expression between the archaic and child-like
forms of art.

create. His feeling of omnipotence was so intensified for the moment
as to give the impression of the more mature vision of a creative
artist.

In John's original scheme for showing the birth of the child from the mother, he had also proposed to make a third figure of the woman in the final phase of giving birth to her child. After an unsuccessful attempt to make the head of the child as it would appear on being released from the mother's body, he abandoned his original intention of creating a woman in childbirth.

While John was unable to carry out this birth cycle to its intended conclusion, such a realization is to be found in an archaic Aztec image of "The Goddess of Childbirth" (Fig. 87). In this compact stone figure, a woman squats upright, with head thrown back and her face and body strained by the anguish she endures as the child is released from her loins.

In the patient's effort to create a pregnant woman and her child, we have a close analogy to this magnificent Aztec figure. For John, in his naively modelled forms, was trying to recapture the same significance of the birth experience. While the patient's attempt to create a woman in childbirth remains foreign to the standards of our imaginatively repressed but verbally articulate culture, it is intimately allied to such a primitive aspect of ancient art as this Aztec figure of "The Goddess of Childbirth."

The Love and Marriage of the Sailor and the Nurse

That moment of inspiration when the patient envisaged the creation of a vast cycle of generations of "human and beast life" came and went before John was able to harness his world phantasy within the limits of plastic form. But the release of creative imagination which occurred in that instant of realization was neither lost nor wasted. For in the following art session John applied his newly-won imaginative power to the creation of a gay, yet earnest phantasy about the love and marriage of a jolly sailor to a beautiful nurse (Figs. 88 and 89). The running commentary that accompanied the spontaneous creation of these two lively figures shows how John's knowledge about the cycle of birth was swiftly sublimated into a saga of the love and marriage of this happy couple.

When the boy had drawn the outline of the sailor in black he filled in his face and costume in appropriate colored chalks. Before making the features he announced that the sailor's eyes would be "large and blue." When they were drawn, he gazed at them with admiration and asked, "Aren't they beautiful?" When the smiling red mouth was done, John told how it was full of white teeth, which he proceeded to make. "The sailor doesn't need a dentist much, because he keeps his teeth so carefully," he commented, as he added the tip of a red tongue between the rows of teeth. Arms were then attached to the sailor's body as semi-circular loops. John threw back his own shoulders and crooked his arms to illustrate the posture he was giving to the figure. "The sailor looks like that — strong," he said. Then to reenforce his assertion, he added, "Oh, I must put more muscle on his arms," and

FIG. 88. THE JOLLY, HANDSOME SAILOR   FIG. 89. THE BEAUTIFUL TRAINED NURSE

These two figures of the sailor and the nurse represent the patient's sublimation of his recently acquired sexual knowledge into an idealized phantasy of love and happy marriage. The sailor in the course of the narration becomes himself and the beautiful nurse, his wife. They marry, are very rich, have four children and live in the Bronx. Food, still important to the patient, is what their wealth is used to purchase. See also color plates V and VI.

two bulges were added. When the naval costume of blue blouse, white trousers and cap, red socks and tie and black shoes was complete, John relaxed with a sigh of satisfaction. "I didn't know," he remarked, "that I could do anything as good as that — Isn't he jolly, isn't he handsome? Don't you wish you could marry him?" To all these questions, the patient received the affirmative answers that he sought.

That the sailor was John's idealization of himself was already clear. But it was only after he had created the beautiful nurse and told of the courtship and marriage of the pair that he attached his own name to the sailor and called the nurse Mrs. John B.

He drew the trained nurse with a white cap and a full skirt; her swelling bosom and small waist accented her femininity. "I'm going to make her beautiful," John announced, as he drew her features. "She's going to have beautiful big eyes — blue eyes." After completing her face and dress, he turned to the writer with a radiant smile and said, "Isn't she beautiful? Her eyes are big and more beautiful than his" (meaning the sailor). "Don't you wish," John inquired, with complete seriousness, "that you were as beautiful as that?"

Asked whether this sailor and nurse were acquainted with each other, he said that they had met in the park. "And they loved each other very much." John then developed the tale of how the sailor and the nurse were married. "They lived in the Bronx and were very rich," he explained. Asked what they did with all their money, he replied, "Oh, they bought things and just said, 'Keep the change.' After a while their money began to go and they stopped doing that." Urged to tell what kinds of things they bought, he said, "Oh steaks, and chops and chicken."

The consummation of the marriage was then dramatized. John did this by picking up the picture of the sailor and placing it face down upon the figure of the nurse in order to have him kiss her. Then the patient reversed the procedure and made the nurse kiss the sailor. After that, as he again covered the nurse's picture with that of the sailor, he said, "Now he's flat on her and squashes her flat." A moment later, reversing the position of the couple, he announced, "Now the nurse is on the sailor and squashes him flat." Asked if the pair were happily married, John said, "Sure, can't you see how jolly his face is?"

At this juncture, John announced that the sailor was himself, Mr. John B. and the nurse was Mrs. John B. He then described and named the family of four children, two boys and two girls, born to this happy couple. Beneath the sailor's picture and that of his wife, the nurse, the writer was asked to inscribe the full names of both Mr. and Mrs. John B. Again he rested his eyes with delight on the portrait of what was now his wife and exclaimed, "Isn't she beautiful!"

There could be no doubt now that John had transmitted his assimilated knowledge of birth and sex into this love phantasy in which he played the important role of the handsome, strong and jolly sailor. In a final phase of the tale, John transformed the beautiful nurse into his own sister. (He had recently described both his half-sisters as beautiful and added, "They let me kiss them because I'm their brother. Gee, how the boys wish they could.") So the love idyll closes with the sister's image as the wife.

Six weeks earlier, John had made a picture of two English pilgrims, which he explained that he had drawn previously in another school. The design was hastily and carelessly produced and only in retrospect did it take on importance as the boy's earliest symbolic representation of his as yet unasked questions concerning the differences between the sexes. The puritan woman, dressed in yellow, wears a white apron; she is shown with a small waist and expansive bosom — feminine characteristics also evident in the later drawing of the trained nurse. The puritan man, garbed in black, wears a high crowned hat; he too, like the modelled father figure to be described, was smaller than the woman. John was troubled by this discrepancy between the size of the two puritans, but this degree of observation did not prevent him from again making the form of the father much smaller than the mother in the cycle of birth.

There is little doubt, therefore, that the two predominant females represent the mother and the two smaller males symbolize the patient. Only in creating the third couple of the sailor and the nurse was the male drawn equal in size to the female. In identifying himself, this time by name with the jolly and handsome tar, John also emphasized the superior strength of the male by adding large muscles to the sailor's arms.

When the boy was preparing to model the father in order to complete the dramatization of the process of birth, he was asked whether he had any other unanswered questions to ask; to this he replied, quietly, "No, I think I understand now."

As he began work on the man, he was somewhat subdued and showed less freedom in his modelling. When it was observed that he had omitted the man's penis, John relapsed into an embarrassed silence. Finally he stated that he did not know how to make it and asked for help. When reminded that he must know how to model it from seeing himself undressed each day, he replied, "I don't know how it is. I don't look at myself. It's dirty." The clue to John's relapse into a sense of shame and guilt about his body came, when he explained, "My father says it's all dirty and he hits me if I talk about it." A little later in the same conversation, he said that his sister also strikes him if he says any of these dirty words. In spite of this temporary return into a family-induced attitude that the body and its natural functions were dirty, he succeeded in finally completing the figure of the man (Fig. 86c). It shows the male as resembling John in both stature and sexual development.

As the patient was modelling the man, he asked his final questions concerning the difference between the sexes. Noting that he must make the "tits" of the man smaller than those of a woman he inquired, "Why should a woman have larger 'tits' than a man?" His tone suggested a resentment against any such possible superiority in woman. As the story of the way in which the mother's breasts supplied milk to the baby was reviewed, he again voiced resistance by protesting that "it's silly."

As John placed his completed figure of the man in the box beside the forms of the two women, he considered his handiwork and pointing to the torso of the woman containing the unborn child, he said, "I like that one best." He then suggested "I ought to name them." After a moment's hesitation, he said, designating the first woman's completed form, "This is *Nothing*." Then, pointing to the man, he announced, "This is *Something*;" and then referring to the woman's torso with the infant, he also called that "*Nothing*." Since these comments followed soon after he had objected to admitting that a woman's "tits" were larger than a man's, it is evident that John, in calling the male figure "Something" and the two female forms "Nothing," was attempting to reestablish his sense of male superiority.

As in his earlier reverie about how he had once been carried within his mother, John now began to recall a childhood memory. "I remember," he recalled, "how, when I was small, my mother used to take me out in my carriage. I had to wait for her outside when she went to buy food. She bought too much food. . I had to wait too long."

John supplemented these childhood memories with the comment, "I sometimes get mad. I don't know why." This was his first reference to temper tantrums. "I love my mother and I love my father, and I love my two sisters," he continued, "I like you best after them. I like you better than my aunt. I hate my aunt. — I am so mad at my father. I'm going to hit him when he comes for me — he didn't get me last week to go home."

After the recall of childhood memories, associated with some of his earliest spells of bad temper, John had now released some of his ambivalent feelings toward his father. While the boy had, as yet, shown no insight concerning the tangled home situation, he was now able to express some of his own resentment against the attitude of various members of the family toward him. This was a distinct advance over his earlier sullen defensiveness which repressed his emotional difficulties and distrusted the approach of any adult.

THE PATIENT AGAIN DRAWS AIR BATTLE SCENES

John maintained a fairly even and happy mood in the art sessions for some time after he had completed the drawings of the sailor and the nurse. But one day he entered the room in a sullen and irritable state. Without saying anything he drew a large picture of a violent air battle between Nazi and British planes. The picture was reminiscent of the previous drawings of war in the air that he had made over three months before (Fig. 79).

The boy made no comment on this war picture, but as soon as he had completed the planes in the sky and the army on the ground he obliterated the entire scene with black crayon strokes, leaving only two British guns to stand guard over the destruction. Pleased with the demolition of his air battle, John laid its smudged remains carefully within his portfolio at the end of the art session.

The sudden reappearance of the patient's expression of hostility, in this and a subsequent war picture, was found to correspond to his chastisement at home for referring to the subject of sex. The patient's relapse into his previous condition of lethargy and resentment was also found to be connected with the growing disagreement between his parents.

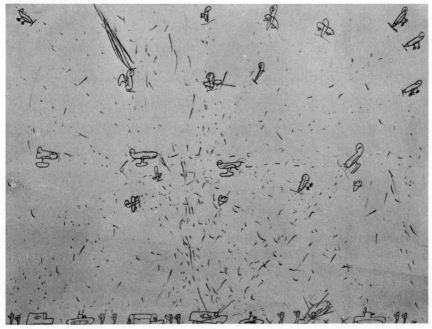

FIG. 90. ANOTHER AIR BATTLE BETWEEN NAZIS AND BRITISH

Drawn 3½ months later than previous war pictures, during a period of regression.

In the next art period, John began to make another air battle scene. He now, for the first time, referred to the complete destruction that he had created in the previous session. About his proposed picture, he remarked, "I'm not going to make it so mussy this time." He then drew a more complicated series of battling planes with clarity and dynamic movement (Fig. 90). In this design both British and Nazis were again in air combat, while on the ground an army, consisting of men, tanks and a red cross ambulance moved across the lower part of the picture. The sounds of battle were again introduced as an accompaniment to the scene of destruction.

In this second scene of war in the air, John continued to release his aggression but found it no longer necessary to obliterate all recognizable aspects of the conflict. Further designs relating to the destruction and violence of war did not reappear during the remaining months of art work.

Since the regressive behavior of the patient was related to home conditions, an effort was made to induce him to comment more freely about his family. When he reported a recent visit from his parents that had given him pleasure, he was asked whether he might not enjoy their visits more if they came separately. After considering this a moment, he said "Yes." This opening was used in order to refer to the conflicting views held by his mother and father about religion and other matters, but the boy still found it necessary to deny to himself, as well as to the writer, that there was disharmony between his parents. For all that John could say was, "My father loves my mother."

Althought the patient recovered from his sulky and difficult behavior and continued to show a degree of imaginative release in his subsequent pictures, the lack of any fundamental cooperation from the home interfered with the continuation of his emotional reorientation through art expression.

THE PATIENT SHOWS THE FIGURES OF THE BIRTH CYCLE TO A FRIEND

While it was not possible, because of family influences, to continue to free John from the strain of the conflicts in the home, evidence was obtained in his responses to another patient that his enlightenment concerning the cycle of birth and sex had made a fundamental alteration in his understanding of this subject.

When the patient asked, after some weeks had elapsed, whether he might show his friend Harry (who also worked with the writer) the box in which he kept his modelling of the mother and child, it was impossible to foresee just how satisfactorily this demonstration would take place. When John opened his box, Harry had no difficulty in accepting the patient's interpretation of the meaning of these three plastecine figures. He praised the way John had executed them and pointing to the female torso with the child, Harry remarked that sometimes such headless figures of ancient statues were found buried in the earth.

When Harry asked about the male figure in the box (Fig. 86c), John explained, "That's the man," and pointing to the form of the first woman, he added, "That's the woman. And the man and woman marry and have a baby." To complete the demonstration, John then referred to the woman's torso, lying between the man and the woman, "There's the way the baby grows inside of the mother," he explained.

Harry accepted all that John told him quite simply and naturally. He did not, however, hesitate to make some critical comments on the inadequate construction of the first figure; Harry thought that what was meant to be the front of the woman's body looked more like the rear. John, however, defended his own creation by explaining that the stomach protruded because the baby was inside.

The atmosphere remained friendly and without strain as John and Harry examined the three human forms and carried on their conversation about the process of birth. No sign of embarrassment or feeling of guilt was evident in the speech or behavior of either patient.

John, pleased with Harry's interested response, told more. "But that's not all. I was going to make a house too, where the baby grows up. But I don't want to make it now." Asked by the writer whether he would not tell Harry about his original plan concerning the life story of that baby, John said, laughing, "When the baby grows up he'll get a ticket to go to the ball game." As John concluded his explanation of the birth cycle with these joking words, he gave the writer a knowing smile which seemed to imply "We know the rest, but that's enough to tell Harry today."

To gauge how the patient now viewed in retrospect his plan to create both "human and beast life," he was asked by the writer whether he still recalled the rôle that his dog and her puppies were meant to play in that scheme. Without hesitation John turned to Harry and explained that he had also meant to include in his story the way in which the baby dogs would grow up and how they in turn would have puppies of their own.

At no time in explaining the birth cycle to his friend did John express any self-consciousness, a satisfying proof that, in spite of the continuing threats of punishment from home, the boy now showed himself able to accept the facts of sexual enlightenment and had incorporated them into his own living, without showing his former reactions of either shame or guilt.

COMMENT

In his art expression, this boy like many other children approaches with caution topics which, in ordinary experience, are not dealt with openly. It is therefore important that one accepts as significant for him whatever subjects he chooses. This applies particularly to matters of sex.

From the beginning, the boy's own sex vocabulary was accepted as emotionally meaningful to him. It was followed by the writer, in order to free John from any sense of self-consciousness about the use of such terms.

As the patient developed more courage in posing his questions about the differences between man and woman, he began to draw upon the phraseology for sexual parts with which he, as a boy, was familiar. Hence such words as "tits," "ass," and "pisser" began to be used. If such terms, when they appear spontaneously in the patient's questions, were to be rejected and treated as obscene, the boy would be liable to relapse into his previous silence and hesitate to make any further reference to problems of sex with the adult. The writer, therefore, accepts without criticism whatever sexual slang is used by a patient, and only goes so far as to suggest that the child's sex lingo is interchangeable with the less familiar, scientific terms that are also introduced into the conversation. This casual acceptance of the forbidden sex words eases tension and alleviates a sense of guilt in these behavior problem children as they struggle to vocalize their long misunderstood sexual questionings.

CONCLUSION

This report deals with a boy of 10 with a marked inability to learn and with no contact with children of his own age group. He was considered obstinate, sullen and uncommunicative at home as well as in school.

In the beginning, John's art expression was exceedingly immature; it was both inhibited and imitative. Although his drawing, painting and sculpture remained naive and crude throughout the five months of art sessions, they gradually developed qualities of spontaneity and originality. Thus, through the liberation of the boy's authentic responses to life, personality difficulties began to be revealed in the language of art long before he could deal with such topics in words.

From the day when John had painted his brown dog until the moment when he had completed his tale of the sailor and the nurse just five weeks had elapsed. The patient had, therefore, telescoped into this brief space of time the entire sequence of sexual enlightenment which it takes most children some six or seven years to traverse. Although John was already 10 years of age, he began his sexual inquiries with the infantile birth theories current among young children. But losing little time over this early childhood phase, the patient was soon able to release his own accurate but long suppressed observations about the sex life of his own dog. The patient then began to verify his own observations and the sexual information he had received, with the help of pictures and scientific diagrams. When anxiety about masturbation and a sense of guilt about his bodily functions had been relieved, the boy gained the courage to produce the sex slang current among his contemporaries. When typical specimens of what adults condemn as obscene language had been used by the patient, he showed considerable ignorance of its meaning. When all John's questions about birth and the differences between the male and female had been dealt with, he was able to say, "Now I think I understand." With a clarification of his sexual conflicts, John was able to transform his sexual knowledge into several creative phantasies; in one he envisaged the cycle of generation of both "human and beast life," and in another he projected in word and picture his dream of future happiness in the love and marriage of the sailor and the nurse.

From the evidence produced in the patient's art expression and his accompanying comments, his first attempts to inquire at home about the birth of children had probably been met with reprimands that made him learn to accept the family prohibitions against looking at his own body or mentioning anything that pertained to sex. The marked improvement in the patient's ability to express his own thoughts and feelings in words as well as art forms, as his anxiety decreased and his confidence in his own creative expression grew stronger, would seem to warrant the conclusion that the contradictory and arbitrary treatment of this boy by quarrelsome and otherwise inadequate parents played a major part in blocking the patient's potential development. What appeared, therefore, as an extreme emotional and intellectual retardation was shown, in the course of the art sessions, to be due, primarily, to the mishandling that he had received from his family. Frightening threats as well as physical punishment had so blocked the satisfaction of this boy's spontaneous and natural curiosity about sex that various aspects of normal development seemed to have been slowed down.

Prohibitions which prevented the boy from satisfying his curiosity about sex also carried over into blocking his intellectual development. The leading complaint from the school authorities, which led to the boy's treatment at the hospital, was focussed on his inability to learn.

As the patient became free enough to ask his questions about birth and sex, he was capable of expressing both feelings and thoughts in an adequate and well organized manner. From an attitude of doubt and suspicion toward the writer, as just another adult whom he could not trust, the boy gradually developed a sense of confidence and friendliness. After testing and questioning the writer, not merely as to the validity of the sexual information she imparted, but also as to her capacity to help him in art, he gradually came to accept her as a stable and mature person who believed in him and his creative powers. As this rapport was established, John found that he was able to obtain answers to all his questions about birth and sex.

In the course of the art sessions, John had also succeeded in overcoming his isolation sufficiently to establish a good contact with his new physician and a boy of his own age on the ward. With the psychiatrist he was able to express himself spontaneously about the cycle of birth that he was modelling in the art sessions. With his friend Harry, he could show and discuss, without embarrassment, the figures of the mother, father and child that he had made. Freed of any sense of shame or guilt on the subject of birth and sex, he could now speak naturally about such matters. For the first time, he was able to meet a boy of his own age as a friend and equal. In spite of the irresponsibility of the patient's family, and their continued misunderstanding of his problems, John had made a rapid advance in the growth and development of his immature ego in the course of the art sessions.

Bibliography

[1] Bruch, Hilde: Obesity in Childhood and Endocrine Treatment, Jl. Pediat., Vol. 18, pp. 36-56, Jan. 1941.

[2] —: Obesity in Childhood and Personality Development. Am. Jl. of Orthopsychiatry, Vol. XI, No. 3, pp. 467-474, July, 1941.

[3] — and Touraine, Grace: Obesity in Childhood: V. The Family Frame of Obese Children. Psychosom. Med., Vol. 2, No. 2, pp. 141-206, Apr. 1940.

[4] —: Psychiatric Aspects of Obesity in Children, Am. Jl. Psychiat. Vol. 99, No. 5, pp. 752-757, March, 1943.

[5] Freud, Sigmund: On the Sexual Enlightenment of Children, Collected Papers, Vol. 2, pp. 36-44, Hogarth Press, London, 1933.

[6] —: On the Sexual Theories of Children, Collected Papers, Vol. 2, pp. 59-75, Hogarth Press, London, 1933.

[7] —: A Phobia in a Five-Year Old Boy, Collected Papers, Vol. 3, pp. 140-287, Hogarth Press, London, 1933.

[8] — : Three Contributions to the Theory of Sex, 4th Edition, Nerv. & Ment. Dis. Mon., New York, 1930.

[9] Klein, Melanie: The Development of a Child, Int. Jl. of Psychoanal., Vol. 4, No. 4, Oct. 1923.

[10] Naumburg, Margaret: Children's Art Expression and War, The Nervous Child, Vol. 2, pp. 360-373, July, 1943.

[11] —: The Drawings of an Adolescent Girl Suffering from Conversion Hysteria with Amnesia, Psychiatric Quarterly, Vol. 18, pp. 197-224, 1944.

[12] —: A Study of the Art Expression of a Behavior Problem Boy as an Aid in Diagnosis and Therapy, The Nervous Child, Vol. 3, No. 4, pp. 277-319, July, 1944.

[13] —: A Study of the Psychodynamics of the Art Work of a Nine-year-old Behavior Problem Boy, Jl. of Nerv. & Ment. Dis., Vol. 101, No. 1, Jan. 1945.

[14] —: Phantasy and Reality in the Art Expression of Behavior Problem Children, Paper in Vol. Modern Trends in Child Psychiatry, Int. Univ. Press, New York, 1945.

THE DRAWINGS OF AN ADOLESCENT GIRL SUFFERING FROM ANXIETY HYSTERIA WITH AMNESIA

INTRODUCTION

This paper will consider a series of abstract chalk drawings done by a fifteen year old girl of Italian parentage who will be designated as Maria. Her condition was diagnosed at the New York State Psychiatric Institute and Hospital, where she was treated for anxiety hysteria with amnesia. Her drawings have significance from several viewpoints; as related to the psychotherapeutic treatment, they show a close parallelism to the problems dealt with by the psychiatrist. As examples of an original and symbolic use of both color and abstract form, they throw light on the behavior pattern of the patient's illness and disclose the presence of recurrent archetypal symbols of which the patient remained completely unconscious.

Before discussing both the conscious and unconscious material presented in Maria's drawings, it should be made clear that although all her pictures are abstract in design she never showed awareness or interest in any modern abstract art that might have influenced such compositions. Her concept of art had, in fact, been conditioned by years of formal public school art teaching which consisted of nothing but tracing and copying. Therefore she came to the introductory art session declaring that she disliked art and could not draw at all. Only when this patient began to realize that art was not a mechanical process but a spontaneous means of expression did she turn with interest to the box of colored chalks. The moment she saw the vivid tones she responded with: "I love color. But I don't like browns. I never get any clothes like that."

Maria was known to be fond of dancing and was recognized as a passionate jitterbug. "I'm crazy about dancing," she admitted. She was therefore made aware in the art class that her interest in dance rhythm could be related to such rhythm as was also to be found in the color and movement in a painting or design. With a love of color and a feeling for rhythm in bodily movement, the problem was to make Maria transfer expression of her own emotional states to paper.

Asked whether she was subject to any sudden variations of mood, she replied, "I should say I am." Could she find which colored chalks might express her happy feelings? Her answer was to select without hesitation a vivid red, strong yellow, bright green and gay blue. These were then set aside in one pile. When asked to choose colors to suit a sad or depressed mood, she immediately selected black, gray and tan shades. These were the three colors that she had previously stated she especially disliked and would never wear.

The possibility was then presented to the patient that pictures could be created from such color combinations to express either her joyous or her depressed moods. She was intrigued with this suggestion and eager to experiment. When asked to decide whether the first picture would represent a sad or happy mood, she said, "I feel happy today, so now I'll use those colors," pointing to the bright ones.

It would have been natural that any preliminary efforts at free expression attempted by a 15-year-old girl, who had, up to that time, only copied or traced pictures, would be somewhat stilted. Her immediate response and quite free and original use of color and design came sooner than the writer anticipated.

At the first session a few suggestions were offered as to ways of using the colored chalks. She was shown how quality of color or of line could be changed by the use of the broad edge or fine end of the chalk; also different methods by which contrasting colors could be mingled or overlaid. She was then encouraged to experiment with the use of a practice-sheet of paper to try out color schemes or ideas. She then drew her first design on a small sheet of paper.

Her initial use of abstract design had not been expected. Nor was it anticipated that, having begun in this way, the patient would continue making abstractions without introducing concrete or realistic subjects in any of her 45 drawings.

Although Maria remained in the hospital for eight months, it was only during the last period of her treatment that the writer was able to carry on any regular art work with her. The sequence of these designs, done during seven sessions which ranged from an hour to an hour and a half in length, emphasize the cyclic character of the patient's behavior, and bring out the nature of her fundamental conflicts with her home environment. Hers is the history of a modernized American-Italian girl whose life was blocked by the severe old world discipline of her Italian parents. In the course of treatment the patient became aware of how her amnesia was an escape from her painful conflict with her parents and in moments of depression she went so far as to threaten to escape again into such a state. Before considering in detail the meaning and significance of the drawings that correspond to various phases in the patient's treatment, a brief clinical summary of the case will be given.

CLINICAL HISTORY

Brief Statement of the Problem

The problem is that of a 15-year-old Italian-American girl who started for school on September 14, 1942, failed to arrive either at school or at home after school. She was located at about 6 o'clock that evening by the police at a local large general hospital where she had been taken following the discovery of her lying beside the road in Central Park. Upon arrival at the hospital she was unable to give any details in regard to her identity. The patient remained at home for one week and was then admitted to the New York State Psychiatric Institute and Hospital, at which time she had recovered some of her memory, but continued to show marked defects. In this hospital her behavior has been extremely cyclic in character. At times she is elated and euphoric; at other times markedly depressed. There has been complete recovery of her memory with only a few exceptions.

Family History

The family on both sides were Italians, middle-class, with no history of mental or organic disease. The father is a barber, exceedingly steady in his habits and fond of his family. The mother is a typical Italian mother, over-protective and solicitous regarding her child. Both parents express their willingness and desire to cooperate, but due to their background it is hard for them to accept their child as a normal American girl who is able to take care of herself. The mother invariably speaks of the child as "my Maria," and will cooperate as long as it does not interfere with her standards of living. There is one brother aged 12, who is described as a normal healthy boy. The collateral lines are negative for mental and nervous disorders.

Personal History

The patient was a wanted child, born 13 months after the marriage of her parents. The child was a healthy baby but was always a poor eater and often vomited if forced or urged to eat. The mother was often told by the doctor that she was too fussy about the baby and was urged to exert less pressure on the child. There was a tonsillectomy at the age of seven, no other severe illnesses. The patient began school at the age of 6½ years, was sent to a parochial school which she disliked intensely. However, she attended regularly and always did acceptable work. She always had many friends, both boys and girls. Menstruation began at the age of 14. There seemed to be no untoward effect, but there had always been some pain and the menses have lasted for as many as eight days.

The mother has always cautioned the patient with such admonitions as the following: "Maria, you must be careful; don't let boys come too near you; be lady-like." The patient had been required to be home each night by 8:30; and if a movie was attended, she was required to sit on the children's side, the mother even going to the extent of asking the matron at the movies to notify her if this procedure was not carried out. The patient has always been sensitive and easily hurt by the slights of her girl friends. Three weeks prior to her present illness, she came home and cried throughout the night later telling her mother that it was due to a quarrel she had had with one of her friends who had criticized her for not being allowed to stay out later at night.

The patient had never been allowed to wear any form of make-up in spite of the fact that all her friends used lipstick and rouge. For the past six months, the patient had complained of dizziness. Three weeks prior to admission, the patient bumped her head, following which she complained of shining images before her eyes and was not able to move for a short period. There was no loss of consciousness. Two days before the onset of the present illness, the patient complained of a feeling of cloudiness in her head. She has attended school regularly, was popular with her teachers and schoolmates and at the present time is in the second year of high school.

Previous Attacks of Mental Disorder

The patient had no previous attacks of mental disorder.

Onset and Symptoms of the Psychiatric Disorder

On September 14, the patient left her home for school. When she did not return at the expected time, the police were notified and at about 6 o'clock that evening she was located at a large general hospital with a complete amnesia for all events prior to the time that she was picked up in Central Park. She had walked from her home in the Bronx to 90th Street and Central Park. This was evidenced by the condition of her shoes which were completely worn out when she was found. The patient remembers nothing of her wanderings except that she had the urge to walk and that she wandered in and out of many large stores on the trip.

Examination at the hospital failed to show any evidence of attack or any physical abnormalities. She remained at home for one week, the first three days of which she slept almost continually. Due to her failure to improve, she was brought to this hospital on September 22nd. At this time, she remembered all events following the fourteenth of September, but only those things prior to that time which had been related to her by her family or friends. She did not feel any close relationship to members of her family and accepted her mother and father as such, only because she had been told they were her parents and it seemed the proper thing to do. She was cooperative, pleasant and at this time showed no evidence of any mental condition except the amnesia.

Physical Status on Admission Including Laboratory Findings

Physical examination showed a well-nourished white girl of 15 years, asthenic habitus, no evidence of any pathology. The electrocardiogram showed a normal rhythm rate 80 per minute; no abnormal complexes. The electro-encephalogram showed a record that might be considered an immature one, or one suggestive, in a mild degree, of a convulsive type of pattern. The Wassermann was negative. Blood chemistry and blood count were normal. Urinalysis was negative. X-ray of the chest showed no abnormality. On September 29, a basal metabolism determination showed metabolism within normal limits. The X-ray of the skull showed no evidence of pathology.

Mental Status on Admission

A psychometric done on October 6 showed the patient's IQ to be 87 with her performance 83.* It is possible that the amnesia present at this time lowered the test to some degree. The attitude and general behavior during the test were excellent. The stream of mental activity was normal in every way. The patient was unable to tell of events that had happened prior to her illness, but was clear and concise regarding recent events. The emotional reaction, affect and mood were normal. The mental trend was also normal. The patient was aware that the parents had been over-severe with her and blamed her present condition, to a marked degree, upon conflict over this. Her sensorium, mental grasp and capacity were all good except for remote memory. The patient showed a poor ability to do problems in arithmetic and when pressed became confused and gave any answer that occurred to her. Her school and general knowledge were fair. Some of the answers were obviously tinged by her loss of memory. Her insight and judgment were good. Her intelligence was average for her age.

Progress and Treatment During Hospital Residence

When the patient first entered the hospital she was hypnotized by the examiner with ease. During her hypnosis, she recalled many events of the past and upon instruction from the examiner she retained these memories after her session. In October an attempt was made to give her sodium amytal intravenously for the purpose of obtaining further subconscious material that might be present. After the injection of less than one gram of sodium amytal, she became markedly hysterical, cried, threw herself on the floor, and for the first time expressed her feelings in regard to her parents. At this time she said: "I don't want to go home. Why should I go home? I was never allowed to do anything that I wanted to when I was there." The next day she apologized to the examiner and expressed her willingness to cooperate if another attempt was made to give her sodium amytal. The second attempt was successful in the administration of the drug, but produced no additional information. After the episode of October first, the patient's behavior changed markedly. She began to present cyclic swings of mood with periods of elation, euphoria and coopera-

*Recent IQ — 10 points higher — 93.

tion, alternating with periods of marked depression and refusal to take part in any of the ward activities.

At this time she expressed her extreme fixation upon the examiner and all attempts to hypnotize her failed. At one time when she was being hypnotized, she suddenly asked how the examiner expected to hypnotize her when she was seething inside. On several occasions, she has refused to go home for the week-end and one week-end upon her return to the hospital from home, it was necessary for the examiner to be called to the ward to talk to her regarding the extreme depressive state which she was in. She frequently refuses to go to school and, although she will go if urged by the examiner, her work on these days is so poor that the time in school is wasted. The patient has felt that there may be periods of short duration in between her two moods in which she is in a dazed condition. She has never been observed to have any form of petit mal nor did carotid pressure produce any change in the patient.

Subsequent Course

During her stay in the hospital the patient had variable moods, with extremes of depression alternating with phases that were almost hypomanic in degree. During her interviews with the examiner, her moods often shifted from one extreme to the other. There were periods of as much as five weeks when the patient refused to go home for week-end visits. Following the longest period of this type — which lasted during the month of February and part of March — the patient asked, in the middle of March, to see the examiner for an extra interview. At this time, she suddenly revealed the fact that she felt her hesitancy in going home had been due to the fact that she was extremely fond of her father and jealous of her mother. She further stated that she felt her main reason for being fond of one of the boys with whom she was going was due to his resemblance to her father. This interview was felt to be markedly influenced by psychological conferences which had been in vogue among patients. This was pointed out to the patient and confirmed by her. Following this interview, the patient remained in a mild depression for several days and then asked if she might be allowed to go home for a visit of one week. This request was allowed, and the patient came back reporting that she had enjoyed her visit and felt better, that her parents were beginning to understand her and were in sympathy with her.

Psychotherapy with this patient has progressed steadily and consistently since her admission into the hospital. She has used varied forms of communicating with the examiner, including a type of free association using the typewriter as the medium. She has written many letters, each bringing out problems that were uppermost in her mind. Psychotherapy was kept on a superficial level at all times with emphasis placed on the family relationship, the patient's jealousy of her brother and her resentment of undue restraint. One week before this report, she suggested to the examiner that she be allowed to live at home while continuing her treatment because she felt that she was being limited by the constant association with the one group of people with whom she came in contact. At the present time, the amnesia has cleared up completely, and as her request was considered logical, she was discharged from the hospital at the end of May with the understanding that she was to return for school daily and for regular psychotherapeutic sessions with the examiner. Her condition was much improved.

DESCRIPTION OF FIRST TWO ART PERIODS
The First Session

The essential quality of Maria's drawings will be more clearly grasped if a detailed description of her work during the first two art sessions be given. This will be followed by a description of the cyclic character of her drawings, a review of the color symbolism and archetypal forms employed, and finally an analysis of the subject matter covered in these designs. Nine small chalk drawings were made during the first hour, in rapid succession. She chose to begin with two successive attempts to express happiness. These she drew with sweeping swaths of bright red, blue, yellow and green that mingled and crossed one another in rhythmic pattern. The first drawing showed a rich and intense use of color. This was followed by a more luminous and delicate design, aspiring in mood, and filled with an upsurge of color. As the drawings developed it was evident that a rising rhythm accompanied a constructive and mounting mood, while a downward swing always went with depression or negation of life. With the achievement of these two "happy" designs, Maria announced, "This is lots of fun." She was now ready to try to create the opposite mood with her black and brown chalks. She had clawed the air with her fingers, releasing sudden and intense emotion, before drawing a depressed state. Seizing the black chalk, she then slashed furiously at the paper, making a series of rhythmic black down strokes; to these she added a mass of terra-cotta brown, which she immediately overlaid with curved and rhythmic black lines. To this picture she gave the title "Vile." "That's just how I feel," she announced. The destructive emotion released in both gestures and drawing was excessive. She was therefore asked when it was drawn whether that mood was completely expressed. "No, I want to do another." This next picture, done only in black chalk, she also called "Vile." In it the charge of emotion had diminished, the lines were more delicate and its rhythm moved upward in flower-like pattern. With this release, the patient placed the two pairs of these designs, the happy and the depressed states, before her for consideration.

She was now asked to recall some actual event which had caused her to feel depressed or angry. "The last time I felt like that was when I went home, a couple of weeks ago. I came home from a party with a boy friend of mine from the hospital and it was 3 in the morning. My father was standing in the street waiting for me. He slapped me in the face. I was awfully upset and embarrassed before my friend. And then when we got inside I screamed and got hysterical and all the neighbors heard. I haven't been home since then."

The next two drawings of the series dealt with this experience. The patient was asked to focus her attention on the recollection of the moment when her father had struck her. Immediately she seized the black chalk and made sudden jagged lines which she supplemented with streaks of red. But one design was not sufficient to release all the pent-up feelings associated with this crisis. So she chose to make yet another picture on the same theme in the same two colors. For the drawing of her hysterical attack, Maria was then asked to close her eyes and recall the exact moment of that experience. Adding a purple chalk to the red, she then drew a somewhat chaotic and shrill design which was surprisingly effective in transmitting a sense of hysteria.

A corroborative note from the psychiatrist's records concerning this same episode follows:

"Three weeks ago the patient returned from a party at an hour which her father thought unreasonable. He was waiting in front of the apartment for her and slapped her in the presence of the boy with whom she had gone to the party. Following this she had hysterics and informed her parents that she hated them and did not intend seeing them again."

The patient now became enthusiastic about her newly discovered ability to express her own feelings through chalk drawings. Her evident ability to express her own moods led to the suggestion that she should now select and draw whatever mood she wished for her next picture, without describing it in advance. The writer would then attempt to guess what the drawing meant. The patient was ready and eager for this experiment, selecting brilliant tones of yellow, orange, scarlet, green and blue she swiftly made a picture. Its pattern stemmed upward from below, spreading open at the top of the page. A bright coral-like red spray reached out from the left side of the design, and a V-shaped angle of deep blue cut up across the centre of the paper, while a mass of moving yellow, orange and green flowed upward from below. There could be no doubt of the elation expressed in the tense brilliance of this picture. The patient was pleased that the intended mood of her design had registered and said, "Yes, that's when I'm high." Unwilling to end the first session with this picture, the patient chose to make a final design (Fig. 91). By its balanced pattern, one side black and the other vivid colors, it left no doubt that it was an expression of the two opposing aspects of the patient's personality.

TREE OR FLOWER-LIKE FORMS — EXPRESSING TWO ASPECTS OF THE SELF (FIGS. 91 AND 92)

The tree or flower-like forms were drawn in symmetrical balance, in contrast to all the other designs that were asymmetrical.

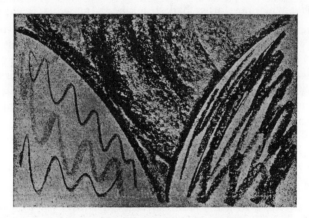

FIG. 91. OPPOSING ASPECTS OF THE PATIENT

In the patient's drawing of two aspects of herself, the lower left triangular space was filled with zig-zag lines of blue, green and orange which represented the elated state; the lower right triangular space with broken black lines represented the depressed state. The central upward-moving form in a series of broad bands of orange, black, red and green, expressed the alternation of moods in the patient's cyclic behavior. See also color plate VII.

In the lower right hand corner, a triangular section was filled with broken black lines, and on the lower left hand corner, a similar triangle was covered with multicolored lines of green, blue and orange. In the centre appeared again an upward growing form that stemmed from a narrow baseline and expanded as it rose, into broad bands of alternating orange, black, red and green. Maria was delighted that the writer understood that, by the central movement of the design, she meant to express the mingling of the various aspects of her self.

The Second Session

The second series of pictures were drawn by Maria two weeks later as she was recovering from the effects of a severe cold. On this day she said that she now felt well and free from depression for the first

time. It was difficult for her to get started with the chalks. Then, as
at other times when she showed severe blocking, it was necessary to
get the girl to talk about herself and her problems in order to uncover
material that she might eventually translate into drawings. Queried
concerning her illness, she spoke of her blue and foggy state while still
in bed, and of how this was followed by a black depression. The
writer asked whether she might wish to experiment with expressing
such moods in pictures. She was ready to try and two somewhat ten-
tative designs in lines of faint gray followed; in the second drawing,
thread-like red lines mingled with the gray ones and were identified as
signs of the return of thought after illness. They were psychologically
significant, but showed no artistic realization in either form or color.

Fig. 92. "I Feel Like That After Seeing My Doctor. Happy or
Depressed . . ."

Another similarly symmetrical tree-like pattern. The upward-reaching black
lines are interspersed with vivid gold, scarcely visible in this black and white
photograph.

In the next drawing came expression of Maria's intense release
from depression on the first day out of bed. Here, then, the patient
began to touch on her inner problem. She volunteered for the first
time: "Then a lot happened. I felt very depressed and then I had a
shock when I realized certain things. And I called for my doctor."

The patient did not at this time refer to the nature of this shock,
which the writer learned later from the psychiatrist concerned her
dawning realization of an over-attachment to her father and her jealousy of her mother. She had no difficulty in beginning the picture
with a mass of heavy black lines for depression. "But how," she
asked, "shall I make shock?" Encouraged to experiment, she decided
on some vivid orange-red gashes flung across the right side of the

page in lightning-like streaks. "This red is the shock, the black is how I felt before the shock."

Just two days before drawing this picture, the patient had spoken to the psychiatrist in a way that will show more specifically her dawning realization concerning the nature of her Oedipus complex. In other pictures and in some conversations with the psychiatrist and the writer that will be introduced later, the clarification of her relation to her parents will be traced in more detail.

Two days before drawing this picture of shock, Maria had said to her psychiatrist: "Even though my father is my father, I know so little about him. I was sitting at lunch with Georgio today." (This is a patient in whom she has been particularly interested at the hospital whose relationship to Maria is shown in many of her later pictures. He was the boy-friend present when the father struck her.) "I was thinking of my father all the time. As a rule I don't feel uneasy with people, but I always do with him. I get along alright with my mother. I actually felt like screaming this afternoon when Georgio put his arm around me. I didn't want him to touch me. At times like this I lose interest in things I really like. Today I hate jazz. I even hate to comb my hair. Do you know I actually feel like I was losing my mind? Something is worrying me and I can't find out what it is." At this point the doctor asked her if Georgio reminded her of anyone. "Yes, Georgio reminds me of my brother and my brother reminds me of my father." This comment has an added interest because Georgio is also the name of Maria's brother, though she never mentions this point of identity.

After explaining how shock had brought realization, Maria also told of the fright that followed, as she considered speaking to the doctor about it. The possibility of using this fright as a theme of the next picture was envisaged. To find colors for this was more baffling than anything yet attempted; but finally white, tan and pale yellow were chosen as descriptive of a state of fright. "It's difficult to express and I'm still not clear." So the subject was dropped for the time being. When, however, it came up again, some weeks later, it was again rejected under slightly different circumstances. How this theme of fright is related to various aspects of the patient's anxiety will be made clear in the last section of this paper.

"I want to do something bright now," suggested Maria, so she chose magenta, turquoise blue, cobalt, yellow, scarlet, orange and green. Without further need of encouragement, she drew a scarlet parabola cutting a turquoise blue arc across a space of undulating magenta, gold and orange. "That's how I feel when I'm happy. But it's kind of mixed up." She was not satisfied and chose to try the same color scheme in another picture. In this design the lower part showed a succession of curving colored bands interspersed with black. "That's the way I've been feeling lately. Sometimes happy, other times depressed, blue or foggy. Then happy again."

Above the denser colors, Maria had drawn a series of radiant shafts of magenta, turquoise, gold and dusty pink, rising upward across the page. "This upper part," she explained, "is when I'm happy and clear, just glad to be alive and young. This picture expresses both sides of me."

For the last picture of this second series, the girl volunteered, "I feel like doing it in yellow and black. I don't know why" (Fig. 92). When the design was finished, it again sprayed open from a narrow centre at the base of the page. The expanding, upward flowing black lines were interspersed with streaks of yellow. The upper centre of the design expanded into a rising spread of gold. "I generally feel like that after seeing my doctor. Happy or depressed, but even in my depressed moments, I always feel everything is going to turn out all right. The centre bright yellow is how I feel right now."

The first two art sessions in which Maria had begun to express herself spontaneously have been described in detail, so as to give a definite picture of the way in which these abstract drawings evolved. This visual commentary seemed necessary as a substitute for the actual presence of all the pictures. The manner in which these early designs came into existence may suggest how the patient was gradually developing her own coherent use of symbolic color and form as she grew more articulate. There is also evidence here of the way in which the subject matter of these drawings was related to the most intimate personal problems of the patient's adjustment. It will now be necessary, however, to examine the cyclic character of this girl's work before giving a more careful consideration to the symbolic levels of their expression.

THE CYCLIC CHARACTER OF MARIA'S DRAWINGS

The drawings already described confirm the description, by the psychiatrist, of the cyclic character of this patient's behavior. Maria constantly showed her awareness of this rapid alternation of mood in the spontaneous remarks that she made at various times about her own work; often she announced, before beginning to draw, exactly what she proposed to express; at other times she offered a running commentary as she proceeded; on some days she would review an entire series of pictures at the end of an art session and then explain exactly what they meant to her. Besides the pendulum-like swing of her moods, the patient also realized, in some of her designs, aspects of the changes taking place in her own development under treatment.

After some weeks of art work she proposed making a picture that would include not only one extreme of her emotional change, but the entire gamut of her cyclic behavior in one design. For this she chose, for the first time, a sheet of black paper. Her drawing, she explained, would show how one of her depressions, symbolized by the dark background, moved upward with increasingly vivid colors, until she reached one of her "high" states, and then would show how she sank back again in descending tones, until she returned to the depressive state of the black paper. Here are her comments as she worked on this drawing: "From the black it goes to gray. White, I feel peaceful with everybody then. Then bright blue happiness, then orange. Yellow when I feel wonderful. Even when I start to get gray, there's a streak of 'high' near places of yellow between all other colors." She drew uneven yellow lines intermingled with faint wavy gray ones. "Gray goes down and when I get very down, then I shoot up. Now, since recently, I've been very quiet. I don't go so up. I feel more low than up. It doesn't ever get 'high.' "

The patient's drawings were done with speed in quick succession, as soon as the cause of blocking was removed. Six to eight drawings, measuring 18 by 24 inches, were the average product of an art period of an hour to an hour and a half. In the more complex, as well as in the simpler patterns, emotion expressive of positive attitudes led the rhythm of the design upwards, while emotion related to negative attitudes drew it downwards. The pace at which these drawings were made precludes the assumption that Maria had planned, either consciously or systematically, to symbolize the direction of her emotions in this fashion. Rather do these contrary-wise rhythmic movements, used consistently throughout her forty-five drawings, suggest that they were a fundamental expression of her unconscious.

Two drawings, made in quick succession during her fourth art period, illustrate this opposing use of rhythm. The patient announced, spontaneously, that she would make a picture of how she felt towards her father (Fig. 98). She drew this rapidly and with an intense release of emotion; it consisted of heavy corkscrew-like red coils, descending rhythmically across the page; to this, aggressive black strokes were added. When it was finished she announced: "Now I'll make a picture of how I feel about my doctor. There won't be any black in this." But immediately, she modified this statement by adding some black to express her disapproval of the psychiatrist, when she was late for an appointment. The movement in this picture was a multicolored, flame-like rhythm, shifting upwards, expressive in the patient's own words of "an outgoing feeling of hope, confidence and affection." There is, in these two sequential designs, a contrasting use of rhythm and color; a negative attitude about her father is expressed by a downward rhythm in black and red; a positive attitude towards her psychiatrist is expressed by an upward rhythm of orange, yellow, blue and violet. The meaning of this color language as developed by Maria, in these and other pictures, will presently be described and analyzed.

In order to release certain repressed emotions into graphic expression, it was necessary to encourage Maria to talk freely of herself and her problems. Whenever blocking was present, it was due to depression. She would ascribe such moods to various circumstances, such as quarrels with her family and friends, or temporary physical disability related to a cold or a menstrual period. Such states were more frequent than the joyous ones at the opening of the art sessions. But once she had verbalized and released emotionally what was on her mind, the sombre pictures were successfully projected and the happier ones were sure to follow. If the art period began with a joyous mood, it was immediately expressed in bright chalk designs, without a moment's hesitation. Such was the case on the last day, when she entered the room, announcing: "I'm feeling wonderful. I've just heard Georgio has a defense job." This mood was expressed immediately in a golden, abstract design that reached upward and outward across the page in a few sure, broad strokes.

COLOR SYMBOLISM

How the rhythmic pattern of these drawings is related to the changing moods of this patient has been described. It is possible, from Maria's own comments, to follow the significance that she attributes to her choice of colors in these compositions. In this work she has developed, as will soon become evident, a consistent color language of her own. Whether her symbolic use of color has a more universal validity would require its comparison with the color symbolism of the past and the art expression of the present, in both normal subjects and mental patients.

The use of black by Maria to express depression and red for anger and rage has already been described. The red of rage or anger was only expressed in isolated red lines in conjunction with black. But red, when related to other vivid colors, was also interpreted as a warm and outgoing emotion. In the drawing concerning her feeling for the psychiatrist, she said, "Red expresses affection." She also stated that "Red means happiness," in relation to several multicolored pictures that dealt with both friends and family.

In a number of drawings the patient spoke of yellow as also signifying happiness; it was usually present in pictures of positive mood. Intense joy was expressed in the yellow design already mentioned. Yellow and black were juxtaposed in another pattern that dramatized the opposition between her depressed state and the new, more confident one which showed her growing faith in recovery through her doctor's help. On two occasions she combined yellow with bright turquoise to express her positive attitude in relation to the boy-friend, Georgio.

The joyous and positive meaning attributed to yellow is again accentuated in one of her loveliest designs. She called the picture "The Perfect Date." It described her emotions concerning what she declared was the most wonderful date she had ever had with any boy. It took place one evening with her hospital friend, Georgio. This is what she said before drawing it: "Saturday is the day that went so well. It will be all happy colors. He acted like an angel, not one quarrel. I made up my mind I'd go home if he acted the same as last time."

Beginning to draw, she commented: "Yellow, starting from down and going up slowly, then orange"; she ran in the wavy band of orange. "And all around the orange, goes yellow; there was that feeling of happiness. Funny way to express how you feel about a fellow! Now wavy bright blue." She made a series of mounting step-like rhythms with the broad side of a turquoise-blue chalk. "Everything went flowing along, just like that. All along here is my yellow. What would I do without yellow!"

Orange too, as used in this picture, was likewise considered a happy color. On one occasion when orange was combined with purple, brown and yellow, in what was a distinctly fetal form, she called orange "comforting."

Maria's color schemes for happiness varied somewhat according to the subject matter. But besides her constant use of yellow, orange and red, bright green, magenta, turquoise or a touch of vivid blue might also be included. But the color combination that gave her the most complete satisfaction occurred in a large rhythmic design of shifting shades; this included magenta, blue and green, accented with hints of orange and of gold. It was the most lyric of all her pictures and contained, although she remained quite unconscious of this, the archetypal uterine symbol that appeared in a number of her designs (Figs. 93, 94, 95 and 96). This drawing, which she said was done in her favorite color scheme, reminded her of summer, which was also her favorite season. It is interesting that the colors which here suggest fertility to the patient are used unconsciously by her to create a fetal form that dominates the whole design (Fig. 93).

In many of Maria's drawings this feminine symbol is to be found; but it appears only in those patterns that are positively creative and full of her personal affirmation of life. It is never present in designs which express her conflict with either family or friends.

FIG. 93. SUMMER (First Fetal Form)

This expressed the favorite season of this patient. It was the most lyric of all her pictures and contained, although she remained unconscious of it, the archetypal uterine symbol. It was drawn in her favorite color scheme of magenta, blue and green, accented with hints of orange and gold. See also color plate VIII.

This patient had usually no hesitation in selecting colors to express the meaning of her drawings. On but four occasions did she hesitate, as to which chalk would be appropriate to fulfill her theme. This resistance to a choice of colors occurred only over the emotionally charged subjects of "Shock," "Fright," "Being Sorry" and the "State of Nausea."

After the repressed episode had been released in words, orange-red was used to express shock. The circumstances which caused shock will be described later in their appropriate relation to the subject matter of these designs. For the condition of fright, the colors arrived at experimentally were white, yellow and tan. How the problem of fright developed will also be discussed later. The need for a color to express "Being Sorry" occurred when Maria tried to make

FIG. 94. ASPECT OF HAPPINESS (Second Fetal Form)
The most complete of the uterine forms drawn by this patient. It was done in a new and untried color scheme of brown, orange, purple and yellow.

a picture of the emotion that she had felt following a fight with her friend Georgio. She had drawn the picture of the fight in black and was now ready to begin her next design. "Back in my room," she said, "I felt angry at Georgio. That's red." And she ran a forceful curving line of red chalk across the page. "But I felt sorry at the same time. I don't know what color to use for sorry." She was urged to try out any possible colors for that emotion, by placing them beside the red on her practice sheet. This led eventually, after a pale yellow orange had been rejected, to the selection of white. "That's more like sorry," she decided. Against the gray ground of the paper, she then drew loops of delicate white interlaced with the heavy strokes of the angry red lines.

The design for "Nausea" was drawn in the last series of pictures. It followed the joyous all yellow design, already described. The resistance to discovering the needed colors for the design of "Nausea" was deeper and more complex than for any of the other drawings and proved to be so profoundly related to the patient's neurotic conflicts that the description of how this picture was finally drawn needs to be combined in the next section with a description of the subject matter that revealed the cause of her state of nausea. This sequence will illustrate the close correspondence between the course of the psychotherapeutic treatment and the art work of the patient.

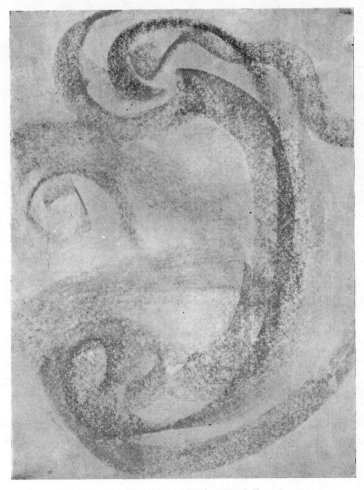

FIG. 95. HAPPINESS (Third Fetal Form)

Another design, fetal in form, made by the patient in the last art session to express happiness. It was drawn in red, violet and blue.

The Subject Matter of Maria's Drawings

The subject matter of this patient's drawings covers the efforts of an adolescent girl to deal with the conflicts that arose from the over-disciplinary attitude of her Italian parents. Maria reached the hospital as a consequence of her attempt to escape from her problem by means of flight into amnesia. On more than one occasion, which will be cited, she voiced her wish in moments of depression or conflict to escape again into amnesia (Fig. 97).

Fig. 96. Happiness (Fourth Fetal Form)

Another of the patient's 11 fetal forms, drawn after Fig. 95 in order to expand further her expression of happiness. It was done in the same color chalks with the addition of some green and orange.

Her pictures can be divided into three groups. Those that deal with her responses to family, with special emphasis upon her attitude to her father; those that deal with her relationship to Georgio, her boy-friend; and two drawings that show the strengthening of her transference to the psychiatrist. While such subject classification may be convenient, it is not one that remains constant; for the problems that centered about family often overlap those that concern the patient's friends, both at home and in the hospital.

Fig. 97. Depression (One of eight such patterns)

This was one of many corkscrew-coil designs, which were, as in this example, sometimes associated with heavy black downstrokes, to express deep depression. Sometimes as many as three all black designs were drawn in one session. Only in the final art period, however, did the patient for the first time draw a series of pictures omitting all black designs in her work.

In the pictures dealing with the familial pattern, the patient gives the relationship with the father a separate place, in just three designs. Otherwise the family is treated, in the drawings, as a unit to which the patient either reacts or belongs. Two of the designs, concerning Maria's response to her father made in the first art session, have already been described. They dealt with that episode in which the father struck her and she reacted with hysteria. The third picture about him she called: "How I feel About My Father" (Fig. 98). In depicting her buried resentment and anger against her father, the patient again drew a large design in red and black. As in the previous father pictures she released at the moment of creating it, an inordinate amount of repressed emotion. An obvious feeling of guilt at having

FIG. 98. "How I Feel About My Father" (One of three designs)

In this red and black design the patient released much buried resentment and anger against her father. The paler corkscrew coil is in vivid red. All the other forms in heavy black. So great was her feeling of guilt about this picture that she immediately forgot what it represented to her.

exposed so much of her true feeling against her father was shown by the way that she forgot immediately the meaning of this drawing. When reminded of what she had said before making this picture about her father, she replied, "When the feeling is out, I forget." But on no other occasion in the making of the other 44 drawings did the patient ever forget the subject of a picture, or the meaning to her of any color employed in a design.

In the first drawing about her response to the family pattern, the patient showed her changing and contradictory feelings in the contrasts between her use of black and bright colors. Pointing to a turmoiled mass of black chalk in the centre of the design, Maria announced, "That black lump is the problem unsolved. Yellow is the hope. Red, I feel good and happy toward them; then I go black, then light again." Now the art work was coming to mean more to the patient, for at this point she commented, "This time is more interesting than ever before."

FIG. 99. "DAYS AT HOME" (One of seven designs)

This represents the patient's response to both family and friends. The quarter circle lower right represents in alternating bands of bright and dark colors her changing relationship with her family. The central zig-zag lines of various colors moving away from quarter-circle of the family represent the patient in her relation to friends. A similar design from this series is found in color plate IX.

The next design about the family came two weeks later, after a week's vacation from the hospital when she had visited her home. The trip had not been as successful as she had anticipated and stimulated the creation of two pictures. The first she called "Days at Home," and the second, "My Past with the Family." Again the colors used to express her family relationships were a mixture of bright and dark. There had been fights, she said, while she was home, and about them she explained, "Of course I couldn't express all my feelings, as they were my parents." Besides her response to family, this picture of "Days at Home" included her relation to her friends in that environment (Fig. 99). Pointing to the streaks of yellow at the left of this design, she interpreted, "Yellow is what I seem to be when I'm with my friends. But that's because I cover what is within." She then drew wavy lines of blue-black and gray that moved out from her centre in the family group towards her friends outside. "The yellow I show with my friends is like being an actress; you know, I cover over the black, blue and red that's me underneath. And I got all mixed up trying to cover myself."

In summarizing the two pictures of "Days At Home" and "The Past with the Family," she stated, "This more or less expresses my life, the way it goes; the curves, the question marks, the colors. It expresses every one of my feelings. In every bit of happiness there is sadness." Again as she worked, she commented, "Fights are blackness at home. When I'm out with friends, I'm happy with them. That's the blue and yellow. I always would be thinking when I'm with them, 'I'm different,' remembering my difficulties at home. At times I cry or get angry or indifferent. But behind this always I kept thinking, 'I'm going to get away.' I felt like killing myself, but I'm too self-centered for that, I found that out in analysis." This wish to escape the apparently insoluble conflicts of home reappears in a later talk with the psychiatrist in which the patient declares that she is "thoroughly fed up. I wish I could go into another amnesia. — I even want to forget who I am, what I've been doing and everything."

Two Unrealized Drawings of Fright

Before analyzing the subject matter of the second group of pictures which deal with Maria's relation to her friend Georgio, it seems advisable to consider how the patient's anxiety and special concern over the problem of her amnesia were related to her two unsuccessful attempts to use "Fright" as the theme of her art work. The strength of the resistance, which made the patient unable to bring this subject of "Fright" into any form of graphic expression, weights it with added significance. (Had it been possible to work more frequently with this patient, it is probable that further material concerning her anxiety would have been obtained in later art sessions.)

The first projected drawing of the subject of "Fright" was planned to follow immediately after the picture of "Shock," which had been drawn to express her growing realization of the nature of her Oedipus complex. She then spoke of the fright she experienced at the prospect of speaking to her doctor about it. In this first attempt to draw "Fright," Maria went so far as to select the colors of white, tan and pale yellow, that she felt appropriate to this picture. She then decided that she was not ready to do it. "It's difficult and I'm still not clear." She was referring to the whole problem of the Oedipus complex, which the previous drawing represented and which she had only just begun to deal with in the sessions with the psychiatrist. The resolving of the dynamics of the Oedipus situation will be taken up more fully in the next section of this paper.

It was more than five weeks later that the possibility of attempting another drawing on the theme of "Fright" reappeared. The patient spoke of having had a gynecological examination because of the too great frequency of her menstrual periods. "I felt awfully depressed each time." Asked about the cause of such disturbance, she replied that she had been trying with her doctor to discover the reason. "I was so frightened, when I had the examination, my heart went back and forth. I was very nervous. We were wondering whether it had anything to do with the last internal examination at the hospital when I was found in Central Park."

It was suggested that the patient attempt to recall that moment when she was examined at this general hospital. She was asked to revive the state she was in when she was examined. Did she remember where she was when the doctor spoke to her? "No, even though I was frightened." She started, however, to draw in black strokes on the paper. "That's the black feeling and then there was gray surrounding it." Following this the patient had planned to make the next picture express the actual moment of fright.

An external circumstance intervened and obliged the patient to leave the ward. By the time she returned, the tension of her mood had been shattered and she was unable to recapture the expression of anxiety or fear on that day. It is impossible to judge whether, at some later time, she might be able to recreate her emotion concerning fright. But the patient's inability to express such a state on two occasions corresponds to the recognition of both psychiatrist and patient that certain deep fears still remained unsolved when the girl left the hospital.

The Rorschach test of this patient also corroborates the existence of such fears and suggests the possibility that "In part at least, the patient's fear seems to be due to anxiety lest a severely repressed psychosexual conflict reappear in her consciousness."

To return to Maria's original concern at having to undergo an internal examination, there is a corresponding dream, reported by the psychiatrist, that the patient had described two weeks before she attempted to draw "Fright" in the art session. "Dr. S. was examining me." (This is the doctor at the Psychiatric Institute who actually did so.) "She had a pair of scissors and said, 'I'm going to cut you.' There were a lot of instruments, all different sizes and she said, 'It is going to hurt,' and I was so afraid."

The dream associations given to the psychiatrist with this dream were as follows: "I'm afraid when I think of that. It brings me back to my examination at the other hospital; I was thinking of my doctor who examined me there. I was screaming, and she told me to relax. That brings me to Central Park and going to the police station, then lying there in the hospital and my father coming for me and I didn't recognize him or want to go with him. Then driving home and all the neighbors staring. The next day at home and my friends came to see me."

When questioned about the inclusion of the instrument table, after much thought the patient said: "I never did much petting before I got sick. With my bringing up there was always too much conflict. Then for one or two months following the amnesia" (when she began to pet freely with boys for the first time) "there was no conflict because I didn't remember anything." A continuation of the patient's sense of guilt over petting with boys, as well as the expression of her anxiety over the problem of birth as it related to kissing, will be discussed more fully in the next section, which deals with the drawings that are concerned with Maria's relation to Georgio.

In the treatment of this patient by the psychiatrist, no attempt was made to undertake a thorough analysis, but only such psychotherapy as might make possible the patient's readjustment with her parents and the home environment. Psychiatric social service helped to modify the attitude of the parents towards the patient. When Maria left the hospital to go home, she had begun to make an adjustment to the home situation while continuing psychotherapy with the psychiatrist.

PICTURES OF MARIA'S RELATION TO GEORGIO

These pictures about Georgio are closely related to those dealing with Maria's father. Immediately after drawing the first three designs about her relation to her friend, she followed them with a red and black design of her feelings about her father.

In the Georgio series, a black design expressing a quarrel was drawn first. Then followed a picture expressing anger and "Being Sorry," which has already been described. The third dealt with Maria's estimate of Georgio, the yellow and turquoise showed her positive attitude: "That's when I'm happy with Georgio." A contorted black and red design on the other side of the page she described as: "That's when we fight and I'm angry."

Maria had announced before drawing the quarrel with Georgio that he was "a father substitute." When she had spoken in similar terms to the psychiatrist, she had admitted a certain resemblance between Georgio and her brother and added that her brother resembled her father. In another interview she explained that "Georgio is like my father in many ways." Georgio also happened to be of Italian parentage and, although the patient never referred to it, had the same name as her only brother.

The next picture concerning Georgio dealt with "The Perfect Date," which has already been described. There followed in the last session the yellow drawing about Georgio's new job. At this point we return again to the design concerning the state of "Nausea," which has already been mentioned in the discussion of the patient's color symbolism. But this picture only gains its rightful significance when placed in correct sequence with the other drawings of that same art session. Seven pictures were made in this final period. Maria had entered the room in an especially joyous mood. First, came the expression of satisfaction about Georgio in the all-yellow pattern. Then she exclaimed that she felt so happy on this particular day, because she had been able to eat all her food, at lunch, without feeling the usual nauseous disturbance. "I want," she announced, "to make a picture of how happy I feel." For this she selected the colors magenta, blue, orange, green and blue-green. But this design for happiness did not develop so easily as she expected. In order to overcome the blocking that ensued, the patient was questioned as to the cause of this recurrent nausea. Maria gave this explanation: "You know how it is when you're a kid and you imagine babies are born through the mouth and that kissing would bring a baby. I always used to get upset because of that idea, whenever a boy kissed me. And then I got that way over my food, too. I just couldn't let a vegetable or potato get mixed up with the meat, or I'd feel this nausea. I've been having talks with my doctor about the reasons for this, and now, today, for the first time at lunch, I could eat all my food mixed up together and I didn't get nauseated a bit."

She was then asked whether she would like to try to make a picture of this state of nausea, before doing the one of her present happy state. As she was unable to imagine what colors to use, she was urged to experiment. Gray she thought would be needed. After trying out many colors and rejecting them, Maria finally decided that yellow-green, a pale orange and whitish-yellow might be usable. As the yellow-green was shrill in tone, she was shown how to mix and modify its color, by varying its value within the color-scheme that she had chosen; the technique of overlaying yellow-green with pale orange or gray and the method of using dull colors as the base to brighter ones was also illustrated. Experiment on the trial paper led Maria to the development of a gamut of tones, running from yellow-green to grayish and orange yellow-green and then on to the more neutral tones of greenish and orange-gray. In weighing this theme of nausea for a design, Maria announced, "It's got to go up and down." And when she finally drew it, this double rhythm was present in the rippling movement of the pattern. When the picture was done, she was much surprised: "I didn't think I could ever make it look anything like nausea, but it really does!" She was right. She had caught the color and feeling within the form. But she had achieved more, for the design contained a strange, essential beauty, due perhaps, in spite of its theme, to the retrospective state of happiness and adjustment from which this picture had been drawn.

Before describing the two drawings of "Happiness," with which the patient ended her last art session, certain supplementary material concerning this deep-rooted problem of nausea should be quoted from the psychiatrist's talks with the patient.

Some time before attempting to draw the picture of "Nausea," the patient made the following remark to the psychiatrist: "It's awful when you feel guilty every time you kiss a boy; you can't go through life feeling like that." As Maria's concern over her nausea continued, the psychiatrist reports that "several sessions were spent in an endeavor to find its cause, through free association. One day the patient related to the examiner what had happened on the previous day. While at a party Georgio was kidding with her and when her mouth was open he stuck his finger between her lips. Immediately the associations of the previous session occurred to her. At this time she recalled that in early childhood she had thought pregnancy occurred through the mouth, and through the ingestion of food. When the finger entered her mouth she became nauseated and immediately thought of a penis. She then remembered some jokes she had heard in relation to fellatio. The period was spent in discussion of her ideas on this subject."

Further resolution of the patient's Oedipus complex took place shortly before she left the hospital. To her doctor she wrote the following, after her recognition of the resemblance of Georgio to her father: "I'm happy with my mother when she is not with my father, yet I hate my father and love my mother, or is it the other way around? When my parents had a fight I was glad that my father was mad at my mother. I like Georgio to kiss me because Georgio can give me what my father never could give me. That's why I've never liked other fellows to kiss me. That's why I don't want to live with my parents. I'm jealous of my mother. I can't believe it. I'm uneasy when my parents are together. That's why I haven't been going home week-ends. I can't believe it's true. It's not true. See your doctor if you want to be well. You must tell her what's on your mind."

Archetypal Forms

No attempt will be made in this paper to do more than suggest the nature and form of the archetypal symbols that were recognizable in the course of the patient's art work; nor will the deeper sexual content of these symbols be discussed within the limits of this paper.

Several distinctly female symbols were repeated by Maria a number of times in her abstract designs. A large fetal or uterine form is most frequently evident in 11 of her pictures. It appeared in a sequence of three or four designs in the course of three different art periods; but it was omitted in all the other sessions. The girl remained completely unconscious of this highly symbolic form throughout all of her hours of art work (Figs. 93, 94, 95 and 96).

Another recurrent symbol is the quarter circle which Maria constructed of a series of successive bands of vivid colors; the bright shades were used to express positive attitudes and happy feelings; while black was interspersed to show phases of depression. Such a quarter circle was usually placed in the lower right hand corner of the paper. Variations on this theme were present in 7 drawings. In four art sessions this design was described as representing the patient's family; the girl's personal reaction to or against this family pattern was on one occasion expressed in zig-zag lines projecting from this quarter circle (Fig. 99). Such a symbol also appeared in three other designs and always expressed, in its alternating strips of black and bright colors, Maria's conflicting emotional attitudes towards her family.

A third unconscious symbol that appeared 3 times in the first two art sessions suggested a tree or flower-like form (Fig. 91 and 92). In contrast to the other symbolic patterns it was always drawn in symmetrical balance. The production of this tree-like form was important as Maria's first expression of a unification of the two opposing aspects of herself. She was able to recognize the meaning of this balanced design as a symbol of the dissociation in her psyche.

Only when these tree-like forms ceased did the uterine symbols begin to appear in the girl's pictures. In contrast to the degree of insight that the patient showed concerning the balanced flower-like symbols as expressing the division in her personality, she never became aware of the unconscious significance of the uterine forms that she began to create in the final art sessions. Such symbolic fetal forms (Figs 93, 94, 95 and 96) broke through at moments when she was attempting to express intimate emotional problems that related to her own feelings about sex and her relation to the boy-friend.

Two other symbolic patterns were in sufficient evidence to warrant description. One was a rhythmic corkscrew scroll or its variant, a tangled network of screwed up coils (Figs. 97 and 98). These two patterns were drawn in red or black, or with these two colors combined. They were used by the patient to express violent emotion concerning quarrels and other personal conflicts. There were five of these corkscrew-coil designs, which were sometimes associated with a group of heavy black down-strokes. Eight of Maria's 45 drawings were made in thick black outlines; such patterns were always used to express her deepest depression.

Conclusion

In the nature of the symbolism created and the colors used by Maria in her pictures, there is a preponderance in the use of either black or red, or black and red in her designs; all of these are expressive of some negative emotional attitude. One and sometimes as many as three pictures, in each art session, were drawn in these two colors. They appeared most frequently at the commencement of a period and were usually replaced later in the hour by designs expressive of more positive and even elated moods.

At the conclusion of the first two art sessions a symmetrical tree-like pattern was developed by the patient, to express the balancing of the two extreme aspects of her cyclic behavior. This design then gave way to the recurrent uterine symbol. Both these feminine, archetypal forms were used by the patient to express moods or changes within herself; they were never chosen to express feelings towards either family or friends.

As symbol of the family, she developed the pattern of a quarter circle, filled with colored bands, interspersed with black; in drawing this the patient again remained unconscious of its archetypal meaning.

At the conclusion of Maria's treatment in the hospital the psychiatrist reported considerable improvement. The patient's art work also reflected a corresponding change. Her improvement was most clearly expressed in the color and subject matter of her final group of drawings. In these Maria omitted, for the first time, all use of either pure black or red. Need of expressing such emotions as anger, rage and depression had altogether disappeared from this final and seventh art session. But the patient showed no active awareness of this change, nor was this transformation to a more balanced and happy state drawn to her attention. She remained as unconscious of the omission of the black and red color in her final pictures as she had been of the use of the uterine symbols in some of her earlier designs. The problem of interpreting to this patient the unconscious symbolism of the fetal forms and the changes in the use of color raises a complex question. Since the art work of Maria covered only 7 sessions before she left the hospital, it was not possible to follow the further evolution of her symbolic expression of her problems. Up to the time where her art expression came to an end, rather unexpectedly, it had not seemed advisable to emphasize the symbolic significance of these abstract designs beyond the patient's spontaneous insight as to their meaning. In some later studies where more complete data are available, showing the art of adolescent schizophrenic girls ranging over periods of 6 months to 2 years, it will be possible to explain more fully the writer's approach to the symbolic art expression of mental patients.

A description of the process by which the patient, Maria, was led to a personal and spontaneous art expression has been presented to fulfill two objectives: first, that it may show the steps by which the patient's unconscious was gradually released through the symbolic speech of art; and second, that it may suggest the possibilities inherent in such a procedure for obtaining valuable material bearing on both diagnosis and therapy.